# THE
# PRINCIPLES
# OF
# PSYCHOLOGY

# THE
# PRINCIPLES
# OF
# PSYCHOLOGY

## SHONA SAUL

SIRIUS

**SIRIUS**

This edition published in 2023 by Sirius Publishing, a division of
Arcturus Publishing Limited,
26/27 Bickels Yard, 151–153 Bermondsey Street,
London SE1 3HA

ISBN: 978-1-3988-3008-0
AD010137UK

Printed in China

# CONTENTS

# INTRODUCTION

## What is Psychology?

There are lots of misconceptions about psychology. Here are some of the things people have said to me when they hear that I am a psychologist:

1. *'So, tell me what he's thinking.'*
2. *'I'd better be careful, you're reading my mind.'*
3. *'You're the same as a psychiatrist then?'*
4. *'Ah, you're a psychoanalyst...'*

The answers are:

A. 1. 'I don't know.'
B. 2. 'I'm really not doing that.'
C. 3 and 4. 'No, I'm not.'

Be assured that a psychologist does not have the power to read your mind, does not observe you as though you are a participant in a study, and does not always want to know what you are thinking! To clarify, psychiatrists and psychologists are not the same: psychiatrists first qualify in Medicine and then specialize in Psychiatry, whilst psychologists qualify in Psychology and then pursue further qualifications to become specialists. Psychologists and psychoanalysts are not the same either (which tends to surprise people who have heard of Sigmund Freud): each profession requires separate qualifications.

Having clarified what psychology is not, let's look at what it is. The British Psychological Society defined psychology as:

### *'... the scientific study of the mind and how it dictates and influences our behaviour...'*

Or, to put this another way, psychologists are interested in the brain, mental processes and behaviour. Since topics which come under these headings are found in the chapters which follow, for now, let's focus on what is meant by *scientific*.

Everyone is an amateur psychologist in that all people try to explain behaviour, whether it be their own, or that of others. In doing this, it can be very tempting to think that what applies to oneself, or to a member of our family or even a friend also applies to others. However, this is not a scientific approach.

Of course, an individual's conscious experience is valuable to that person. It also provides a psychologist with information regarding that particular person's impression of an event, such as how they feel they went about putting a name to a familiar face. Yet, a single, *subjective* reflection

*A psychologist at work.*

upon an experience does not necessarily provide an accurate picture of what actually occurred and can easily be misleading. Consequently, psychologists gather information *objectively*, via carefully designed studies, which collect data from multiple people.

Carefully designed studies allow behaviour to be measured appropriately. Taking data from many people means the measurements are representative of what actually occurs psychologically, compared with relying upon one person alone, or just a few people. Statistical analysis of the resulting data reveals whether chance could satisfactorily account for these results. If it is highly unlikely the results are the product of chance, it is inferred that something meaningful has been found. The psychologist must now determine what this is using current knowledge and their specialized expertise.

Most psychological research involves people whose brains are intact but it can also involve people whose brains are impaired. In fact, it's possible to explore why we behave in the way we do without a detailed appreciation of what's taking place in the brain. Indeed, for many years it simply wasn't possible to study the brain directly except after death, through a post-mortem. Hence, the effects of brain injury and brain disease had to be relied upon to glean important information. Today, however, it is possible to conduct informative research without investigating the brain *and* to study what's happening in the brain of a living person. Imaging techniques such as Computerized Axial Tomography (CAT scan), Positron Emission Tomography (PET scan), Magnetic Resonance Imaging (MRI scan) and Functional Magnetic Resonance Imaging (fMRI scan) have been added to the psychologist's investigative tool box.

## Becoming a Psychologist

In Britain, becoming a psychologist would typically involve taking a degree in psychology and then a postgraduate qualification (often a second degree), to become a Chartered Psychologist. Although academic and applied psychology can be distinguished, they are not entirely separate entities: some academic psychologists work within applied fields (e.g. clinical psychology) and applied psychology will draw upon academic research relevant to its field.

## EXAMPLES OF ACADEMIC AND APPLIED PSYCHOLOGY

| ACADEMIC PSYCHOLOGY | APPLIED PSYCHOLOGY |
|---|---|
| Academic psychologists teach and conduct research in universities in the applied areas opposite, in one or more of topics such as those below. | **Clinical Psychology** – Helps with mental and/or physical health issues, e.g. depression, anxiety, addiction. |

**Biopsychology** – Biological factors in psychology, e.g. how behaviour is affected by the brain and other parts of the nervous system, hormones, heredity, drugs.

**Cognitive Psychology** – Mental processes such as memory, perception, language, problem-solving and reasoning.

**Developmental Psychology** – Biological, cognitive, social and emotional change over the human lifespan.

**Evolutionary and Comparative Psychology:**

**Evolutionary Psychology** – theory is applied to account for thoughts, emotions and behaviour. This involves combining biology and psychology.

**Comparative Psychology** – similarities and differences are compared between different animal species to understand evolutionary relationships. Study of non-human animals can provide valuable information about the human animal.

**Individual Differences** – How people differ from each other, e.g. in terms of personality, intelligence and mental disorder.

**Social Psychology** – Behaviour within a social context, e.g. forming impressions about other people, relationships, conformity, obedience, prejudice, aggression.

**Counselling Psychology** – Helps with mental health difficulties arising from life circumstances, e.g. trauma, bereavement, domestic violence.

**Educational Psychology** – Helps children and young people with issues such as social and emotional difficulties, complex developmental disorders, learning difficulties.

**Forensic Psychology** – Employs psychology in the contexts of criminal investigations, psychological issues and crime, plus treatment of offenders.

**Health Psychology** – Psychology is used to help people who are physically ill, to promote wellbeing and improve healthcare systems.

**Neuropsychology** – Helps those who have a brain injury, tumour, stroke, neurodegenerative disease, and toxic and metabolic disorder. Links to neuropsychological issues considered in biopsychology.

**Occupational Psychology** – Helps to improve job satisfaction and effectiveness of organizations/corporations.

**Sport/Exercise Psychology** – Sport psychology relates to sports related roles, e.g. helping athletes psychologically in relation to training, competition and injury. Exercise psychology involves helping the public to take up exercise and maintain an exercise regime, for example.

## This Book

This book covers topics from both academic and applied psychology. As a discipline, psychology encompasses a great deal of thought – far more than can easily be captured in a book of this size. I have tried throughout to mention leading practitioners and theories for you to follow up, if anything particularly sparks your interest.

In the following chapters, you will find that different psychological approaches have addressed the same issue(s) and thus provided alternative accounts of the same phenomenon. What happens when we have different explanations for the same thing? Often in psychology there is a dominant view until new thinking and/or new research offers different perspectives and new ideas become the standard position. An example of this is Freud's psychoanalytic approach which had a substantial influence on the discipline for some years. Over time, though, as people disagreed with his ideas and new explanations came along, his views lost their prominent position.

Different explanations can also be useful because it can be beneficial to draw from a variety of relevant perspectives. Clinical psychology, for instance, is a broad area that recognizes the value of different approaches.

Shifts in perspective occur because psychological ideas, concepts, studies, theories etc are critiqued: this is one of the ways in which any scientific discipline progresses.

In this book I have endeavoured to cover a variety of topics for the interested, but uninitiated reader. This has meant trading between breadth and depth and comes at the expense of review and critique. Most of the studies and theories you will read about are well-established or have provided a foundation that others have built upon. As with all disciplines, psychology has been subject to historical circumstances and the biases of its practitioners along such lines as race, gender, sexuality and class. I would encourage you to seek out further reading for the topics that interest you and explore these issues for yourself.

My hope is that something in this book further arouses your interest and acts as a springboard to take you further into the world of your mind and behaviour.

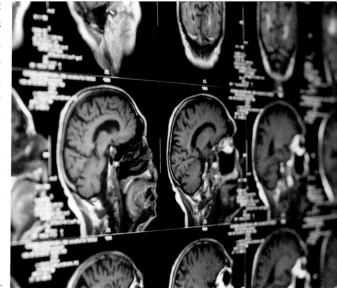

*A CAT scan of the brain.*

# COGNITIVE PSYCHOLOGY

Cognitive psychology examines how our higher mental processes operate, such as memory, perception and language. Typically, cognitive psychologists learn about these issues by conducting experiments with neurologically intact participants. However, sometimes people experience brain damage and when this occurs, it is possible to investigate the neurologically impaired person's cognitive functions. What the person now can or cannot do sheds light upon how a given function may operate.

## A Brief History of Cognitive Psychology

Interest in the higher mental processes began in the 19th century, one contributor to the area being Hermann Ebbinghaus, who explored how memories are formed and how forgetting occurs. Between the 1920s and 1950s though, consideration of cognitive processes waned. During this period, *Behaviourism* – although by no means a very great influence in Europe – held sway in the USA. Behaviourist Burrhus F. Skinner believed psychology's proper focus was directly observable behaviour and quite simply, the higher mental processes could not be directly observed.

In the 1950s, however, information processing psychology began and Donald Broadbent discussed how information gleaned by the perceptual system progressed into memory if it received attention. In the same decade, Allen Newell and Herbert Simon developed computer programs which could solve problems in a way which resembled a human's performance and Noam Chomsky introduced important concepts relating to language.

By the 1960s, research and understanding of higher mental processes was progressing significantly. In 1967, Ulric Neisser published a review of the current state of knowledge, drawing together research on attention, memory, perception, pattern recognition and problem-solving. His book, *Cognitive Psychology* – giving its title to the field of study – helped initiate the 'cognitive revolution' and Neisser became regarded as cognitive psychology's founding father.

As research developed, analogies were drawn between computer processing and humans' higher mental processes: for instance, knowledge regarding the operation of memory grew and was captured in models such as Richard C. Atkinson and Richard M. Shiffrin's Multi-Store Model of Memory.

As knowledge increased about cognitive function and the effects of cognitive loss, models reflected this information (e.g. Vicki Bruce and Andy Young's functional model of face recognition). Particular brain structures were associated with cognitive functions and more advanced computer-based models which resemble brain functioning were proposed for areas such as memory, language and perception.

# Memory

## WHAT IS MEMORY?

Put very simply, in order to remember, we have to put something into memory, keep it there and then access it later, when needed. More technically, incoming information from the senses must be coded in order to enter memory and the *encoding* type depends upon which sense originally detected the data. Next, the encoded information must be retained, or *stored*, after which, when it is needed, it has to be retrieved. Memories are retrieved in two ways, recognition and recall. Recognition involves encountering something and remembering that you've met it before, such as, you see a face, hear a tune, smell a scent and recognize it as familiar. Recall, on the other hand, consists of searching through memory, for example, for the name belonging to a face, a tune's title, or a perfume's name. Often, we are only aware of these retrieval processes when there is a problem, such as 'blanking' someone because we've failed to recognize a familiar face, or the embarrassing situation of misrecognizing an entirely unfamiliar individual as somebody known to us! With a recall failure, we simply cannot access the information we want and are aware that we know, like the name of a recognized face, or the title of a recognized tune.

## TYPES OF MEMORY

Have you ever done any of the following?

A.  'Drawn' with a sparkler or created zigzags with a torch?
B.  Realized what someone has just said immediately after asking for the words to be repeated?
C.  Worked out if your change is correct at the shops?
D.  Read a book, magazine or paper?
E.  Drawn a diagram from a textbook or board at school?
F.  Recalled where you went on holiday, or the name of the Prime Minister?

| 1. ENCODING | 2. STORAGE |
|---|---|

Information is coded into memory.

Information is retained.

| INFORMATION | ENCODING TYPE |
|---|---|
| Seen | *Visual* |
| Heard | *Acoustic* |
| Taste | *Gustatory* |
| Touch | *Haptic* |
| Smell | *Olfactory* |
| Meaning | *Semantic* |

**Sensory Memory**

When we see, hear, taste, touch or smell something, this information is held briefly in the sensory store relevant to the type of stimulus encountered. Being able to 'draw' with a sparkler/torch, for instance, indicates there must be a visual (*iconic*) sensory store since we see a visual trace despite the light source having moved. Similarly, Question B's experience demonstrates a sound (*echoic*) store. Despite sensory stimulation continuously reaching our senses, only some of it receives attention (active consideration).

**Short and Long-Term Memories**

Collectively, many studies have indicated a distinction between short-term memory (STM) and long-term memory (LTM). They differ in capacity, duration and preferred form of encoding. Additionally, neurological evidence has revealed STM can be damaged whilst LTM remains intact, and similarly, LTM may be damaged whilst STM remains intact.

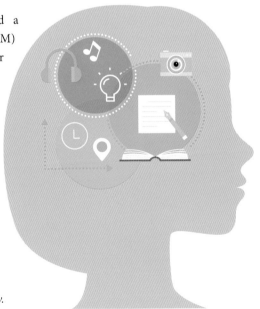

*Types of memory.*

## 3. RETRIEVAL

Memories are accessed by either recognition or recall.

| DIFFERENCES BETWEEN STM AND LTM | | | |
|---|---|---|---|
| Memory type | Capacity | Duration | Preferred encoding (when letters/words are presented visually) |
| STM | strictly limited to 5–9 chunks (e.g. letters, words) dependent on chunk size | brief (seconds) without *rehearsal* (repetition) | acoustic |
| LTM | unlimited | can be a lifetime | semantic |

Neither LTM (discussed below) nor STM is a single store. If STM were one store, it would be impossible to complete two short-term tasks simultaneously – one task would fully occupy STM – yet, a visual task can be performed successfully alongside a language task. Furthermore, neurological evidence has shown parts of STM can be damaged whilst others remain intact, which also indicates STM is not a single store.

**Working Memory**

Try the following:

*Task 1* – Calculate: 30 x 2 and then take off 45. What is your result?

*Task 2* – Read this: It was a hot day, that last Thursday in May, and everyone at Number 4 Acorn Terrace had decided it would be a good idea to have a splash-about in the river's cooling water.

Psychologically, Tasks 1 and 2 are similar, respectively, to Questions C and D. Task 1 involves working out 30 x 2, then holding the result (60) followed by calculating the difference between 60 and 45 (15). Task 2 involves holding the words and their order for them to make sense. Both tasks are easy but cannot be done without temporary storage. After 15 is calculated the stages to arrive at this figure aren't needed and once the meaning of the sentence is acquired, all the words and their order don't have to be stored. We use working memory for both tasks.

Working memory (proposed by Alan Baddeley and Graham Hitch and developed again by Baddeley) contends short-term memory constitutes different systems that both store and actively process information. The *visuospatial sketchpad* and *phonological loop* are subsystems whilst the *central executive* is in overall control. The visuospatial sketchpad stores visual and spatial information for manipulation; it is used when drawing, for example. The phonological loop is sound-based; it stores word order and is involved in speech perception and production. Auditory information automatically enters the loop's *phonological store* which remembers speech sounds and their order. This information is lost rapidly unless rehearsed (repeated) by the *articulatory process*. The articulatory process also transforms text into phonological code when we read, thereby visual language can also access the phonological store. The phonological loop also holds information required to produce speech.

The central executive is the most important component. It isn't a memory system and instead functions like attention. It decides which subsystem should be used, controls the visuospatial sketchpad and phonological loop and is used in most cognitive tasks. More specifically, the executive determines what is or isn't given attention; divides time between the subsystems when both are needed; allows us to switch between different kinds of information that must be retrieved and it activates long-term memory to supply necessary information. Finally, the *episodic buffer* allows links between the subsystems and between the central executive and long-term memory.

Problems with working memory can give rise to difficulties at school with reading, spelling, maths and science. A dysfunctional central executive has been linked to Alzheimer's Disease symptoms.

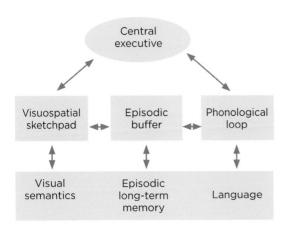

*Baddeley and Hitch's working memory model.*

## Long-Term Memory (LTM)

Larry Squire divided LTM into *declarative* (explicit) and *nondeclarative* (implicit)

*Larry Squire.*

memory. Declarative memory involves conscious recollection and is divided into *episodic memory* (i.e. personal events, e.g. going to a party, meeting someone for lunch) and *semantic memory* (world knowledge, e.g. Wellington is the capital of New Zealand; 2022 was Elizabeth II's Platinum Jubilee year; lemons are yellow and bitter). Semantic and episodic memories may or may not consist of two separate systems: they are different but also clearly related since semantic memories begin episodically. For instance, knowledge about Wellington would begin as a learning episode but we may not recall the time(s) we learned this information.

Nondeclarative memory involves retrieval from LTM through performing an action without conscious recollection, e.g. riding a bike, skilled typing.

*Remembering going to a party or being on the Mall for Queen Elizabeth II's Platinum Jubilee are episodic memories. Knowing the year of the Queen's jubilee is a semantic memory.*

**Forgetting**

Due to its limited capacity, it has been proposed STM forgetting occurs through *displacement*: when full, new information pushes out older material. LTM theories of forgetting include *interference* and *retrieval failure*.

We often organize our lives systematically, with routines for going to work or school, for caring responsibilities or shopping etc. We design these systems to make us more efficient but they mean that we create many similar memories which can interfere with each other. When new information prevents retrieval of similar older memories, this is called *retroactive interference*; e.g. a teacher might be unable to recall the given name of a student they taught previously because the given name of the younger sibling currently being taught is recalled. When older information prevents retrieval of similar newer memories, this is called *proactive interference*; e.g. entering a previous password instead of the new one.

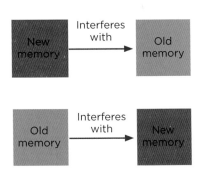

*Retroactive and Proactive Interference.*

When information is stored but can't be accessed, this is called *retrieval failure* or *cue-dependent forgetting*. That is, a memory isn't retrieved because an appropriate *cue* (memory jog) present at encoding (e.g. physical context, mood, emotional state) is missing at retrieval.

**Amnesia and LTM**

*Amnesia* is characterized by permanent or temporary damage to memory. Neurological amnesia's causes include stroke, severe head injury, encephalitis (brain inflammation; possibly due to viral infection), Korsakoff Syndrome (severe Vitamin B1 deficiency typically due to prolonged alcoholism), anoxia (lack of oxygen to the brain) and ageing effects (e.g. Alzheimer's Disease). In *retrograde amnesia*, old memories from before the brain damage are lost, whilst with *anterograde amnesia*, new memories can't be formed after the brain damage.

In the 1950s, Henry Molaison underwent major brain surgery which resulted in anterograde amnesia. He could remember events before his operation but could not establish new episodic or new semantic memories. Interestingly though, Mr Molaison was able to acquire implicit memories such as the ability to draw an image whilst looking at its reflection in a mirror. Clive Wearing, however, contracted a viral infection that led to encephalitis. Since this illness, he has been unable to create new memories (anterograde amnesia) and recalls little of his past (retrograde amnesia). Mr Wearing repeatedly believes that he has just recovered his consciousness because his memory lasts only seconds.

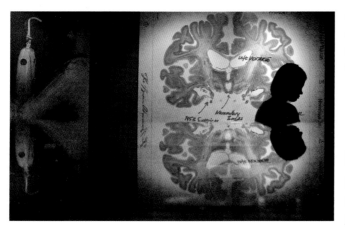

*An image of HM's (Henry Molaison's) brain. HM could not develop new episodic or new semantic memories.*

## Perception

### SENSATION AND PERCEPTION

*Perception* derives from sensation but not every *sensation* produces perception. Sensation results from specialized *neurons* (nerve cells) responding to sensory information in the environment and is physiological. Perception is instead psychological: it involves adding meaning to sensations through information selection, organization and interpretation. Perception can result from *bottom-up* or *top-down processing*.

### VISUAL PERCEPTION: SEEING AND COLOUR VISION DEFICIENCY

When we see, light waves hit edges, surfaces and textures and pass through the eye's transparent *cornea* which focuses the waves. Light next goes through the *pupil;* muscles connected to the *iris* control its size, constricting it when light is bright to limit how much light enters the eye and expanding the pupil to increase light to the eye when light is low. The *lens* focuses light onto a part of the *retina* (the eye's light sensitive lining) called the *fovea*. The fovea contains light-detector cells called *cones* which function best in bright light, are sensitive to detail and are also involved in colour perception. Another type of cell, *rods*, are found in the rest of the retina; they help us see in low light conditions and to perceive movement in peripheral vision. The *optic nerve* takes retinal information to the brain.

**TOP-DOWN PROCESSING**
Knowledge, experience, expectations used to interpret incoming information and create perception.

**PERCEPTION**

**BOTTOM-UP PROCESSING**
Sensory information from the environment used to build perception.

*Top-Down versus Bottom-Up Processing.*

Colour is detected firstly at the retina which has three different types of cone: red, green and blue. That is, one kind of cone responds to red's light wavelength, another to green's and the third to blue's light wavelength. All colours can be detected by combining the activity of these cones. (This is the *trichromatic theory* of colour vision). After the retina, cells respond differently, working in opponent pairs: yellow-blue, red-green and black-white. This means that cells which become active to yellow also become inactive to blue and vice versa, with a similar pattern occurring across red-green and black-white. This is called the *opponent process theory*.

Colour vision deficiency (colour blindness) is rarely characterized by a loss of all colour perception such that only shades of grey are experienced. When it occurs, there is a complete absence of cone cells meaning red, green and blue light wavelengths cannot be detected. Red/green is the most common colour deficiency and difficulties arise with any colour which has a red or green element; e.g. blue and purple may be confused because purple consists of red and blue. Less commonly, issues arise with shades relevant to blue. In both cases, colour perception is impaired due to one or more relevant cone types being absent or dysfunctional.

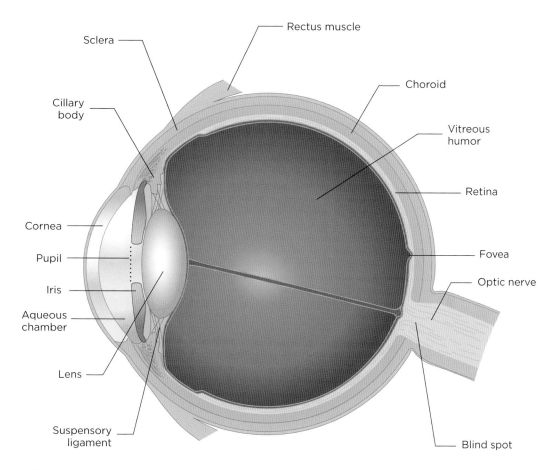

Sclera

Cillary body

Cornea

Pupil

Iris

Aqueous chamber

Lens

Suspensory ligament

Rectus muscle

Choroid

Vitreous humor

Retina

Fovea

Optic nerve

Blind spot

*The anatomy of the eye.*

## VISUAL PERCEPTION: DEPTH CUES, CONSTANCIES AND VISUAL ILLUSIONS

Depth/distance can be detected using information from both eyes (*binocular cues*) or from one eye (*monocular cues*). For example, *binocular disparity* refers to each eye having a slightly different view; (open and close each eye alternately to experience this). When objects are near, the disparity is larger than when they are far away and this provides distance/depth information.

Monocular clues include *occlusion* occurs when one object partly overlaps another and the overlapped object is perceived to be more distant. *Perspective* is derived from parallel lines such as railway tracks which converge in the distance: the tracks' horizontal separation is larger

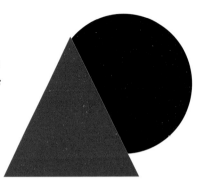

*The red triangle occludes, or overlaps the black circle and this information is used to determine that the circle is further away than the triangle.*

near to the viewer than farther away. *Texture gradient* refers to the way in which texture detail is greater close to the viewer but diminishes with distance such that far away, individual pebbles, for example, 'disappear' and become smooth. *Relative brightness* signals depth because nearer objects appear brighter than further ones. *Motion parallax* is another instance of a monocular cue. When looking out of a car window as the vehicle goes down a motorway, near objects appear to move quickly but those further away appear stationary or to move very slowly. Your movement produces position changes and the speed at which objects cross the retinas is used to judge distance.

Perceptual constancies such as size and shape are also used in visual perception. If a double-decker bus passes close to you and when you look at it again it is far down the road, its retinal image will alter from large to small. However, your perception is not one of a shrunken bus due to *size constancy*: the perceptual system allows for increased distance so that perceived and actual size remain constant. A closed door is rectangular but when opened its projected shape varies but the perceptual system employs *shape constancy* and ensures we still perceive a constant shape.

*Although the projected shape of this door changes as it moves from being closed to open, shape constancy ensures that we perceive the door as having a constant shape.*

*Imagine that these three identical buses are one and the same. When the bus is far away its retinal image size is small but increases in size as the bus gets nearer. However, we do not perceive the bus as having grown larger; size constancy ensures we perceive the bus as having a consistent size.*

*Relative brightness: in this image there are two sets of hills, ones on the skyline that are dark and others in the mid-ground which are brighter. The difference in brightness between the two sets of hills signals depth – the brighter hills are nearer.*

*Texture gradient: here, the extent of the pebbles' textural detail signals depth. Those pebbles near to the viewer have the greatest texture but this detail diminishes the further away the pebbles are from the viewer.*

*Perspective: the horizontal width of these railway lines is larger nearer to the viewer and decreases as the lines get further away. The information that the lines are converging signals that this point is further away.*

A visual illusion occurs when perception of a stimulus doesn't match its physical characteristics and Richard Gregory proposed four types of perceptual illusion. *Ambiguous figure* illusions offer two potential interpretations; each is equally plausible and thus we 'switch' between the two, e.g. Edwin Boring's old/young woman illusion.

*Distortions* or *geometrical* illusions involve perceptions distorted in terms of, for example, length, size, position.

The vertical-horizontal illusion's lines are the same length, yet the vertical line is perceived as longer due to it bisecting the horizontal line. This may be contributed to by environmental factors since the illusion is stronger for those living in cultures with urban (angular) environments than those in rural cultures. In the Ponzo illusion the upper and lower lines produce the same retinal image sizes but the converging lines are interpreted as linear perspective signalling

*In this image we switch between perceiving a young woman and an old woman. If you are struggling to see the two, they are both wearing the same coat. The white, pointed area between the coat's lapels is the old woman's chin and the horizontal line above this, her mouth; the other white, pointed area above the mouth, to the left, is her nose and her eye nearest to us is found just beneath the curly hair. In the young woman, the area between the lapels is her neck and the horizontal line a necklace; the pointed area to the left is her jaw; she is facing away, towards the wall. The old woman's eye is the young woman's ear.*

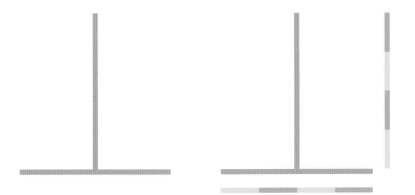

*Looking at the stimulus on the left, the vertical line is perceived as longer than the horizontal line. Yet, as illustrated by the stimulus on the right, they are both the same size*

 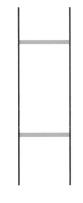

*As the stimulus on the right illustrates, the blue horizontal lines in the left stimulus both produce the same sized retinal image. The convergence of the railway lines causes the upper line to be perceived as being longer.*

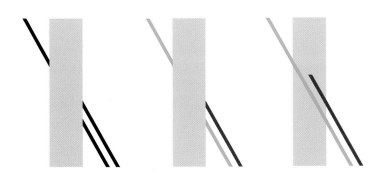

*In the first stimulus, a grey rectangle obscures a black line. It appears as though the segment on the left is continued by the uppermost of the two segments to the right of the rectangle. Similarly, in the second stimulus, the red line appears to be the continuation of the blue line on the other side of the rectangle. However, as can be seen in the final image, the blue sections either side of the rectangle are actually continuations of the same line.*

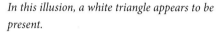

*In this illusion, a white triangle appears to be present.*

*If you look carefully, despite appearing to be a solid object, the triangle cannot exist as such.*

distance. The only way a further object can cast the same sized retinal image as a nearer object is if it is bigger, hence the upper horizontal line's size is perceived as greater. In the Poggendorff illusion, a line is obscured by a rectangle. A segment of this line protrudes from the left of the rectangle and two segments protrude from the right. Although it appears as if the uppermost of these right-side segments forms the line, this is an illusion. This percept is related to the acute angles between the lines and the rectangle being expanded by the viewer.

Fictions occur when a shape is perceived although it isn't present, whilst *paradoxical figures*, or *impossible objects* cannot exist in reality. In Kanizsa's triangle, an illusory white triangle appears present. The wedges cut from the three solid circles create an illusory contour and this, coupled with their spatial positions and those of the 'V' elements, create an uppermost white triangle. Penrose's triangle is paradoxical because the tribar is an impossible solid object despite its existence in a perspective drawing.

## AUDITORY PERCEPTION: HEARING

Hearing involves the outer, middle and inner parts of the ear. When we hear, the *pinna* (the visible part on the side of the head) helps direct sound waves along the *auditory canal* to the *tympanic membrane* (ear drum) making it vibrate. This vibration causes changes in the middle ear: movement occurs in three extremely small bones known as the ossicles: the *malleus* (hammer), *incus* (anvil) and *stapes* (stirrup). The inner ear is affected because the ossicles' movement causes the stapes to press on the *oval window* belonging to the fluid-filled *cochlea*. The oval window is a thin, flexible membrane, which, when pressed by the stapes, causes the cochlea's fluid to move which produces vibrations in the *basilar membrane*. These vibrations cause changes in the basilar membrane's *hair cells* (auditory sensory receptor cells) which send information along the *auditory nerve* to the brain.

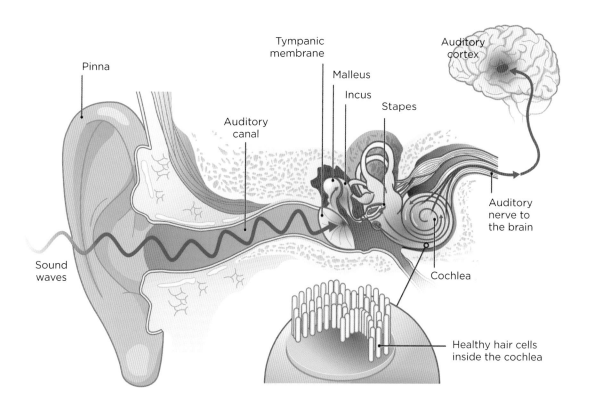

**AUDITORY PERCEPTION: LOCALIZING SOUND AND PERCEIVING PITCH**

Sound can be localized using information from one or both ears (*monaural cues* and *binaural cues* respectively). Monaural cues allow us to tell whether sound is coming from in front, behind, above or below. They are created due to the ear pinnae's folds and bulges filtering sound waves differently according to a sound's origin and these differences being employed by the auditory system to localize sound.

Binaural cues operate horizontally. The *interaural level difference* cue refers to the ear nearest to the sound receiving stronger vibration due to any sound being more intense in the nearer rather than the farther ear. The *interaural time difference* cue relates to the brief time difference between the arrival of a sound at the ears. The ear nearest to the sound receives it marginally sooner than the further ear and this difference is then used by the brain to determine where the sound is localized.

High pitched sounds are associated with high frequency sound waves whilst low pitched sounds are associated with low frequency sound waves. A wave's frequency is determined by how many waves pass a specified point in a given time, with long waves generating low frequencies and short waves high frequencies. According to the *temporal theory*, a sound wave's frequency influences the timing of a hair cell's activation and this yields pitch perception. The *place theory*, however, maintains that areas of the basilar membrane respond differently according to sound wave frequency; i.e. its base vibrates more to high frequencies, whilst its tip vibrates more to low frequencies and these differences produce pitch perception.

## Language

### WHAT IS LANGUAGE?

Language = words + rules (these govern how words must be used to express meaning).

All languages have their own *lexicon*, or dictionary. Each word is constructed from *phonemes* (i.e. the individual sounds that exist within a particular language), which, when

---

### EXAMPLES OF LANGUAGE COMPONENTS

**Phonemes**

Say the following English words: *bath, think, that* and *either*. The letters '*th*' are the same in each but the phoneme relevant to '*th*' for ba*th*/*th*ink is different for *that*/*ei*ther. Now say *eight* and *ate*. The words may be different but their two phonemes are not. Sometimes meaning is altered by one phoneme alone, e.g. dine versus fine.

---

**Morphemes**

| | |
|---|---|
| one morpheme | consume |
| two morphemes | consume + able |
| three morphemes | un + consume + able |

Other morphemes include: pre-, dis-, anti-, -ly, -er, -ist and the past tense -ed and plural -s.

---

**Semantics**

Words have meaningful properties or features, e.g.

| | |
|---|---|
| baby | human, young |
| hen | animal, not human, female, not young |

---

combined, construct *morphemes,* or the smallest, meaningful units of a language. *Grammar* refers to the rules of meaningful word use and it consists of *semantics* (associating meaning with morphemes and words) plus *syntax* (the rules of sentence formation and structure).

## SPEECH PRODUCTION

Speech production is extremely complex but a flavour of how it operates is given below using the kind of mistakes you may have made yourself. That is, a selection of *slips of the tongue,* or speech errors.

Whatever we wish to say starts as a concept to be expressed. Since both word and root morpheme exchanges (Examples 1 and 4) frequently occur within, rather than between clauses, this indicates that speech uses clauses as planning units. Given that intended words can be replaced by ones which share a similar concept ('time' in Example 2a) or ones which are phonemically similar (Example 2b), the lexicon must store words according to both meaning and sound. *Spoonerisms* are named after the Reverend W. Spooner (Example 3 is attributed to him) and involve the reversal of either two consonant phonemes or two vowel phonemes. This kind of slip shows speech planning occurs before articulation and that words are not planned phoneme-by-phoneme. Before being spoken, 'missed' and 'history' must both have existed as collections of phonemes otherwise the /h/ and /m/ sounds could not have exchanged. In Example 4, the root morphemes 'arm' and 'shirt' exchanged, whilst the plural morpheme (or inflection) 's' kept its position but changed its sound (say the intended expression and the slip out loud to hear the difference). This tells us something about the order of speech planning because the alteration in the inflection's sound to fit the morpheme-error indicates it must have been attached after root

| EXAMPLES OF SLIPS OF THE TONGUE | | |
|---|---|---|
| **Intended to Say** | **Slip** | **Type of Error** |
| 1. A piece of pie | A pie of piece | Word exchange |
| 2a. She arrived too late | She arrived too early | Word replacement (meaning) |
| 2b. Don't take that attitude | Don't take that altitude | Word replacement (sound) |
| 3. You have missed all my history lectures | You have hissed all my mystery lectures | Spoonerism (phoneme exchange) |
| 4. The arms of the shirt | The shirts of the arm | Root morpheme exchange |

morphemes exchanged. Ultimately, speech planning can be summarized thus:
semantics – syntax (grammar, word order) – morphemes (vocabulary) – phonology.

## READING

As you are reading this book, it can be assumed you are a skilled reader of English and reading familiar words has become automatic. Reading familiar words automatically is demonstrated by the Stroop Effect. Participants take longer with the incongruent list compared with the congruent one. They cannot prevent themselves automatically reading the words and this interferes with colour naming in the incongruent stimuli.

When reading, it might be assumed that the eyes track smoothly left to right but they do not. Instead, they make rapid jerks (*saccades*) and *fixations*. Saccades' speed is 20–30ms, covering eight letters/spaces; the majority are forwards but others are backwards (*regressions*) to permit re-fixation. Information is taken in during fixations (200–250ms); 80 per cent of which are on content words (nouns, verbs) and 20 per cent on function words (e.g. 'the'). Up to 15 letters are fixated to the right and 3–4 to the left before each saccade. Fixations are required because reading needs detailed vision; information must be sent to where it can be best detected and this is at the fovea due to its density of cone cells.

### EXAMPLES OF STIMULI THAT COULD BE USED TO DEMONSTRATE THE STROOP EFFECT

With each list, the participant has to name the ink colour and is timed. In a full experiment the lists would be longer and more colours might be used. To prevent order effects, (such as practice or fatigue), all participants would not complete the different types of stimulus lists in exactly the same order. Instead, presentation order would be balanced across the participants.

| Control | Congruent | Incongruent |
|---------|-----------|-------------|
| ■ | BLUE | PURPLE |
| ■ | RED | BROWN |
| ■ | GREEN | ORANGE |
| ■ | PURPLE | GREEN |
| ■ | BROWN | BLUE |
| ■ | ORANGE | RED |

## SUMMARY

- Memory involves encoding, storage and retrieval (recognition, recall).

- Information detected by the senses is held in the sensory store.

- Short-term memory (STM) and long-term memory (LTM) can be damaged separately; they differ in terms of capacity, duration and preferred form of encoding.

- Working memory consists of the central executive, phonological loop, visuospatial sketchpad and episodic buffer.

- LTM consists of declarative and nondeclarative memories.

- Forgetting can occur through displacement (STM) and interference, retrieval failure (LTM).

- Retrograde and anterograde amnesia are associated with LTM.

- Perception involves adding meaning to sensation.

- Seeing involves the eye's pupil, iris, lens, fovea, cone cells and rod cells.

- Depth/distance are detected via monocular and binocular depth cues.

- Visual illusions include ambiguous figures, distortions/geometrical illusions, fictions and paradoxical figures/impossible objects.

- Hearing involves the outer, middle and inner parts of the ear.

- Sound is localized using monoaural and binaural cues.

- Pitch detection has been accounted for using temporal theory and place theory.

- Language consists of words and rules.

- All languages have a lexicon, phonemes, morphemes and grammar.

- Slips of the tongue provide information on how we produce speech.

- Reading familiar words is automatic; reading occurs using saccades, fixations and regressions.

# NEUROPSYCHOLOGY

**Neuropsychology can be thought of as the point where psychology and neurology meet. That is, the study of mind and behaviour meets the study of the nervous system and its disorders: the nervous system being the means by which information is processed and transferred by the body's nerve cells.**

To help understand how neuropsychology works, please do the following:
- Tap your left foot three times.
- Draw a circle with a finger of your right hand.

You may have found the tasks above very easy, however they are more complicated than you might think. To read requires using vision, language ability and memory. You've probably considered how big or small the circle should be and different kinds of movement are required for foot-tapping and circle-drawing. If we want to understand how functions such as vision, language, memory, movement, sensory stimulation, emotion, thinking and self-control work, we have to explore the relationship between mind, behaviour and the nervous system (part of which is the brain). This is what neuropsychology does. It puts us in a position not only to describe how a person is behaving but to explain why, and then ways can be found to help someone who has impaired functioning such as memory or language problems.

Neuropsychological knowledge has often been drawn from individuals with brain injury:

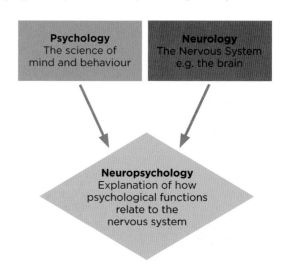

*Neuropsychology: a meeting point between psychology and neurology.*

their pre- and post-injury abilities being compared and linked to damaged brain areas. It is these kinds of studies that will be concentrated upon below, but it would be wrong to fail to point out that modern imaging techniques (discussed in the Introduction), along with electrical recording techniques have permitted the study of both injured and intact brains.

## A Brief History of Neuropsychology

Physiological psychology began with Franz Joseph Gall, who, in the early 19th century linked behaviour to mental functions located in particular brain regions. He assumed that development of a mental function would be reflected in brain development, which in turn, would be reflected in the skull. A highly developed mental function, Gall believed, would produce a raised area, or 'bump' on the skull, whilst an under-developed function would not do so. Gall's assistant, Johann Spurzheim, popularized the ideas and called them *phrenology*. However, the notion that bumps on the skull revealed brain size and associated mental function was incorrect and phrenology was later discredited by Pierre Flourens.

By 1836, Marc Dax had associated language with the left half of the brain. Later, in the same century, Paul Broca linked language to a frontal region in the left half of the brain, whilst Carl Wernicke discovered there was more than one language area and that brain regions are connected. Additionally, John Hughlings Jackson concluded part of the brain controlled muscle movement and the brain was organized vertically, with low, middle and high level centres.

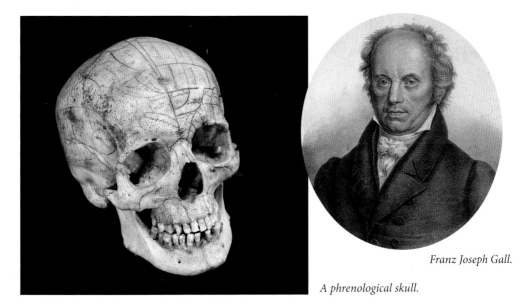

*Franz Joseph Gall.*

*A phrenological skull.*

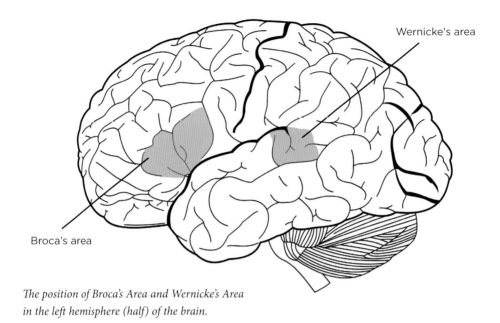

Wernicke's area

Broca's area

*The position of Broca's Area and Wernicke's Area*
*in the left hemisphere (half) of the brain.*

The 20th century saw Korbinian Brodmann map the cell architecture of the brain and Wilder Penfield map the functions of regions of the brain.

However, it is Donald Hebb who is often considered to be a principal founder of neuropsychology because it is he who merged psychology with neuroscience, largely through his 1949 work, *The Organization of Behaviour: A Neuropsychological Theory*. From the late 1950s Roger Sperry was exploring what occurred to behavioural abilities when the two halves of the brain were disconnected. In the 1960s and 1970s, Norman Geschwind explored how nerve damage associated with the brain's halves affected behaviour, along with investigating the different functions of the two halves.

Brenda Milner has made substantial contributions to neuropsychology. A well-known example is her research, in association with William B. Scoville, on the relation between memory loss and the brain (Henry Molaison – Patient HM, 1957). However, in a very long career, she has also contributed to our understanding of the brain's frontal region plus the specialization of, and interaction between, the halves of the brain.

As other patients are referred to below, it is sensible to explain at this point why some individuals are referred to by their name, whilst others are called 'Patient…', both of which we see in the case of Henry Molaison – Patient HM. It is customary to preserve a patient's anonymity by using initials and this is how Mr Molaison was identified for many years: only in 2008, after HM had died was his full name revealed. In this chapter, you will find that those people who are referred to by their full names provide historic rather than recent information.

## The Nervous System

To reiterate, the nervous system consists of the body's nerve cells and it subdivides into the *central nervous system* (CNS) and *peripheral nervous system* (PNS).

The CNS comprises the *brain* and *spinal cord*. The brain receives messages from the senses and other areas of the body and it sends messages back to the body. It controls movements carried out consciously (e.g. tapping your foot, waving to a friend); processes information that has been received from the senses and controls memory, language, thinking etc.

At the bottom of the brain is the brain stem which connects to the spinal cord. The brain stem regulates many essential processes such as breathing, heartbeat and swallowing.

The spinal cord runs down the back, ending at a point just under the ribs. It carries messages from and to the brain and also controls automatic processes (*reflexes*), such as the knee-jerk reflex. The spinal cord is organized in segments. Each segment connects – via the peripheral

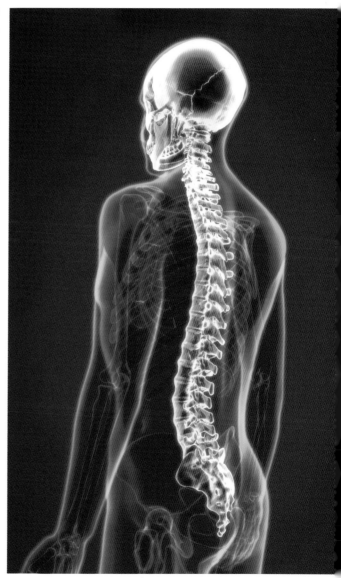

*The brain and spinal cord.*

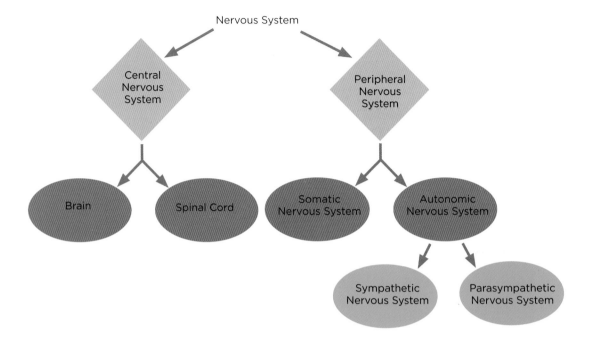

nervous system – to a particular part of the body. Damage to the spinal cord causes paralysis; the higher the damage, the greater the paralysis as all lower segments cannot now communicate with the brain.

The peripheral nervous system comprises nerves which connect the CNS to muscles, sense organs and glands on the body's periphery. The peripheral nervous system has two parts: the *somatic nervous system* and the *autonomic nervous system*.

The somatic nervous system sends information to and from the CNS. *Sensory* information (i.e. from the senses) is sent to the CNS whilst *motor* information is sent from the CNS with instructions for the skeletal muscles. This allows us to move consciously, or voluntarily. If nerve cells in the sensory route are damaged, sensation can be lost in the body part connected to those cells. Similarly, motor nerve cell damage can lead to paralysis of the body part connected to those cells.

The autonomic nervous system controls those bodily processes that do not need conscious effort and are typically out of voluntary control. It connects the CNS to glands and 'smooth' muscles thereby influencing the internal organs. For example, the autonomic system regulates heartbeat, breathing, digestion and urination.

The autonomic nervous system divides into two branches: the *sympathetic* and *parasympathetic* nervous systems. The sympathetic system prepares the body for stress-related behaviour and expending energy. The parasympathetic system restores the body to its usual, customary state where bodily energy is conserved. Together, the sympathetic and parasympathetic systems keep our bodily processes in equilibrium. For example, if we find ourselves in a threatening or stressful physical or psychological situation, the sympathetic system activates so we have sufficient resources to deal with the threat (e.g. energy, strength, speed). This is an acute (i.e. severe but of short duration) stress response. Once the threat has gone, the parasympathetic system dampens down bodily activation to usual levels.

The autonomic system's action is valuable when faced with a 'one-off' emergency like those our early ancestors might have faced, such as an animal attack. However, modern life can produce psychologically stressful situations which recur. For instance, a stressful job may repeatedly produce circumstances where stress is severe and persistent rather than short and this can lead to illness.

| EXAMPLES OF BODILY CHANGES BROUGHT ABOUT BY THE SYMPATHETIC AND PARASYMPATHETIC NERVOUS SYSTEMS IN RESPONSE TO STRESS ||
|---|---|
| **Sympathetic** | **Parasympathetic** |
| Eye pupil dilates | Eye pupil constricts |
| Breathing increases | Breathing decreases |
| Heart rate increases | Heart rate decreases |
| Digestion slows/stops | Digestion increases |

## The Brain

If you look at a brain from directly above it resembles a walnut half. The outer surface of the brain has ridges (*gyri*) and grooves (*sulci*) and is called the *cerebral cortex*. It consists of grey matter.

Along the brain's midline is a deep groove (the *longitudinal fissure*) which separates the two halves of the brain: the *left* and *right* *hemispheres*. Each hemisphere has four lobes: the *frontal*, *parietal*, *occipital* and *temporal*

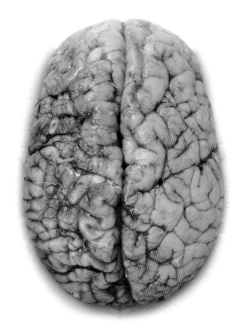

*The brain from above.*

## NEURONS, GREY AND WHITE MATTER

Nerve cells (*neurons*) consist of a *cell body* and a tail (*axon*). Cell bodies (*soma*) look light grey, and because the cortex consists of cell bodies, it is grey matter. The axon which tails-away from a cell body is sheathed in a fatty substance, *myelin*, which is whitish. Hence, white matter is found beneath the brain's grey matter. Reduction in grey/white matter impacts mental abilities such as memory, reasoning and language.

Neurons carry messages which travel away from the cell body along the axon. Messages travel as an electrical signal with the axon conducting that signal. The axon's end has multiple divisions and at the end of each of these is a *terminal button*. The multiple divisions mean an axon has the opportunity to communicate with a number of other cells rather than just one.

To transfer a message from one cell to another, the communication has to cross from a terminal button to a close-by *dendrite* on the other cell. Dendrites are little branches which extend from a neuron's cell body. When a terminal button is located close-by a dendrite, the location is known as a *synapse*. There is a tiny gap between the terminal button and dendrite (the *synaptic cleft*) and for a message to transfer across the gap, it has to become chemical. Once the chemical message is received by the dendrite, the communication again becomes electrical.

The chemicals which travel across the synaptic cleft are called *neurotransmitters*. Low levels of the neurotransmitter *dopamine* are linked to

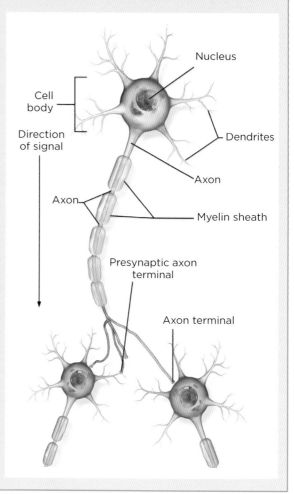

*Parkinson's Disease,* whilst high levels have been linked to *schizophrenia*. Another neurotransmitter, *serotonin*, has been linked to *depression*. The neurotransmitter *glutamate* is associated with memory and learning.

Sensory neurons communicate incoming messages concerning external stimuli (smell, taste, light, sound, temperature, pressure information). Motor neurons communicate outgoing messages to the muscles about what sort of behaviour or movement should be made. Interneurons integrate sensory information and behaviour.

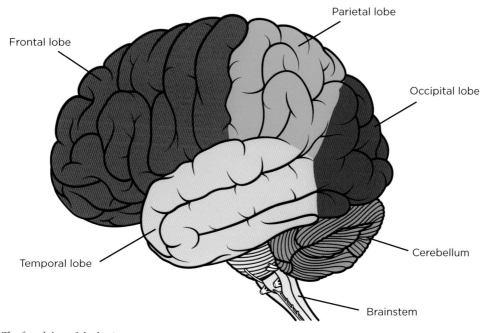

*The four lobes of the brain*

lobes. Different functions such as language, reasoning, movement, sensation from bodily areas and vision are associated with different lobes.

Remember tapping your left foot and drawing a circle with your right finger? When you performed these actions, you did so by moving muscles. You probably also felt a firm sensation in your foot too. Once the command had been given to move your muscles, the *primary motor cortex/area* was responsible for sending information to the relevant muscles to perform the desired movements. The *primary motor cortex* in your right hemisphere's frontal lobe moved your left foot and the *primary motor cortex* in your left hemisphere's frontal lobe moved the finger in your right hand. Information about the sensation in your left foot travelled to your right hemisphere's *primary somatosensory cortex/area* in the parietal lobe. Similarly, any sensation in your right finger would have travelled to your left hemisphere's *primary somatosensory cortex*, again in the parietal lobe. The somatosensory cortex receives information about sensations from the body such as touch, temperature, pressure, pain and taste.

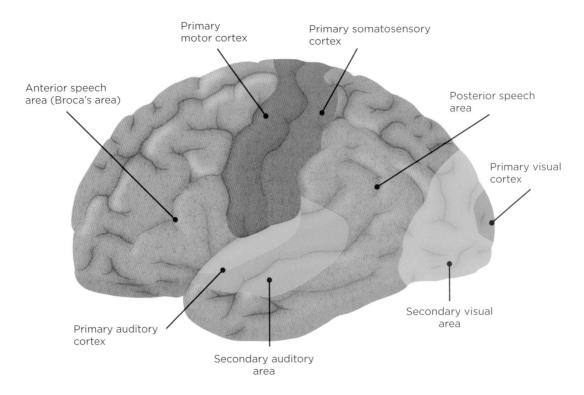

*Areas of the brain including the primary motor cortex, primary somatosensory cortex, primary visual cortex and the primary auditory cortex.'*

This crossing over between one side of the body and the opposite hemisphere is called *contralateral* organization (see box). Contralateral organization means that if a hemisphere's primary motor cortex is damaged, this will result in a paralysis in an area or areas on the opposite side of the body, as can be observed in a stroke, for example. Similarly, damage to a hemisphere's

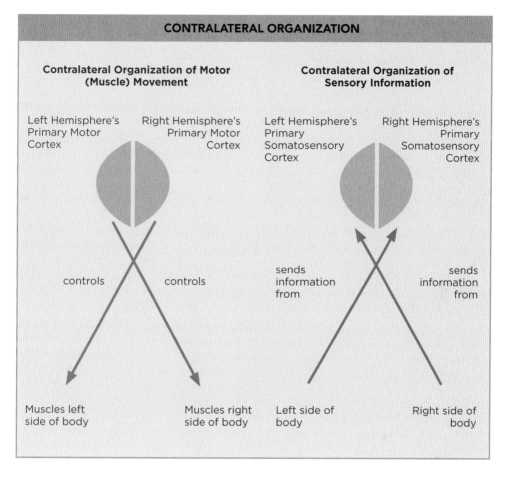

**CONTRALATERAL ORGANIZATION**

**Contralateral Organization of Motor (Muscle) Movement**

Left Hemisphere's Primary Motor Cortex

Right Hemisphere's Primary Motor Cortex

controls

controls

Muscles left side of body

Muscles right side of body

**Contralateral Organization of Sensory Information**

Left Hemisphere's Primary Somatosensory Cortex

Right Hemisphere's Primary Somatosensory Cortex

sends information from

sends information from

Left side of body

Right side of body

primary somatosensory cortex can lead to a loss of sensation in a body part or parts on the opposite side of the body.

Thanks to neurosurgeon Wilder Penfield, we know that the primary motor and somatosensory cortices have particular topographies related to the body parts. They appear as if a *homunculus* (or little man) is draped along each cortex. Notice that different parts of each homunculus are dedicated to different bodily regions. Notice too, that lower body parts appear towards the top and higher body parts towards the bottom. In the primary motor cortex, those body parts requiring finer control have more cortex devoted to them: e.g. we need more refined movement in our hands and lips than in our elbows. In the somatosensory cortex, those body parts with greater sensitivity have more dedicated cortex: compared again with the elbow, the upper and lower lips have more cortex, for instance.

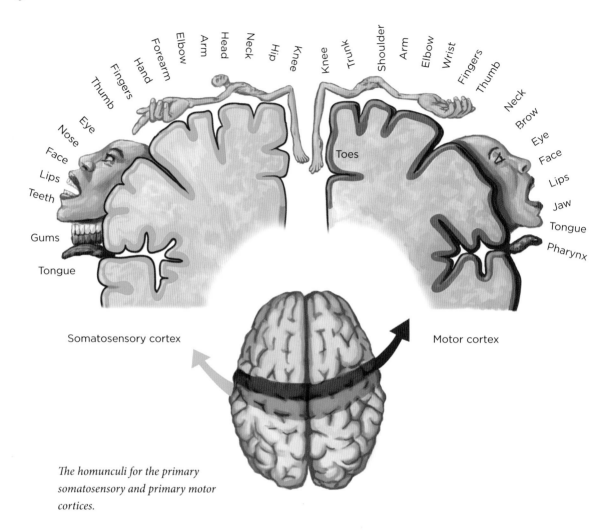

*The homunculi for the primary somatosensory and primary motor cortices.*

Now, please look directly ahead of you. As you keep looking straight ahead you will be aware of detecting information to the left of your fixation point and information to the right of your fixation point. The box above shows how that visual information travels to the *primary visual cortex* found in the hemispheres' occipital lobes.

Note that information transfers from the visual fields to the hemispheres contralaterally. That is, the left visual field maps to your right hemisphere and the right visual field maps to your left hemisphere.

Colour, shape, size and movement information are processed in the primary visual cortex. This isn't the only area involved in visual processing; an estimated 30 other brain areas are

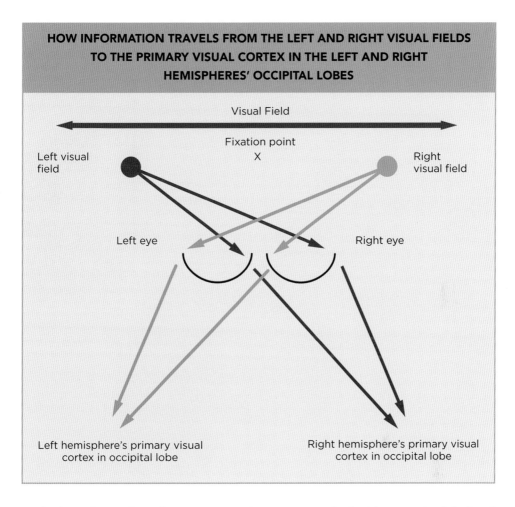

## HOW INFORMATION TRAVELS FROM THE LEFT AND RIGHT VISUAL FIELDS TO THE PRIMARY VISUAL CORTEX IN THE LEFT AND RIGHT HEMISPHERES' OCCIPITAL LOBES

Visual Field

Fixation point
X

Left visual field

Right visual field

Left eye

Right eye

Left hemisphere's primary visual cortex in occipital lobe

Right hemisphere's primary visual cortex in occipital lobe

involved too. Routes from the primary visual cortex are involved with processing 'what' and 'where/how' information. The 'what' route travels to the temporal lobe and is so-called due to its role in processing objects. Typically, it leads to conscious awareness of the visual environment. The 'where/how' route travels to the parietal lobe and processes movement information. It is used to visually guide action and grasp objects and isn't often associated with conscious awareness.

Damage to the primary visual cortex can lead to blind areas in the visual field. If the damage is in one hemisphere, there will be a problem with the relevant visual field in both eyes. For example, if the right hemisphere's primary visual cortex is damaged, the right and left eyes will both have a left visual field defect. As a result, objects to the left are difficult to see without moving the eyes. How much vision is lost depends on how much cortex is damaged.

## BLINDSIGHT AND ANTON SYNDROME

**Blindsight** – Larry Weiskrantz worked with Patient DB who had undergone necessary surgery to his right primary visual cortex. The operation resulted in both of DB's eyes being unable to see in their left visual field: when shown a spot of light in this part of space, DB reported seeing nothing. Nevertheless, despite his left visual field blindness, he could point accurately to objects presented in this visual field. When a stick was presented, although he could not see it, he was extremely good at identifying whether it was horizontal/vertical. DB also reported that now and again he had a feeling that an object was smooth/jagged or that it was moving towards or away from him.

DB's condition was called 'blindsight'. The blindness came from damage to his primary visual cortex, part of the route to vision which allows us to be consciously aware that we are seeing an object. His 'sight' came from another, intact, visual pathway which transmits sufficient visual information to guide actions unconsciously. (This involves transmission to the *superior colliculus* and onwards to other regions).

**Anton Syndrome** – Blindness resulting from damage to the primary visual cortex in both occipital lobes is associated with Anton Syndrome. Anton Syndrome is characterized by *visual anosognosia*; that is, the individual denies being blind despite clearly being so. The denial is accompanied by *confabulation* (making-up/filling-in what's missing) and reliance on being able to describe the surroundings. A person with Anton Syndrome might walk into objects, try to walk through a closed door or wall, or describe elements in their surroundings/people who aren't present. Even though such behaviour provides good evidence of blindness, the individual will still not accept s/he is blind.

Hearing involves various brain areas including the *primary auditory cortex*. The primary auditory cortex is found in the temporal lobe of both hemispheres. Auditory information's route from an ear to the primary auditory cortex is predominantly contralateral but some information also travels to the cortex on the same side as the ear (the *ipsilateral pathway*). This arrangement helps the brain compute where a sound is coming from and interpret its quality. Different pitches of sound are detected due to the front region of this cortex responding to high frequency sounds whilst the rear part responds to low frequency sounds. Damage to the primary auditory cortex can lead to impaired sound localization, impaired ability to discriminate the pitch of sounds and problems recognizing certain aspects of sound related to speech.

## THE FINDINGS OF PAUL BROCA AND CARL WERNICKE

In 1861 Louis Victor Leborgne was admitted for surgery at the Bicêtre Hospital, Paris due to a gangrenous leg. His surgeon, Paul Broca, was curious about his patient's speech because it almost exclusively consisted of the expression 'tan, tan' and hence, Monsieur Leborgne was known as 'Tan'.

Broca learned that at age 30, Leborgne had lost his power of speech. Ten years later, a right-sided paralysis presented in his right arm and then right leg. He understood what was said to him; his intelligence was unaffected; Leborgne could indicate the time and how long he'd remained at Bicêtre using left hand gestures. The problem wasn't associated with movements necessary for speech. Yet, his verbal responses remained 'tan, tan' accompanied by gestures, which, if not understood could be added to with the phrase 'sacré nom de Dieu' (literally, in God's sacred name).

*Paul Broca.*

After Leborgne's death, Broca conducted a post-mortem on his brain. The crucial abnormality discovered was an egg-sized depression caused by tissue loss in the left hemisphere's frontal lobe. Broca found other patients with the same kind of symptoms and damage as Leborgne and thus language production became associated with a region of the left frontal lobe: *Broca's Area*. Ultimately, the kind of verbal behaviour manifested by Tan and others became known as *Broca's aphasia*.

Later, in 1874, Carl Wernicke reported patients with different symptoms. Their speech was fluent, with good pronunciation but it was also meaningless and there was poor language understanding too. Post-mortem revealed damage to a region in the left hemisphere's temporal lobe which Wernicke connected to comprehension and meaningful speech content. The region is known as *Wernicke's Area* and the pattern of symptoms as *Wernicke's aphasia*.

In the time since Broca and Wernicke, their respective areas' exact locations have been reconsidered and understanding of aphasia has advanced.

*Carl Wernicke.*

Typically, language is associated with the left hemisphere, although this does not apply to all people. There is no single language centre, but historically, speech production was linked to *Broca's Area* and the meaningfulness of language to *Wernicke's Area*. Damage to the brain such as stroke or head injury can lead to *aphasia*, a condition in which spoken, written or other forms of language can no longer be expressed, understood and/or otherwise communicated as before the brain impairment.

---

### THREE EXAMPLES OF APHASIA

**Broca's Aphasia** – Typically, symptoms can include problems with fluency, articulation, word-finding, repetition and producing complex grammatical structures. Comprehension generally remains unaffected but can be problematic if the grammar is complex. Issues can arise in both speech and writing. Tan's type of symptoms are found in those individuals with a more severe form of Broca's aphasia.

**Wernicke's Aphasia** – Symptoms include speech that doesn't make a lot of sense but it is fluent, spoken at a normal rate and possesses intonation. There's usually a serious loss of language comprehension ability. Reading and writing are often severely affected. The Wernicke's aphasic may not be aware that they have a problem with language.

**Anomic Aphasia** – Language comprehension and fluent speech are present. Relevant nouns cannot be recalled and are substituted by more general terms, e.g. rather than identifying items, they could be referred to as 'stuff'.

---

The front part of the frontal lobe is called the prefrontal cortex. If damaged it can lead to a number of issues such as difficulties with problem-solving, making plans, taking decisions and behaving with a view to long-term objectives. Personality changes can be observed too, along with an inability to maintain self-control. A famous early example of this was reported by Dr John Harlow.

---

### PHINEAS GAGE

In 1848, Phineas Gage was a foreman for a railroad company in Vermont, USA. The job involved blasting rock: a hole was drilled, powder plus fuse inserted and sand poured. A metal tool called a tamping-iron was then employed to force the blasting components carefully into the hole. The tamping-iron was a rod 109cm (3ft 7in) long; it weighed a

---

little over 6kg (13lb) and tapered from over 2.5cm (1in) to about 6mm (¼in) in diameter.

One day, Gage accidentally used the rod before the sand had been poured; the rod caused a spark and an explosion resulted. This caused the tamping-iron to be propelled through Phineas's head. It first penetrated under his left cheekbone, then behind his left eye-socket and out of the top of his skull, landing a distance away.

Before the accident Phineas held a very responsible job. He was reliable, conscientious, efficient and energetic at fulfilling his plans. He used appropriate language and was well-regarded by both his employers and the men to whom he was foreman.

*Phineas Gage.*

After the accident Gage was unable to formulate and stick to his plans; he frequently changed his mind, became impatient if things did not go his way and used inappropriate language. The rod had damaged Phineas's frontal lobes: the part of his brain that controlled thinking, planning and choosing what might be the best course of action.

Yet, despite the extent of the injury, at some point after 1850 but before 1859, Phineas Gage once again was employed in a responsible job where organization and dealing with people was involved. Phineas, therefore, also provides an example of recovery potential after brain injury.

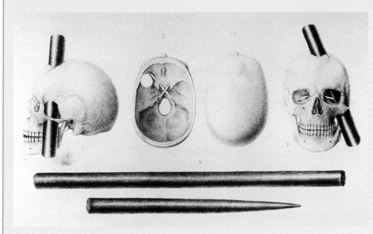

*These images show the the route of the tamping rod from entering through the left cheek bone to exiting at the top of the skull.*

Beneath the cerebral cortex, deep within the temporal lobe, is a structure called the *hippocampus* (Greek for 'seahorse' because it looks somewhat like this creature). There are actually two hippocampi, one in each hemisphere. The hippocampus is important in learning and memory. It is where memories are created and organized for later and where learning is consolidated to long-term memory. If damaged, problems with long-term memory follow, such as remembering new information. The hippocampus is also important for spatial memory which allows us to navigate familiar environments. Consequently, damage can lead to an inability to remember directions. It is the earliest and most severely affected region in Alzheimer's Disease which is associated with memory loss and disorientation.

Of course, many other brain regions have fundamental roles to our functioning as well.

*Location of the hippocampus.*

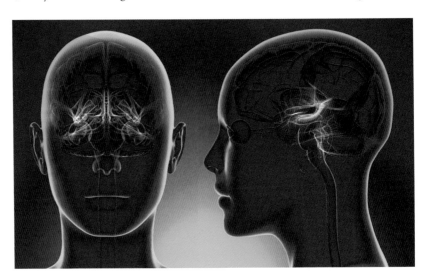

### TWO STUDIES ON THE HIPPOCAMPUS

**Brenda Milner's Investigation of Henry Molaison's Memory**

Henry Molaison (historically known as Patient HM), had experienced epileptic seizures since youth, but by age 27 they led to his being unable to lead a normal life. His neurosurgeon, William Scoville, offered experimental surgery, and with the agreement of HM and his family, damaged brain tissue was removed including hippocampal tissue. After the operation HM's memory was profoundly affected and this led to Brenda Milner's investigations. (Both HM and Milner have made major contributions to our understanding of memory.)

Amongst many findings, Milner discovered that the day's events were rapidly forgotten. For example, although HM could hold a conversation and accurately repeat a list of 6–7 digits he'd just been given, if his attention were taken elsewhere, he would forget that the conversation and memory test had taken place. Indeed, although he learned how to trace a star-shape whilst looking at it in a mirror and even maintained the memory of how to do this over a three-day period, he could not recall ever having completed the task. Furthermore, despite his success with mirror-drawing, HM's ability to learn new material was greatly restricted. Faces and designs could not be mentally repeated over and over like a list of numbers and they were forgotten in less than 60 seconds. Additionally, even if he had just been introduced to someone, HM forgot their name.

As a result of Milner's and others' research, the view is now that the hippocampus is involved in creating new memories. That is, it can take-in, index and temporarily store information which is then moved to long-term memory.

### Eleanor Maguire and Colleagues' Studies of London Taxi Drivers

To be licensed, London taxi drivers must learn the fastest routes between A-B within a 9.6km (6 mile) area. It requires knowing thousands of streets and hospital, tube station and hotel locations etc. In other words, a London cabbie must acquire very many spatial memories. Eleanor Maguire and colleagues discovered that compared with controls who didn't drive taxis, cabbies' hippocampi were bigger towards the back (they had more grey matter), and smaller towards the front. The rear part of the hippocampus is thought to store spatial memories: cabbies had to hold many of these and thus their posterior hippocampi expanded to accommodate the information. Interestingly, when reliance on spatial memory lessens because a cabbie has retired, the hippocampus changes: retired drivers were found to have less grey matter volume in the posterior hippocampus compared with older, full-time drivers.

*Eleanor Maguire.*

## EXAMPLES OF OTHER BRAIN REGIONS AND THEIR FUNCTIONS

**Forebrain**

| | |
|---|---|
| Thalamus | Apart from smell, all sense information travels to the thalamus and then is sent to other brain regions for processing. |
| Amygdala | Plays a role in experiencing emotion. Links emotion to memories. |
| Hypothalamus | Involved in maintaining a stable internal environment, e.g. blood pressure, temperature, hunger, thirst regulation. |

**Midbrain**

| | |
|---|---|
| Reticular Formation | Involved in regulating alertness/readiness, sleeping/waking bodily rhythm, motor activity. |
| Substantia Nigra<br>Ventral Tegmental Area | Involved in movement and production of neurotransmitter dopamine; damage to these areas is observed in Parkinson's Disease. |

**Hindbrain**

| | |
|---|---|
| Medulla | Controls autonomic nervous system processes; e.g. heart rate, breathing, blood pressure. |
| Pons | Involved in controlling sleep cycles, breathing, reflexes. |
| Cerebellum | Involved in movement, balance, coordination, posture, breathing and cardiac activity, for example. |

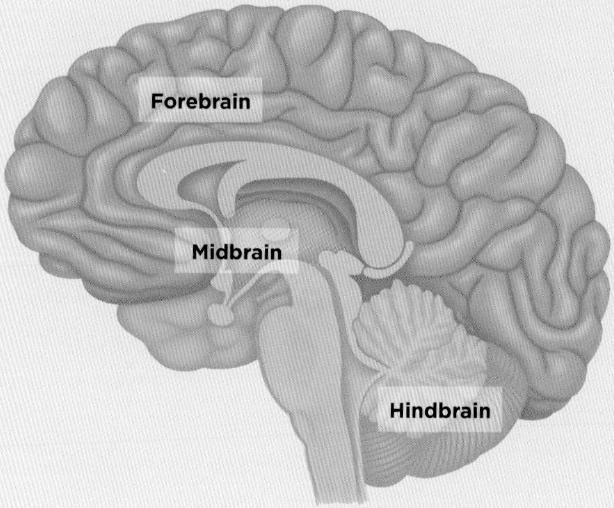

Forebrain

Midbrain

Hindbrain

## THE CONNECTED AND DIVIDED HEMISPHERES

The hemispheres are connected by fibres called the *cerebral commissures*; the main one of these being the *corpus callosum* which consists of approximately 250 million axons (different authors supply different figures). Consequently, without our being aware of it, the hemispheres rapidly share information and interact with each other.

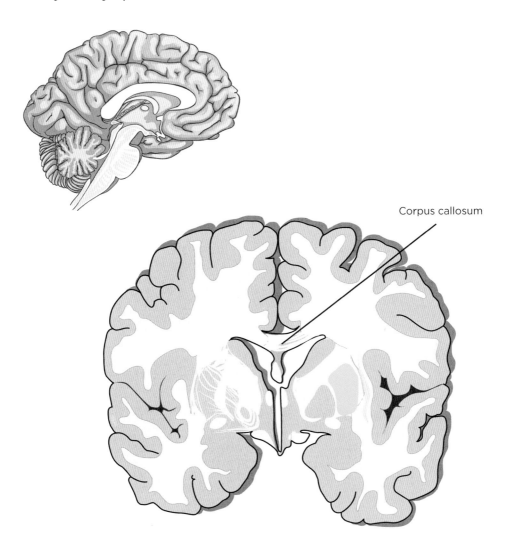

Corpus callosum

*The corpus callosum.*

However, interesting patterns of behaviour are observed when the hemispheres are disconnected. *Commissurotomy* is a treatment of last resort for very severe, life-threatening epilepsy and it involves surgically severing the corpus callosum. This helps control seizures by containing them within one hemisphere and thereby preventing the involvement of many brain circuits. The operation produces what is known as a 'split-brain'. The split doesn't cause any problems: normal eye movement ensures both hemispheres receive all visual information and behavioural issues can only be detected using a special method, devised by Michael Gazzaniga, called the divided-field technique. It uses the fact that the right visual field projects to the left hemisphere and the left visual field projects to the right hemisphere. Roger Sperry discovered that if stimuli are presented very briefly, to prevent eye movement, a stimulus can be projected to one hemisphere alone. Essentially, the participant sits in front of a screen, focuses on the fixation point and stimuli are flashed in the right/left visual fields. The participant can reach under the screen but cannot see their hand as they do this.

Patient NG was shown a picture of a spoon in the left visual field/right hemisphere. NG said she had seen nothing. The mostly nonverbal right hemisphere could not respond 'spoon' and the verbal left hemisphere had indeed seen nothing. However, when asked to use touch to select the appropriate object from a number of items behind the screen, NG's left hand/right hemisphere could hold up the spoon. (The left hand sent sensory information to the right hemisphere and the right hemisphere controlled the muscles of the left hand). When asked what it was, the verbal left hemisphere still didn't know and guessed 'pencil'.

*Roger Sperry.*

## FUNCTIONAL RECOVERY AFTER BRAIN TRAUMA

Earlier, we saw how, despite his extensive brain injury, Phineas Gage experienced some recovery. Phineas is not the only example of functional recovery after brain damage but the extent of recovery can vary *substantially* from one person to another.

Recovery takes place through *neuroplasticity*. You have already encountered neuroplasticity in the London taxi drivers discussed previously: their brains changed in response to environmental input. After damage, neuroplasticity helps a person to regain function and some examples of the ways in which this can be fostered in rehabilitation are given below.

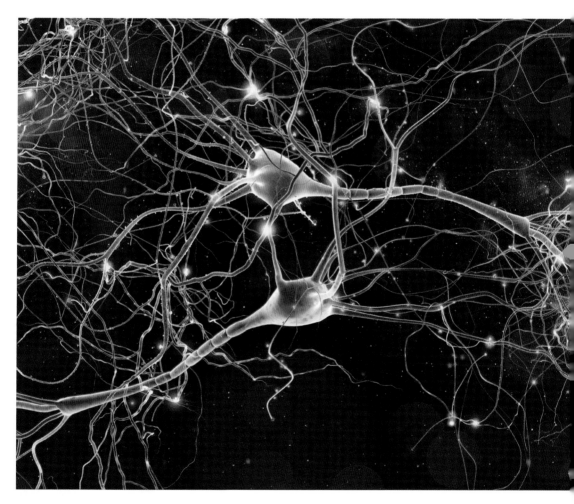

*Neuroplasticity allows the brain to change in response to its environment.*

New blood vessels can form from pre-existing ones (*angiogenesis*). This increases blood flow to damaged areas and thereby provides them with increased oxygen and glucose (for energy). Physical exercise encourages angiogenesis.

In some cases, if a neuron is damaged, other axons which are already connected to that neuron sprout extra connections (*axonal sprouting)* and increase the number of synapses for communication. Additionally, the number of dendrite spines (see box on page 36) can grow so more information can be acquired from other neurons (*dendritic arborization*). This form of brain rewiring also increases the number of synapses. When new synapses are formed through axonal sprouting and dendritic growth, this is known as *synaptogenesis*. Synaptogenesis, along with strengthening of existing synapses, can lead to rearrangement in the brain. For example, in the motor cortex, topographical changes may occur where an adjacent motor area compensates for the damaged one. Cognitive exercises and rehabilitation exercises designed to improve movements in affected body parts can both be used to rebuild bridges between disconnected neurons.

However, neuroplasticity can also lead to unwanted results such as seizure, chronic pain, learning and memory interference. Consequently, rehabilitation seeks to promote beneficial neural connections and to prevent undesirable ones.

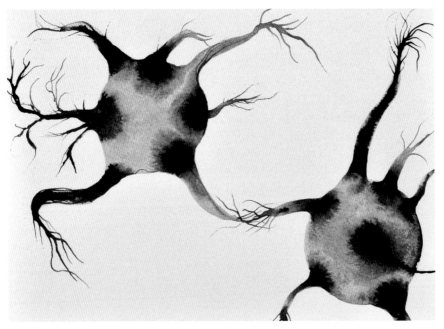

*Neurons may develop new connections in a process called 'axonal sprouting'.*

## SUMMARY

- Neuropsychology may be regarded as the point where psychology and neurology meet. It helps us explain why a person is behaving as they are and thus means to improve impaired functioning can be found.

- The nervous system consists of the central nervous system (brain and spinal cord) and peripheral nervous system (somatic and autonomic systems). The autonomic system subdivides into the sympathetic and parasympathetic systems.

- The brain has two hemispheres each with four lobes.

- The primary motor cortices are in the frontal lobes; the primary somatosensory cortices the parietal lobes; the primary visual cortices the occipital lobes and the primary auditory cortices the temporal lobes.

- Touch pain, taste, pressure and temperature information are sent contralaterally to the brain; the right and left visual fields also send information contralaterally.

- The brain controls the body's muscles contralaterally.

- Broca's Area (left frontal lobe) is connected to speech production and Wernicke's Area (left temporal lobe) to the meaningfulness of language.

- The prefrontal cortex is associated with executive functions.

- The hippocampus is associated with reading, indexing and consolidating memories for long-term memory.

- The hemispheres are constantly in touch with each other via the cerebral commissures, especially the corpus callosum. Severing the corpus callosum produces interesting behavioural patterns.

- Neuroplasticity permits the brain to recover functions; rehabilitation fosters beneficial new neural connections.

# CHAPTER 3

# DEVELOPMENTAL PSYCHOLOGY

Developmental psychology examines how humans change physically, mentally and socially across their lifespan. In the discussions below, although some consideration is given to adolescence and adulthood, greater focus has been placed on infancy and childhood because arguably, development is more obvious during these periods.

## A Brief History of Developmental Psychology

Early child developmental research exists from the 19th century in Charles Darwin's observations on his son and in Wilhelm Preyer's *The Mind of the Child*. In the 20th century, cognitive development was examined by figures such as Jean Piaget and Lev Vygotsky and is continued today by many others including Renée Baillargeon. Lawrence Kohlberg built upon the work of Piaget and explored moral development. Research into attachment was conducted by John Bowlby, Mary Ainsworth and Michael Rutter and racial consciousness research is found in the work of Mamie Phipps Clark and Kenneth Clark. Contributions to our understanding of language acquisition have been made by Patricia Kuhl. Psychosocial development across the lifespan was discussed by Erik Erikson and the number of investigations considering the different aspects of adult development in early, middle and late adulthood continue to expand.

## Perception

Although newborn babies have an immature visual system, their perceptual abilities and those of older infants (ages 0–2 years) are more competent than might be anticipated. As described in Chapter 1, adults possess *size* and *shape constancy* which allow for consistent perceptual experience of the world. That is, objects are appreciated as remaining the same in terms of size and shape despite their movement creating changes on the retina (the light sensitive part of the eye). Size and shape constancy are both present at birth. Research demonstrates that newborns base their responses to objects upon that object's real size and real shape despite shifts in viewing distance altering an object's retinal size and manipulating its orientation changing its shape.

Infants are also capable of detecting depth. In their famous study, Eleanor Gibson and Richard Walk created a *visual cliff*. This consisted of a glass-topped table with, on the shallow side, a check pattern a short drop from the glass, and on the deep side, the same pattern far beneath the glass. In the middle of the apparatus was a central platform. Infants ranging from 6–14 months were placed on the platform and were encouraged to one side or the other by their caregiver. All 27 infants crawled to the shallow side but only three went onto the deep side. Evidently, the infants had detected the difference in depth between the two sides.

Gibson and Walk considered depth perception and avoiding the brink as inborn abilities. Subsequently, other researchers proposed depth perception may be learned as a result of an infant being able to move by her/himself. Similarly, brink-avoidance was accounted for in terms of self-produced movement: the infant learns about the consequences of heights, and fear of heights leads to their being avoided. More recently, however, it has been proposed that self-produced movement allows an infant to learn what is practical at a brink. That is, infants learn what is possible and impossible for them to achieve based upon the environmental circumstances coupled with their present level of bodily competence.

Faces are very important social stimuli and face processing abilities are found early in development. For example, newborns prefer their mother's face over other unfamiliar female faces. This shows that based upon relatively little visual experience, newborns are able to learn, recognize and discriminate between different faces. Furthermore, adults process faces *holistically* (as a whole) and by three months, infants also do this, though some studies indicate holistic processing isn't fully mature until four years.

*Charles Darwin and his eldest son, William, in 1842.*

## EXAMPLES OF THE WAY IN WHICH INFANTS' PSYCHOLOGICAL ABILITIES CAN BE STUDIED

Very young infants are limited in the responses they can make to stimuli. Of course, they can't use language, nor do they have the muscle control required to press a response switch. Consequently, techniques have to be used which allow psychologists to explore infant behaviour without requiring their participants to engage in sophisticated responses.

*Habituation* – This technique is based on the way in which infants typically look at a new stimulus for some time. As time passes, however, they grow accustomed to, or bored with it and so they look at it less and less; that is, they become *habituated* to the stimulus.

   Habituation allows us to determine if two different stimuli can be discriminated. For example, suppose we want to know if the infant can distinguish a circle from a square, or if they can distinguish Face A from Face B. If a square cannot be distinguished from a circle, it should only be looked at about as much as the circle was by the time the infant was habituated to that stimulus. On the other hand, if the square is looked at much more (i.e. the infant *dishabituates* to the square), s/he must be able to tell that a circle and a square are not the same. Similarly, if the infant dishabituates to Face B, they can tell that this face is different from Face A.

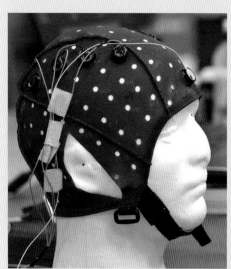

*An electrode cap.*

*Heart Rate* – heart rate has been used to detect attentional and emotional change in infants. Heart rate decreases with increased attention but increases as attention reduces. Heart rate also increases when an infant hears their mother's voice but decreases to the voice of a stranger.

*Event Related Potentials (ERPs)* – ERPs measure the brain's electrical activity in response to a stimulus.

   The infant is fitted with a cap which stretches to fit comfortably on the child's head. The cap has electrodes at strategic points which measure brain activity when a stimulus is presented. For example, if the psychologist is interested in brain activity in response to faces, a number of faces would be shown mixed with other, control stimuli. Specialized equipment then transforms the electrical measures into waveforms and allows detection of a wave that is characteristic in response to faces.

Adults also process upright faces much better than they process inverted faces. We encounter upright faces far more frequently than inverted ones and thus our perceptual skills develop accordingly. The effect of inversion is found early: four-month old infants' face recognition abilities are affected by facial inversion. Greater exposure to a female/male face according to the sex of the primary caregiver affects facial preferences at 3–4 months. If raised mainly by a female, infants have been found to prefer female over male faces. Likewise, if mainly

*An infant on the visual cliff apparatus. The child is on the central platform looking over onto the deep side. Behind can be seen the shallow side of the apparatus with the check pattern a short distance from the glass.*

raised by a male, infants have a preference for male faces. Similarly, at 3–4 months a preference emerges for faces from infants' own ethnic group – unless there is frequent exposure to, and social contact with, members of another ethnic group.

## Language

A newborn baby makes different sounds but does not produce language. Yet communication still occurs through crying to signal states such as hunger or pain. Afterwards, babies follow a sequential pattern of language acquisition, although there are considerable differences between individuals regarding when a given milestone is reached. Indeed, different authors associate similar, but not identical ages with the sequences: thus, any specific ages supplied here are not intended to be taken as hard and fast rules but to indicate 'around this time… it could be sooner or later.'

Babies will *coo* within the first months of life. Characteristically, cooing involves production of vowel sounds such as 'ooo', but the tone of cooing differs according to the language to which the baby is exposed in the home. The sounds of English are different from French and these are different from Urdu, for example.

At six months, *babbling* begins in which the child's vocalizations are focused on the sounds of the language around them. One syllable repetitions occur such as 'ma-ma', 'da-da', 'ba-ba', 'goo-goo' and 'boo-boo'. Picking-up the sounds associated with a given language is important

*Parent and baby.*

## LANGUAGE STAGES

| 6 months | 12 months | 18 months | 2 years | 3 years | 5 years | 7 years |
|---|---|---|---|---|---|---|
| babbling stage | holophrastic stage – single word utterances | multi-word utterances – telegraphic speech | utterances resemble complete sentences | sentences | rhyming, defining words and questioning word meanings | fluent speech, slang and clichés |

### WHAT'S HAPPENING IN THE INFANT'S BRAIN AS LANGUAGE BEGINS TO BE LEARNED?

All newborn babies can discriminate the sounds of all languages. By the age of one year, however, this is no longer the case; the sounds the infant now discriminates belong to the language(s) to which s/he has been regularly exposed. For example, a child exposed to the sounds of English will be able to distinguish r and l as in *rake* and *lake* and th as in *this* and *that*.

Patricia Kuhl's research indicates that babies take statistics from the language(s) they hear as to how often sounds occur. For instance, in an English-speaking environment, English's /r/ and /l/ sounds are heard every day but this isn't the case in a Japanese-speaking environment. Consequently, a baby hearing English learns to distinguish English's /r/ and /l/ but a Japanese baby doesn't. In a bilingual environment though, let's say with one parent speaking English to the baby and the other parent speaking Japanese, Kuhl suggests two sets of statistics are taken, one for each language. Hence, at a year-old, the child can detect the sounds associated with both Japanese and English.

What then is taking place in the infant's brain if s/he begins by discriminating the sounds of all languages but by one year of age this ability has changed?

The brain's auditory cortex (see Chapter 2) is responsible for producing the subjective experience that you have heard particular spoken sounds such as /r/ and /l/. If a baby hears only the sounds of English, the brain circuits belonging to that child's auditory cortex become dedicated to only English's sounds. For example, every time /r/ is heard, particular brain cells respond and after /r/ has been heard sufficiently often, cells in the auditory cortex will become specialized to this sound. Once the auditory cortex is wired to the sounds of a given language, it is committed to the sounds of that language and loses sensitivity to the sounds of other languages.

for being able to hear and speak that language: if, after the first couple of years of life, you have not been exposed to a particular phoneme (see Chapter 1), it becomes harder to hear and say that sound. This explains why it can be difficult for the speakers of one language to produce the sounds of another language. During babbling, the infant also picks-up the intonation or *prosody* of the language to which they are exposed. This gives rise to babbles which follow the language's intonation pattern and so 'sound like phrases', based upon the prosody alone.

At one year of age, the single word, or *holophrastic* stage occurs. A *holophrase* refers to a single word being used to represent a phrase. For example, when the word 'milk' is spoken, it can be used to intend several different meanings such as, 'Is there any milk?'; 'I want some milk'; 'milk is there'; 'spilled milk'; 'where's the milk?' The holophrastic stage is also associated with over-generalizations in which one word is used in relation to the item it represents and also to other similar items. 'Doggy', for instance, may be used in association with a dog but also with other four-legged animals; 'dada' may be used to refer to daddy and also to other men. At this point, the infant has a very limited vocabulary so it's unsurprising that there isn't greater precision.

At 18 months, multi-word utterances appear beginning with two-word combinations (e.g. 'doggy bark') and then *telegraphic* speech, in which very short expressions are used which contain just key words. For example, 'Mummy light off' instead of 'Mummy, the light has gone off'; or 'Anna Daddy gone' for Anna and Daddy have left.

By two years, utterances resemble something like complete sentences including grammatical features. However, over-generalization can appear here too, in which a rule that applies in one circumstance is generalized to another, where it does not apply. For example, 's' is often added to nouns to make plurals (cats, dogs) and regular verbs take -ed in the past tense (walk, walked): however, some plurals do not follow the -s rule (mouse, mice) and irregular verbs do not take -ed (drink, drank). Generalization, though, leads to 'drinked' and 'mouses': other examples could include words such as 'broked' and 'sheeps'. Albeit these are errors, they nevertheless indicate that language acquisition is advancing because rules are being learned.

Beyond these years, sentences appear (age three), rhyming, defining words and questioning word meanings (age five), with fluent speech, slang and clichés appearing later (age seven). Between 2–6 years words are learned quickly and vocabulary expands, though the number of words understood does not automatically translate into number of words spoken.

## Cognitive Development

Piaget's stage-theory of cognitive growth has been hugely influential. Although it is no longer regarded as wholly accurate, it is nevertheless worthy of consideration due to its impact and the considerable research it has generated.

Piaget's theory proposes children's thinking progresses through four different stages Between the ages of 0–2 years objects are learned about by being grasped, shaken, or put to the mouth. Between 8–12 months, an infant will look for a completely hidden object: s/he realizes that the object is permanent; it continues to exist even if not in sight. Stranger anxiety, or fear of unfamiliar people emerges about the same time as object permanence.

*Jean Piaget (left).*

| PIAGET'S STAGES OF DEVELOPMENT | | | |
|---|---|---|---|
| **Stage** | **Age (years)** | **Characteristics** | **Features** |
| Sensori-motor | 0–2 | World knowledge from senses and actions. Internal mental representations emerge. | Object permanence. Stranger anxiety. |
| Pre-operational | 2–6/7 | Symbolic thought develops, e.g. in play, language and image use. | Imaginative play. Language develops. Egocentrism. |
| Concrete-operational | 6/7–12 | Understands concrete, immediate experience; capable of logical thought within these parameters. | Conservation of mass, volume, length and weight. Takes others' perspective more readily. |
| Formal-operational | 12– | Start of abstract reasoning: ideas can be manipulated in the mind. | Logical reasoning. Moral reasoning. |

The stranger does not fit with the infant's established mental framework which helps him/her understand and predict their world.

From 2–6/7 years, symbolic thought increases. This is exhibited in language use, drawings, play with building bricks/constructional toys or using a ruler as a sword, for example. However, the child is influenced by how things look rather than by logical thinking/operations. Another feature of this stage is *egocentrism*; that is, the child sees the world from their own viewpoint and cannot see things from another's perspective.

By 6/7–12, children's thought is not dominated by appearance. Now, when an object changes its appearance, it is appreciated that other qualities are unchanged (this is *conservation*) and that the object can return to its original state (*reversibility*). From age 12, abstract reasoning begins; ideas can be manipulated in the mind, hypothetical thinking and deductive reasoning can take place.

Piaget's theory covered a long timespan and huge areas of development. Importantly, it spurred many, many investigations, which, with the passage of time, have highlighted the theory's inaccuracies and thereby increased our knowledge. For example, we now know:

A. cultural context affects the rate of stage attainment;

*A child playing with building blocks – an example of increased symbolic thought.*

**Conservation of Mass**

A & B are the same sized plasticine balls.

B is rolled out into C. Only at 6/7–12 years old is it understood that C's mass still matches A's; the pre-operational child thinks C has a greater mass.

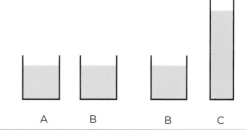

**Conservation of Volume or Liquid Quantity**

A & B contain the same quantity of liquid.

B's liquid is poured into C. Only at the concrete-operational stage is it understood that C's quantity matches A's; the pre-operational child thinks C has a greater quantity/volume.

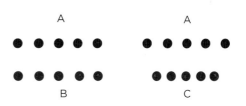

**Conservation of Number**

Lines A & B have the same number of counters.

B's counters are transformed into C. Before the concrete-operational stage it is not understood A and C's number of counters are the same; the pre-operational child thinks A has more counters.

*Examples of conservation.*

B.  some object permanence can be found at 3–4 months;

C.  conservation of length and number can occur in pre-operational children;

D.  adjustment to others can occur sooner than Piaget's egocentrism allows.

# Attachment

Attachment, or the creation of an emotional bond to another person, begins during infancy. Most research in this area has concentrated upon mother–infant attachment because mothers have historically been the primary caregiver; the person who provides a secure base from which a shared attachment relationship can grow. However, attachment is not limited to mother–infant; it can exist with other consistent caregivers too, such as the father, or a grandparent (often the maternal grandmother).

Attachment style is not identical for all infants. This is known from the work of Mary Ainsworth who measured infants' security of attachment using the *Strange Situation* (SS) procedure. The procedure involved a standard setting and exposing an infant to eight different episodes over 25 minutes. The episodes explored the infant's reaction to being with mother, a stranger, with both, or being alone. As mother left and returned at strategic points, the infant's reaction to being separated from and reunited with mother could be appraised. Ainsworth's results led her to propose infants' attachment styles belonged to one of three broad groups: *secure, anxious-avoidant* and *anxious-resistant/ambivalent*. Again, using the SS, Mary Main and Judith Solomon later added a fourth style, *disorganized*.

Evidence indicates that compared with insecure styles, secure attachment leads to attributes such as more positive self-concept, stronger friendships with peers, more advanced emotional understanding, and can influence cognitive development by freeing-up the child to explore the environment.

*Mary Ainsworth (wearing spectacles).*

Other attachment styles are not automatically caused by conscious, intentional acts on the part of the caregiver. Although these can occur, there are many other reasons why a secure attachment style may not evolve. For example, the parent may suffer from psychological distress; be poorly emotionally equipped for parental responsibility; or live in stressful circumstances which markedly impact upon childcare.

## Adolescence

Adolescence begins at puberty and ends as the individual moves into adulthood. The age of adulthood varies according to culture; figures for Western culture are approximately 18–20 years. A number of psychological changes occur during adolescence including cognitive, social and neurological adjustments.

During adolescence, cognitive changes occur such as improved attention, information processing and memory. More complex and abstract thinking emerges; new ideas form/develop; opinions emerge on different topics which can be further considered and discussed. There is also an increase in perspective-taking so that others' positions can be appreciated.

Adolescence is also marked by growing away from parents and the increasing importance of peer groups. Parents often worry their adolescent may engage in risky behaviour and be encouraged to do so by peer pressure. Whilst such concerns are realistic, a teenager's behaving in these ways is not a straightforward rebellious choice or 'attitude'. Instead, behaviour can be linked to brain development.

The front part of the brain is responsible for planning, making judgements and governing impulsive behaviour (see Chapter 2). However, during adolescence this part of the brain isn't mature: it's roughly on a par with a child's brain. Yet, those parts of the brain linked to the rewards we get from pleasure-seeking are as active as in an adult. Hence, it is more likely that an adolescent will take risks. Furthermore, Leah Somerville and colleagues have suggested why teenagers may be more prone to risky behaviour when with peers. The researchers noted the connection level between brain regions responsible for socially motivated behaviour and responsible for putting motivation into action. The connectivity level led to the proposal that when being appraised by peers, adolescents are impelled to action, even if this action involves dangerous behaviour.

Peer relationships can be beneficial, though. Good peer relationships provide friendships and social support (e.g. emotional support, support with self-esteem and supplying advice), and this kind of positive relationship is associated with happier adolescents.

Just as parenting plays a role before adolescence, it is important during this period too. As Roger Kobak and colleagues have pointed out, adolescents are not, of course, identical;

| THE STRANGE SITUATION (SS): INFANTS' BEHAVIOUR, ATTACHMENT STYLE AND PARENTAL CAREGIVING BEHAVIOUR FROM THE RESEARCH OF AINSWORTH AND MAIN AND SOLOMON | | |
| --- | --- | --- |
| **Infant's Behaviour in SS** | **Attachment Style Classification** | **Association with Mother's Caregiving Style** |
| • Comfortable whilst mother is there.<br>• Prefers mother to stranger.<br>• Mother used as secure base for exploring surroundings.<br>• May cry when mother leaves; wants to be close when she returns.<br>• Is happy; quickly calms upon mother's return. | Secure | • Sensitive and responsive to child's needs.<br>• Child learns support will be available when needed so looks to mother if upset. |
| • May not be comfortable in SS.<br>• Doesn't react very differently to mother versus stranger.<br>• Doesn't use mother as secure base.<br>• May cry when mother leaves; closeness not sought on her return, instead actively avoids proximity. | Anxious- Avoidant | • Insensitive caregiver, unresponsive to child's needs. |
| • Wishes to be close to parent but also resistant to interacting with her.<br>• Desire for proximity means surroundings go unexplored.<br>• Distressed on mother's departure; when reunited, infant not easily calmed – resistance to contact may be particularly noticeable. | Anxious-Resistant/ Ambivalent | • Inconsistent responses to child. |
| • Typically brief, unpredictable behaviour.<br>• Behaviours may include: child appears to both approach and avoid caregiver; odd movement patterns (e.g. jerky movement; freezing). | Disorganized plus also categorized as one of the above | • Frightening/frightened behaviour.<br>• Dissociative and helpless or withdrawing behaviours. |

1. After a mother and infant have settled, a stranger enters and sits quietly on the free chair.

2. After an interval, the stranger starts talking with the mother and, after a while, starts to play with the child.

3. Then a little later, the mother gets up and leaves the room.

4. The stranger stays and tries to interact with the child.

5. After a period, the mother then re-enters. The stranger leaves.

6. After a further interval, the mother leaves again, leaving the child alone.

7. After a period, the stranger enters, offers comfort to the child if necessary, and tries to play with the child.

8. The mother returns, the stranger leaves, and the mother and child remain in the room for a few minutes.

*The Stange Situation Procedure. This involves a researcher observing the reaction of an infant to being with their mother, a stranger, with both, or alone.*

*Parent and teenager.*

differences exist in many ways such as personality, temperament and presence of mental health issues. Likewise, parents are not equally equipped in ability to adapt to their offspring's increasing independence whilst both preserving their adolescent's safety and taking into account her/his individual qualities. A variety of factors can have an impact, including stressful events and economic circumstances. This said, Kobak and colleagues have also identified three ways to achieve *sensitively attuned* parenting across adolescence.

- Parents' *positive engagement* with adolescents (which includes elements such as being supportive, showing affection, good family relationships), leads to the adolescent being assured that their parent will provide help and comfort, and s/he builds in self-confidence. The presence of positive engagement can be seen in the shared respect and positive feeling that exists when parent and offspring interact.
- Having fairly accurate information about an adolescent's actions allows for appropriate *supervision and guidance.* Essentially, having a pretty good idea as to what the adolescent

is doing means the amount of independent decision-making permitted, and the quantity of supervision supplied, can both be tailored according to whether the adolescent makes suitable decisions and engages in suitable behaviour. From this approach, the adolescent acquires both independent decision-making skills and control of their behaviour.

- *Open communication* increases both an adolescent's ability to communicate and to see matters from another's point of view. When differences arise over independence, open communication is characterized by parent and adolescent working together to resolve the issue. To be successful, this feature requires that the parent: listens and pays attention to what the adolescent says; gives attention to how the adolescent is behaving; properly grasps what the adolescent says and does; empathizes and responds in a way that shows s/he has understood.

An important issue relevant to Point 2 above is *psychological control*. Amongst several other negative effects, parental psychological control limits development of independent decision-making. It does this by invalidating the adolescent's feelings and exerting pressure to think in certain ways via manipulation of, and intrusion into, the feelings and thoughts of the adolescent. In this way, the adolescent is controlled psychologically, and the parent holds power over them. Brian Barber and Elizabeth Harmon have highlighted that psychological control may be achieved by removing affection, making the adolescent feel guilty and/or manipulating the parent–child relationship. Furthermore, a psychologically controlling parent is unable to see matters from their adolescent's position.

## Adulthood

From the early 20s to approximately 60 years, cognitive abilities are comparatively steady. From 60 onwards though, cognitive decline can be noted, for example in terms of memory and reasoning. Cognitive abilities can also be affected too by issues which affect brain health, such as dementia, as well as psychological factors such as loneliness, depression and anxiety.

However, those aged 60+ are not automatically on a fixed road to decline! The older brain benefits from stimulation and keeping active. One way to do this is by engaging the brain in frequent cognitive activity such as reading, completing crosswords, learning a new language or a different kind of skill. Driving, engaging in intellectually stimulating tasks – such as taking on responsibilities – are beneficial too. All these examples set assorted challenges such as having to draw upon different kinds of memory and thinking. Physical exercise also helps to maintain the brain, as does social interaction (e.g. joining a club; volunteering; meeting friends) and the extent of your social network (the number of relatives and friends who you are in touch with regularly).

*Physical exercise like playing tennis can help maintain the brain.*

Other factors which influence decline include being open to new experiences, conscientiousness, purpose in life and optimism. For example, conscientiousness may well keep you exercising, learning a new skill and being a reliable volunteer, whilst being open to new experiences may start you on that new skill, or mean meeting new people.

Keeping the older brain active affects the brain directly. This is because it is not fixed; it still has *plasticity*, which means it can adapt to new input. Adapting to the stimulation it receives means more connections can grow as a result of keeping it fit. The higher the number of connections that exist, the greater the opportunities, or brain routes, for dealing with cognitive challenges.

## SUMMARY

- Size and shape constancy plus face processing ability are present at birth.

- Infants detect depth; between 3–4 months further face processing abilities and preferences can be noted.

- Spoken language acquisition progresses through: cooing, babbling, single words, two words, telegraphic speech, sentences and fluent speech.

- Piaget had four developmental stages: sensori-motor, pre-operational, concrete-operational, formal-operational.

- Four different attachment styles have been described: secure, anxious-avoidant, anxious-resistant/ambivalent, disorganized.

- Cognitive improvements occur in adolescence; changes to the adolescent brain are linked to the ability to plan, make judgements and take part in risky behaviour. Peer relationships can provide support. Sensitively attuned parenting is associated with positive engagement, supervision and guidance plus open communication, all of which assist with the adolescent's increasing independence. Increasing independence is limited if the parent exercises psychological control.

- Cognitive abilities remain comparatively steady through adulthood until 60+ years; cognitive decline can be mitigated by stimulating the brain, physical exercise and social involvement. Psychological risk factors such as loneliness, anxiety and depression can speed cognitive decline.

# SOCIAL PSYCHOLOGY

**Social psychology examines how people affect each other's thoughts, feelings and behaviours when we are in social situations; that is, in groups of two or more people. Social situations can include family, friends, work colleagues; sports, political, national and religious affiliations; memberships of associations or clubs and those we meet online. Within social situations, different influences exist such as culture, group type (e.g. sports team, older/ younger, ) and social role or status (e.g. parent/child, employer/employee).**

Broadly speaking, social psychological research addresses attraction, attitudes, social influence, social cognition (the way we think about others), peace and conflict.

## A Brief History of Social Psychology

Social psychology's history can be traced to Norman Triplett, who, in the late 19th century reported that the presence of another led to cyclists riding faster and to children performing a simple task more quickly. In the first half of the 20th century, Kurt Lewin (often thought to be the founder of social psychology) proposed behaviour is the product of personal and environmental characteristics and that groups affect the behaviour of their members. In the 1950s issues such as conformity (Solomon Asch) and obedience (Stanley Milgram) were investigated. Later in the 1990s, researchers such as Alice Eagly and Shelly Chaiken focused on attitudes and attitude change.

## Liking Others: Interpersonal Attraction

If you think about social situations in your own life, you will be able to identify people you like or dislike and those people who you love. Interpersonal attraction research seeks to explain what kinds of factors cause us to like or love another person.

Before we can form a friendship or closer relationship, we first have to meet someone and this is determined by their *proximity*. Physical nearness to or distance from another determines whether we are able to initiate any kind of relationship. For example, if we travel to different geographical locations for work or study, this increases opportunities to meet

*A race of the League of American Wheelmen, c. 1890. Norman Triplett observed that cyclists rode faster with the presence of another cyclist.*

new people. The geography of where we live in relation to others has an influence too. People who live nearer together are more likely to bump into each other and form friendships. If this also creates a greater number of opportunities for meeting different people, the more likely it is you will have more friends. Indeed, just repeatedly encountering someone can increase how much you like them: psychologically, we tend to like and feel safe with whatever we encounter more frequently. When a person is new to us – let's call him Andrew – his characteristics are unknown: he is a potential threat. As we meet him again and again, however, that threat diminishes, and we become more favourably disposed towards him, maybe even regarding him as one of 'our group'.

On that very first meeting, though, it is likely that the only information available to us about Andrew, or any other individual, is what we can glean from their appearance and facial attractiveness plays an important role. Before reading further, please complete the task associated with the four faces, in the box overleaf.

Based on data from African hunter-gatherers, and men and women from Australia, Great Britain, Japan and North America, the more average a face is (i.e. the closer it is to the majority of faces from which it is drawn) the more attractive it is perceived to be. For example, how much a young adult female face is like most other young adult females etc.

Why average faces are thought to be more attractive has also been accounted for in terms of increased familiarity leading to liking. When any face becomes familiar, we store its structural appearance in memory and as we see faces all the time (in real life, films, television, advertising, social and other media) many of them become familiar to us. This repeated experience allows us to establish a familiarity with 'averageness' and so when a face meets our unconscious criteria for averageness, its familiarity renders it more attractive.

Please compare the two male faces with each other. Which do you find the most attractive, the one on the left or right?

Now compare the two female faces. Which do you find the most attractive, the one on the left or right?

Do you think you used different criteria in deciding about the attractiveness of male faces versus the attractiveness of female faces?

If you were to draw a vertical line down the middle of each face, would you say the different features in the two halves are very similar or quite dissimilar? That is, do you think the face is symmetrical or asymmetrical?

What were your criteria for making your decisions about the faces in the box? If you considered the skin, this is unsurprising: flawless skin (smooth, even skin tone) is considered attractive. Were the faces that you thought most attractive symmetrical? Symmetrical faces are regarded as more attractive. Average faces are generally more symmetrical, so again, attractiveness can be connected to a facial structure we find more familiar.

Evolutionary accounts propose that we (unconsciously) want to increase the chances of our genes surviving and therefore endeavour to select an individual who would be a good reproductive mate. A symmetrical face and healthy-looking skin are taken to signal underlying health and therefore reproductive fitness. Moreover, since an average face's features align with the majority of faces from which it is drawn (e.g. young adult males), this signals the presence of genetic variety. Such variety is beneficial because it promotes the possibility of our genes surviving.

Did you find the more attractive female face more feminine? Feminine female faces are deemed more attractive across different cultures. With males the evidence is more mixed: some research reports more feminized faces are more attractive and other research that more masculine male faces are regarded as attractive. Of course, what and who is considered to be attractive does not remain fixed. For example, when Jane Austen wrote *Pride and Prejudice* (published in 1813)

an attractive woman would have had a rounder, plumper face with pale skin and a fuller, curvier figure compared with the kind of looks favoured today.

Fortunately, physical attractiveness is not the only criterion for interpersonal attraction. Albeit that men seek more youthful partners and women are drawn to social status, traits such as dependability, kindness, humour, sociability, intelligence and similarity are important too.

*The painting of Victoria, Duchess of Kent, by George Dawe in 1818, exemplifies the different standards of attractiveness of this era.*

Shared values and beliefs increase the likelihood that a relationship will both develop and be maintained. Factors which play a role in this include age, intelligence, education, socioeconomic status, religion, race, attitudes and sense of humour. When two people match in these ways, their similar thinking, attitudes and what they want from life increases agreement and the number of times they will make each other feel good. Consequently, the couple's relationship is likely to run more smoothly.

However, even if you and the other person are similar in all of the above aspects, the potential relationship must be reciprocal. No relationship can exist if only one party exhibits liking or friendship. Relationships depend upon give and take so that balance or *equity* is reached: it is impossible to have a successful friendship with someone who isn't friendly to you. Equity must be present in other ways too; e.g. if one person brings high social and financial status and the other person does not possess these, s/he must balance the relationship in some other way.

## Love

There are different kinds of love, e.g. love between a parent and child, between siblings, between friends and between romantic partners.

Robert Sternberg has proposed a *Duplex Theory of Love* which draws together his *Triangular Theory of Love* and his *Theory of Love as a Story*. The Triangular Theory contends that there are eight kinds of love produced by different combinations of intimacy, passion and commitment. However, before reading further, it should be noted that these distinctions are not meant to imply that all relationships can be neatly slotted into one type of love. The nature of love in a relationship is unlikely to be so clear-cut and can also change over the duration of the relationship.

*Nonlove* lacks intimacy, passion and commitment, whilst *consummate love* possesses all three and it is also the type of love sought by adults in romantic, permanent relationships. *Liking* involves intimacy and can be found in true friendships; *infatuation* comprises passion alone whilst *empty love* constitutes only commitment. *Companionate love* consists of intimacy and commitment; *romantic love* has intimacy and passion and this form of love may precede a long-term relationship before commitment is added. *Fatuous love* possesses passion and commitment and is less likely to be successful due to the absence of intimacy.

When intimacy, passion and commitment are equally balanced, they are represented by an equilateral triangle. (A triangle where all sides are the same length and all internal angles are the same size.) Additionally, the more love there is, the bigger the triangle. However, since love's components aren't always equal, the triangles which represent this inequality aren't equilateral

## INTIMACY, PASSION AND COMMITMENT

Intimacy – feeling close to, connected with and bonded to the other person such that you experience a warm loving relationship. Caring and emotional support are involved. Intimacy is typically stable over time and plays a greater part in long-term relationships than short-term ones.

Passion – unique to romantic love; physiological and emotional changes occur associated with physical attraction, romance and sex. Passion plays a medium role in long-term relationships but a higher one in short-term relationships.

Decision/Commitment – cognitive processes are involved in deciding that you love someone and also in committing to maintaining that love long-term. However, decision and commitment do not always appear together. A person can decide that he or she loves but not be committed to that love. A committed love can be present but undeclared. Commitment is typically stable over time and plays a substantial part in long-term relationships and is slight or absent in short-term ones.

*The Triangular Theory of Love proposes that different combinations of intimacy, passion and committment produce different kinds of love.*

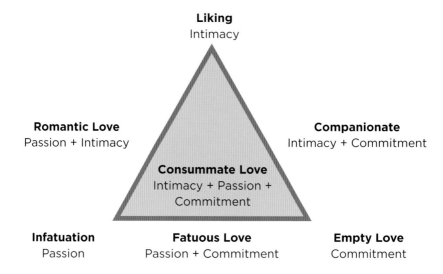

and have different configurations. Furthermore, the triangles representing the love of two members of a given relationship will not necessarily be identical, reflecting that they do not love in precisely the same way.

The triangles are created from the stories about love that we encounter. The term 'story' refers to the way in which we learn about love through real-life and from fictional accounts. We may learn from the way in which others talk about their relationships and we can note the nature of the love between friends and relatives. Information can be taken too from books, magazines, television, films and so forth. Collectively, all this information allows us to create our own stories or representations of love. Once these are established, their standards are applied to whether we begin, maintain or end a relationship. Where people have formulated dissimilar stories, love will not be understood similarly, and a close relationship is less likely to be successful. In contrast, when similar stories exist, love will be understood in similar ways and a close relationship is more likely to be successful. Or to put this another way, two people are more likely to be happy together when the size and shape of their respective triangles are broadly similar.

## Attitudes

According to Alice Eagly and Shelly Chaiken, an attitude is present when a favourable or unfavourable evaluation is made based upon a psychological tendency. In other words, an attitude involves positive or negative feelings (emotion or *affect*) and thoughts/beliefs/ knowledge (*cognitions*) about a target, or *attitude object*, which are manifested in our *behaviour*. Targets of attitudes are various; for instance, they can involve individuals (e.g.

*An illustration from* Romeo and Juliet.

friends, relations, politicians, actors, our boss, a specific animal, product or food); groups (e.g. political parties, followers of a religion, sports teams/supporters, types of animal) and concepts (e.g. freedom of information, terrorism, the death penalty). Attitudes help us to decide what to do or avoid doing and to predict what may happen; e.g. we might decide to stroke a cat (cute, friendly pet, may purr) but avoid proximity to a lion (probably dangerous; could attack).

The contribution of emotion, cognition and behaviour in relation to an attitude is not the same for all attitudes we hold. Even if two people hold the same attitude, this does not mean their attitudes comprise identical weighting of emotion, cognition and behaviour. In the box

*Examples of different kinds of targets of attitudes.*

The Death Penalty

**Attitudes**

Celebrity

Teams

below, different people have different attitudes towards swimming; Angus and Calum both find the activity fun, yet Calum's cognitive component is different from Angus's, and their behaviours are driven differently.

Angus and Calum answered quickly but Bruce took time to think, producing a quite slow response. This indicates that Angus and Calum hold a strong attitude towards swimming because their views were readily available, whereas Bruce's attitude is weaker as it needed consideration. Furthermore, given that all three elements of Angus's attitude agree, he will hold a stronger attitude towards swimming than Calum because Calum's cognitive element (pool accessibility) means all attitude elements do not align. Interestingly, now that all three have been asked about swimming, their respective attitudes will have been strengthened further: simply thinking about or stating an attitude can make it more available and thereby stronger. Angus and Calum have positive experiences when swimming because they find it fun and it has fitness benefits; positive experiences also strengthen attitudes. Indeed, the opposite is true too: a negative experience can also strengthen an attitude; e.g. a frightening experience of falling into water and having difficulty getting out could produce a negative attitude towards swimming.

Angus and Calum's strong attitude towards swimming means that they will probably have a strong intention to swim and thus will swim. Strong attitudes towards an attitude object and having the intention to perform a behaviour make it much more likely that the behaviour will occur. In contrast, Bruce's weak attitude and probable weak intention means a swim is unlikely.

However, albeit that Angus has the strongest attitude towards swimming, this does not mean the activity will necessarily always be pursued when an opportunity presents itself. If

| ATTITUDES TO SWIMMING | | | |
|---|---|---|---|
| | **Angus** | **Bruce** | **Calum** |
| Emotion | It's fun. | I don't like it much. | It's fun. |
| Cognition | It's good exercise; keeps me fit. | It's time-consuming; easier to walk or cycle. | Good exercise, keeps me fit but accessing a pool is hard. |
| Behaviour | Swims regularly. | Swims very rarely. | Swims whenever possible. |
| Speed of Reply | Quick | Quite slow | Quick |

*Positive feelings towards swimming coupled with positive thoughts/beliefs/knowledge about the activity will be evident in a person's behaviour - s/he will swim. On the other hand, if negative feelings and cognitions towards swimming exist, this will be evident in a person not swimming.*

Angus is amongst friends who do not favour swimming or perhaps are disinclined to physical exercise, he may feel under pressure to fit-in with the others. If he is keen to fit-in and thus be liked more by his friends, swimming may be skipped. On the other hand, if Angus is the sort of person who doesn't adapt to this social influence, a swim is more likely to take place.

Of course, attitudes aren't always positive. Prejudice involves having a negative attitude and feeling towards another, and prejudiced attitudes ('us' and 'them') can arise from social categorization.

Henri Tajfel proposed that we get our sense of identity from group membership (*Social Identity Theory*). Group membership can be variously defined, such as race, gender, nationality, sexuality, education, social class, our family, work, political, religious or sporting affiliations etc. and therefore, we belong to more than one group at a time. For example, two of Angus's groups are 'male' and 'swimmer' whilst two additional groups could be 'fit' plus 'member of a swimming club.'.

When Angus encounters people, he will categorize them according to the different groups to which he belongs, such as family/non-family; male/female; 'fit'/'unfit'; his swimming club/a different swimming club. Once he has categorized himself as belonging to a group, such as his swimming club, Angus will feel as though he belongs to this group; his behaviour will fit with or conform to the way other members of the club behave and his self-esteem will be associated with club membership. Additionally, Angus will compare his club with other swimming clubs (*social comparison*) and for his self-esteem to remain intact, his in-group will be perceived as better. He will perceive his club more positively; its members will be regarded as possessing many similar characteristics whilst other clubs will be seen as different, viewed negatively and differences will be emphasized.

When we hold positive/negative beliefs about any group we possess *stereotypes* about them. That is, we make over-generalizations which guide our conclusions/decisions/ behaviour towards group members, often without being consciously aware that we are doing this. For example, Angus could hold the negative stereotype that all members of a particular swimming club are poor swimmers. If taken to extreme, unjustifiable negative attitudes can develop towards an out-group – *prejudice* – such that it becomes associated with negative feelings such as: dislike, disgust, fear, hatred. Stereotypes coupled with prejudice can create *discrimination*, i.e. unjustified negative behaviour towards out-group members. For instance, Angus might dislike members of the other swimming team because they are 'poor swimmers' and go on to treat them in a disparaging manner.

Prejudice stemming from in- versus out-group membership has consequences. It can lead to out-groups not being given opportunities, bullying, vilification and genocide. Genocide was witnessed during the Holocaust and more recently in Rwanda: in both instances, an in-group deliberately killed an out-group.

Discriminatory, prejudiced attitudes can be addressed. We often have little or superficial contact with out-groups; yet, evidence indicates that imagining positive interactions with those of a different group can produce an increase in their perceived

*Group membership can provide us with our sense of identity*

positive attributes and a more positive attitude towards them. Furthermore, greater inter-group contact which moves people closer together instead of farther apart, fosters appreciation of the out-group as individuals; inter-group similarities rather than differences can be seen and new beliefs can be created about the out-group. Finally, prejudice can also be dealt with by confronting it when it arises.

## Conformity

1. Imagine that you are attending a funeral and whilst listening to the eulogy you have occasions when (a) you agree very much with what is said and (b) you vehemently disagree with what is said. Would you cheer for (a) and boo for (b)?

   It's highly unlikely that you would do either. There is no law to prevent you (laws are explicit *social norms* governing behaviour) but there are unwritten rules (implicit social norms) that it is inappropriate, undesirable and unacceptable to cheer or boo.

2. Suppose you are trying to decide whether to visit a particular place but you wonder whether it is worth the expense and if the weather will be suitable. A reliable friend has visited recently. Would you:

   • Ask your friend whether the place is worth visiting?
   • Ask if undercover options are available should the weather be bad?
   • If the friend recommends going, would you check weather forecasts beforehand?

In the box above, a group pressure is present to be respectful to the bereaved, deceased and to the religious or other circumstances of the funeral: you *conform* to the group's expectations. Often, social norms smooth everyday functioning: chaos would ensue if drivers did not stick to the appropriate side of the road or if people refused to queue at checkouts, for example.

According to Morton Deutsch and Harold Gerrard groups produce conformity in two ways. The first scenario in the box above is an instance of *normative social influence* which involves complying with the group's expectations, perhaps to fit-in, gain acceptance or approval even though there's some private rejection of the views that were expressed. *Informational social influence*, on the other hand, involves reference to others as a source of information. Their actions are used to guide our understanding so that our opinions and behaviour are appropriate.

This kind of conformity can arise from different sources such as professional experts, friends, family and colleagues. We may request information or seek it out (see the box's second scenario) or compare our opinions/behaviour with those of others (*social comparison*). Both of these types of conformity emerged in the laboratory, in classic experiments by Solomon Asch. Before continuing, please read through the box overleaf which discusses Asch's conformity research.

When Asch's participants did not want to appear different from the others, normative social influence occurred. When they became uncertain about what they were actually seeing, informational social influence was used to help the participant resolve their difficulty. In everyday life, although both types of social influence operate together, one of them can predominate.

Asch's experiment related to *majority influence* because apart from the participant, everybody else in the group was a confederate with the same opinion as to which test line matched the standard line. As majorities increase in size by about 3–5 people, the greater are the effects of normative and informational social influence. However, further increase in group size does not increase conformity because what was a collection of individuals with their own views is now perceived as a group with a group view.

*Social influence: our behaviour is affected by others.*

## SOLOMON ASCH'S CONFORMITY EXPERIMENTS

Asch had 18 experimental trials in his study. In each trial, participants were presented with a perceptual problem like the one below. On the left is a standard line and on the right three testlines. The participant had to decide which test line, A, B or C was the same length as the standard line. Different sets of test lines were used on each of the 18 trials.

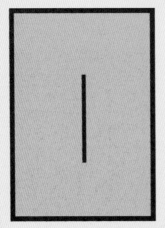

**Standard line**

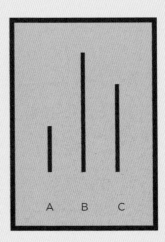

**Test lines**

Between seven to nine men were tested at a time but unknown to each participant, the others in the group were confederates of the experimenter. On 12 out of the 18 trials, it was prearranged with the confederates that they would give a clearly inaccurate, shorter answer. For example, with the lines above, the response would be 'A'. Everyone was seated in a semi-circle and one after another the men gave their responses. As the participant was seated in the penultimate position, he had heard the majority of the responses before he gave his.

A total of 123 participants were tested: nearly 76 per cent of them conformed and gave the inaccurate answer at least once. Out of all the responses made by participants to the 12 key trials, 37 per cent were conforming and 5 per cent of men conformed on all 12 key trials. However, 24 per cent of the men never conformed.

It is easier to resist social pressure if somebody else shares your opinion, or even simply fails to agree with the majority. Conformity to the majority drops markedly when just one person agrees with you or has a different opinion from both you and the majority. Having someone in agreement reduces normative social influence as your dissenting opinion no longer stands out so much. Additionally, it becomes less likely that the majority is correct and so informational social influence decreases. If a person dissents from the majority but does not endorse your opinion, this still confirms you are right to disagree with the majority's view.

Majorities can be influenced by minorities: *minority influence*. Elements which lead to successful minority influence include: consistency between members; consistency over time; flexibility; compromise; operating from a principled position and majority identification with the minority.

## Obedience

Obedience occurs when a person with greater power issues an order and an individual with less power complies with that authority. Sometimes this is beneficial; parents may prevent their children taking an unwise course of action and teachers may insist important study is completed, for example. Orders are issued by a variety of sources such as police officers, lifeguards, sports officials, work superiors etc and, of course, the military. Please now read the box overleaf which describes the obedience research of Stanley Milgram.

Milgram conducted many obedience experiments which manipulated different aspects of his original study. This research led to the conclusion that obedience is influenced by the social situation which includes the status and power of the authority figure. The original study was conducted at Yale University's interaction laboratory and the experimenter wore a grey technician's coat and adopted a rather stern appearance; thus appearing as an impressive scientist. However, in subsequent

*Stanley Milgram.*

## STANLEY MILGRAM'S OBEDIENCE RESEARCH

Under the Nazis millions were put to death. At the Nuremberg trials after World War II, the 'following orders' defence was used but rejected. The judges' position was that unless a moral choice was unavailable, individuals had responsibility for following an order that was illegal under international law. An obvious psychological question was why individuals were prepared to obey orders which led to the Holocaust and deaths of Jews and of other groups such as Roma, Slavs, homosexuals, communists, and those deemed to be defective.

To understand what happens in the presence of an authority figure, Milgram investigated whether participants would follow commands from an experimenter. Each participant was introduced to another person and informed that the experiment concerned the effects of punishment upon learning. Via a rigged draw, the participant

*Judges at the Nuremberg trials.*

became the 'teacher' and the other person the 'learner' because in reality, the learner was actually a confederate of the experimenter. It was explained that the teacher would read out a list of pairs of words and the learner had to remember the pairs for the subsequent memory test. Upon testing, every time the learner made an error he was to be punished.

Punishment was to be an electric shock delivered by an electrode strapped to the learner, and the teacher received a demonstration shock to illustrate the shocks were genuinely painful. Of course, the learner did not receive any electric shocks and to ensure the teacher did not realize what was happening, teacher and learner were in different rooms. In the test room there was a shock generator device with 30 numbered switches. The first switch supposedly delivered a 15 volt shock, with each subsequent switch having a 15 volt increase until the final one delivered 450 volts. Labels on the shock generator read: slight, moderate, strong, very strong, intense, extreme intensity,

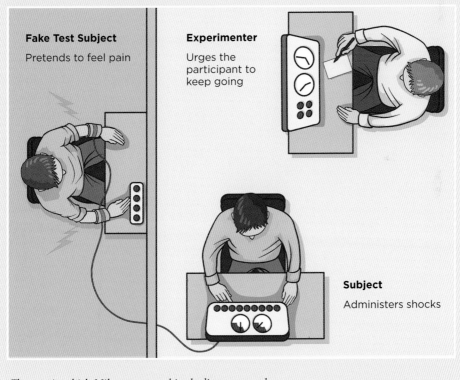

**Fake Test Subject**
Pretends to feel pain

**Experimenter**
Urges the participant to keep going

**Subject**
Administers shocks

*The way in which Milgram set-up his obedience research.*

danger: severe shock, XXX 450 volts. With the learner's first error, the first switch was to be thrown, with the second error, the second switch, and so on such that every extra error led to a stronger shock.

During 'learning', the learner played pre-recorded answers which the teacher could hear. The answers contained many mistakes. After the first few shocks, the learner was heard to be in discomfort; at 120V he said he really hurt; at 150V he reported having heart trouble, his heart was bothering him, he refused to go on and wanted to be released; agonized screaming was heard at 270V onwards, along with demands for release. At 330V there was silence: silence had to be considered an error. Appeals to the experimenter by the teacher received scripted, graded replies: *please continue/go on*; *the experiment requires that you continue*; *it's absolutely essential that you continue* and *you have no other choice: you must go on*.

Although some participants refused to pursue the experiment after about 150V, 65 per cent showed total obedience and went to 450V.

studies, Milgram found obedience declined as experimenter authority decreased. Given the options of not administering a shock, or choosing their own shock levels, few shocks were given. Obedience reduced when the experimenter spoke to the teacher by phone or if a student-confederate of the experimenter issued instructions. It also declined with two experimenters, one of whom was in favour of shocking and the other against the procedure and if a participant-confederate refused to continue administering shocks before the actual participant was asked to give them.

Philip Zimbardo expanded on Milgram's work by exploring the effects of different situational variables on behaviour. He reproduced the physical circumstances of a prison with participants being assigned to be 'guards' or 'prisoners'. Two days into this experiment, the prisoners rebelled and guards used physical and psychological abuse to quash the uprising (e.g. food, water and sleep deprivation, removing prisoners' clothes and putting bags over their heads). The intended two-week experiment had to be terminated early. Zimbardo concluded that it was the situation that produced behaviour.

More recently though, Alex Haslam and Stephen Reicher have challenged the conclusions relating to Milgram and Zimbardo. They argued that Milgram's findings can be accounted for in terms of the extent to which participants identified with the scientific research. Haslam and Reicher drew attention to the way participants typically refused to administer a shock if given the order 'you have no other choice: you must go on' but would typically do so if told 'the experiment requires that you continue'. They contended this latter statement encouraged

*Philip Zimbardo.*

belief that what the participant was doing was significant, such that there was a greater commitment to / identification with, the experiment and experimenter compared with the learner. Furthermore, the reduction in obedience across Milgram's different social settings can be accounted for in terms of how much participants identified with the experimenter: the more participants identified with the experimenter, the more they were prepared to shock the learner.

Regarding Zimbardo's results, Haslam and Reicher claim that although Zimbardo did not supply the guards with direct orders, he nevertheless indicated how they were expected to behave. Yet, subsequently, all guards did not behave in the same way: some were harsh whilst others were not. Hence, the guards' behaviour wasn't the product of simply conforming to the situation; instead, harsh behaviour was associated with guards who responded enthusiastically to Zimbardo's behavioural expectations.

In their BBC prison study (early 21st century), Reicher and Haslam found participants didn't simply conform to being a guard or prisoner. Behaviour according to group membership was dependent upon how much that group was identified with, and the prisoners' group identification led to them successfully challenging the guards' position to establish a more equal regime. However, this regime did not last: a group developed who were unhappy with the arrangement and were motivated to produce an alternative, harsher social order. This group possessed the following characteristics: shared social identification, an imaginative and inventive leader plus a dedicated set of followers.

Reicher and Haslam's results and their reconsideration of Milgram's and Zimbardo's findings led them to the conclusion that the social situations did not bring about behaviour. People do not simply 'follow orders' and go along with the roles they have been given by authority. Instead, conformity and obedience to authority are brought about when a person identifies with authority and believes that authority to be right.

With reference to the Nazi regime, it can be demonstrated that the Nuremberg defence of

*The Adolf Eichmann trial.*

'following orders' does not stand. At his trial in 1961, Adolf Eichmann, logistical architect of the *Final Solution*, argued he had no authority in the Nazi hierarchy and had no choice but to follow orders. Yet, historical analysis demonstrates that his utmost efficiency went beyond the role of simple bureaucrat. As Haslam and Reicher point out, Eichmann knew what he was doing and believed it to be right.

## WOULD THE MILGRAM AND ZIMBARDO STUDIES BE CONDUCTED TODAY?

Are you asking yourself whether a social psychologist would be able to repeat Milgram's and Zimbardo's experiments in exactly the same way that they were conducted in the 1960s (Milgram) and 1970s (Zimbardo)?

The investigations took place in the United States and today, it would not be possible to complete them in their original format: the American Psychological Association's (APA) detailed code of conduct for psychologists (Ethical Principles of Psychologists and Code of Conduct) – which includes research and publication – would not permit this.

Similarly, in Britain, it would not be possible to replicate the original studies. The British Psychological Society (BPS) has a Code of Human Research Ethics which describes how research ought to be conducted with human participants.

Both Codes are available online.

## SUMMARY

- Social psychology examines how people affect each other's thoughts, feelings and behaviours in social situations.
- Interpersonal attraction involves proximity and is affected by a number of factors including facial attractiveness, shared values and reciprocity.
- Love depends upon the balance between intimacy, passion and commitment.
- An attitude exists when a favourable or unfavourable evaluation is made based upon a psychological tendency. This involves emotions and cognitions about an attitude object which lead to behaviour.
- People sharing an attitude do not have identical weighting of emotion, cognition and behaviour.
- Prejudice involves having a negative attitude and feeling towards another and prejudiced attitudes ('us' and 'them') can arise from social categorization.
- Groups produce conformity through normative social influence and informational social influence.
- Social pressure comes from majority influence and minority influence.
- Obedience occurs when a person with greater power issues an order and an individual with less power complies with that authority.
- Milgram argued obedience is influenced by the social situation which includes the status and power of the authority figure. Zimbardo proposed that it is the situation that produces behaviour.
- Haslam and Reicher concluded conformity and obedience to authority are brought about when a person identifies with authority and believes that authority to be right.
- Ethical codes are in place to ensure research is conducted appropriately with participants.

# CHAPTER 5

# PERSONALITY PSYCHOLOGY

Personality is what makes each of us different. It comprises enduring, relatively stable elements which make us think, feel and behave in particular ways which are evident when we interact with others. Different kinds of personality theory have been proposed: *psychodynamic, behaviourist, humanistic, biological, trait, social cognitive* and *evolutionary*. Under these headings, various people have contributed ideas and theories. Consequently, what follows is highly selective and is not intended as an exhaustive account of all personality theories.

## A Brief History of Personality Psychology

Hippocrates (460–370 BCE) proposed that four humours, or fluid substances, are present in the human body. To be healthy, an equilibrium was required between blood, phlegm, yellow bile and black bile; too much or too little in one or more humours led to illness. Subsequently, Galen (129–216 CE) expanded these ideas to personality, arguing that there are four temperaments, each linked to one of the humours.

The first modern attempt to capture personality in its entirety was Sigmund Freud's psychoanalytic theory. His theory enjoyed some longevity and attracted followers, perhaps most famously, Carl Jung and Alfred Adler, both of whom went on to propose their own theories after disagreeing with Freud. Other psychodynamic accounts include those of Erik Erikson and Karen Horney, for example; Horney addressing the heavy male emphasis found in Freud's arguments.

Behaviourism, or learning theories followed such as Burrhus Skinner's operant conditioning, whilst other psychologists added elements of social learning to personality (e.g. Julian Rotter, Albert Bandura). Humanistic psychology, on the other hand, proposed personality results from motivation to meet needs (Abraham Maslow) and to self-actualize, or become a fully functioning person (Carl Rogers).

Trait theories captured personality in terms of characteristic behaviours and included the work of Gordon Allport, Raymond Cattell plus Hans and Sybil Eysenck. Today, current trait theories include the 'big five' traits of OCEAN plus Kibeom Lee and Michael Ashton's, six trait theory, HEXACO.

Walter Mischel disagreed with the idea of fixed personality traits and linked personality

*The Four Humours.*

to situations, whilst Albert Bandura proposed cognitions, behaviour and social context all interact to produce personality. Although linking personality to biology is not new, recent approaches of this sort have addressed brain biochemistry (Richard Depue); genetics and temperament (Alexander Thomas and Stella Chess; Arnold H. Buss and Robert Plomin) as well as the effects of evolution (David M. Buss).

| THE HUMOURS, TEMPERAMENTS AND EXAMPLES OF PERSONALITY CHARACTERISTICS | | |
|---|---|---|
| **Humour** | **Temperament** | **Personality Characteristics Examples** |
| Blood | *Sanguine* | optimistic, cheerful, joyful, popular |
| Phlegm | *Phlegmatic* | calm, consistent, reliable, thoughtful |
| Yellow bile | *Choleric* | passionate, ambitious, energetic, quick tempered |
| Black bile | *Melancholic* | reserved, creative, anxious, unhappy |

## Psychodynamic Theories

Built from his clinical cases, Sigmund Freud's theory of personality was all-encompassing. It addressed the nature of personality, its development, and how defence mechanisms can yield particular behaviours.

Freud proposed that personality has *conscious, preconscious* and *unconscious* aspects and comprises three elements, *id*, *ego* and *superego* which are all engaged in a dynamic relationship. Entirely unconscious, the id is present at birth and is the source of all motives. Containing

*Sigmund Freud.*

| FREUD'S CONSCIOUS, PRECONSCIOUS AND UNCONSCIOUS STATES OF AWARENESS | |
|---|---|
| **State of Awareness** | |
| Conscious | The conscious part of awareness relates to what's occurring at the moment, including thoughts and feelings. Perhaps about 10 per cent of our awareness is conscious. |
| Preconscious | Preconscious content isn't currently conscious but is readily available to be so, such as what you had for lunch. This content won't remain permanently conscious. |
| Unconscious | This content isn't easy to access; it includes anxiety-provoking material that has been pushed out of consciousness, (repressed) because it is disturbing and unwanted (e.g. aggressive impulses, sexual impulses). |

our drives, the id controls basic biological urges related to hunger, thirst, warmth and sex, for example. The id operates on the *pleasure principle* and therefore, demands immediate gratification of its urges.

Between about one to three years old, the ego emerges from the id and is effectively the subjective self. The ego is largely unconscious; some of it is preconscious and the rest (the smallest part) is conscious. In this way, the ego protects us from fully grasping the motives behind our behaviour. The ego is also the rational part of personality, which has to balance the desires of the id and the requirements of the superego in a realistic fashion: it operates on the *reality principle*.

From the ages of about three to five, the superego develops from the ego. It is the smallest part of personality and is also unconscious, preconscious and conscious. The superego corresponds to our conscience and consists of the rules learned from our parents and society; it makes us strive towards ideals but it is often too strict.

A healthy personality follows from an ego which can satisfactorily balance the id's demands plus the superego's conscience. However, if balance cannot be achieved and one personality element dominates above another, problems follow. A too-dominant id can lead to an impulsive, narcissistic personality, whereas a too dominant superego can produce an overly controlled personality, in which the person becomes so restrained that their level of denial is too high. A too weak, or non-existent superego can also bring about personality issues such as psychopathic behaviour.

*The id, ego and superego are in a dynamic relationship; the ego attempts to balance the id's desires and the superego's conscience*

When the ego cannot achieve a satisfactory balance between the id and ego, anxiety arises. This is unpleasant and so the ego uses unconscious *defence mechanisms* to protect itself. Defence mechanisms distort internal/external reality and although this may be helpful in the short-term, it is not a long-term solution because it may give rise to unhealthy behaviour.

Freud also contended that personality develops during childhood and becomes firmly established during this time. This occurs as we pass through *psychosexual stages*. Each stage not only has its own challenge, but if over-gratification, or under-gratification, occurs during a stage, *fixation* occurs. This means that the behaviour patterns associated with the relevant fixation stage persist into adult personality.

**Cautionary Note** – Before going further, it must be pointed out that what follows may be found offensive by some readers. To reiterate, Freud's developmental model possesses *psychosexual stages* and, as the term implies, this means each stage is associated with sex, as in sexual gratification. THE THEORY IS CONTROVERSIAL. Freud's ideas were questioned even at the time he proposed them and his emphasis on sex was disagreed with by others who had been influenced by Freud.

| EXAMPLES OF DEFENCE MECHANISMS | |
|---|---|
| **Defence Mechanism** | **Description** |
| Repression | A disturbing, unwanted memory, wish or feeling is driven from the conscious to the unconscious; e.g. being unable to remember an argument with a relative shortly before s/he died. |
| Sublimation | A valued activity or goal is substituted for an unacceptable impulse; e.g. redirecting a desire into sport, or into a creative activity such as music or a piece of art. |
| Denial | Refusing or failing to accept something which is real but unpleasant; e.g. refusing to accept smoking is producing ill health despite evidence to the contrary. |
| Displacement | Urges/feelings/behaviours are moved from the real target to a substitute; e.g. a person who is angry with their boss takes it out on a subordinate by yelling at them. |
| Regression | Retreating to a behaviour associated with an earlier stage of development; e.g. comfort eating to feel better. |
| Reaction Formation | Adopting thoughts or feelings which are the opposite of what you really think or feel; e.g. encountering someone you dislike intensely but being extremely nice to them. |

Each psychosexual stage is associated with a particular body zone that is linked to an urge for pleasure that originates from the id. During the first, or *oral stage* (birth to age 18 months) pleasure is derived via the mouth, tongue and lips. This involves sucking (feeding, dummies, thumbs) and mouthing objects, for instance. The conflict during this stage is being weaned off milk and oral fixation can lead to characteristics such as: an adult's habitual pen/pencil sucking, smoking, overeating, dependency, passivity/resistance, credulousness/suspiciousness.

Between age one to three years is the *anal stage*, a time when the emerging ego starts to control the id and conflict emerges from toilet-training. This is because bladder and bowel movements are the source of pleasure, yet these id urges to soil must be controlled. If caregivers over-gratify the child and do not successfully encourage appropriate self-control, fixation produces an *anal-expulsive* personality. Conversely, if the child is made to fear soiling, so that

*An image of Oedipus from a 2nd century CE fresco from the so-called 'House of Oedipus' at the site of Tuna el-Gebel in Egypt. In Greek mythology, Oedipus did not know his birth parents. Circumstances led to him killing his father and marrying his mother.*

s/he engages in excessive control, fixation yields an *anal-retentive* personality. Examples of the associated personality characteristics include: anal-expulsive – untidy, disorganized, generous, flexible; anal retentive – neat, orderly, stubborn, parsimonious, excessive self-control.

At the *phallic stage* (approximately 3–6 years old) the sexual organs become central. Conflict arises from 'romantic' feelings arising towards the opposite-sex parent. This is called the *Oedipal complex* in boys and the *Electra complex* in girls. Boys wish to replace their father but fear being punished for their feelings. Identification with the father resolves this anxiety; it is an unconscious way of attempting to win the mother's attention and additionally, father will not harm someone who is like himself. Identification also means that the father's behaviour and notions of right and wrong are taken on too. Girls, on the other hand, notice they don't have a penis, are angry about this, blame their mother and move their affection to their father. Girls identify with their mothers to put themselves in a better position to have the desired relationship with their father and in doing so, a girl takes on her mother's values. Taking on the ideas/values of the same-sex parent leads to the development of girls' and boys' superegos. Phallic stage adult personality characteristics include vanity/modesty and cautiousness/rashness.

From 6–12 years, the *latency period,* personality doesn't develop as sexual feelings are quiet due to girls' and boys' focus being elsewhere, as they learn about the world around them. Finally, the *genital stage* occurs between adolescence–early adulthood. Now, sexual interests appear which are directed towards the opposite sex. If all the other stages have been completed without fixation, a healthy adult emerges who can enjoy adult sexuality responsibly.

The first person to break away from Freud was Alfred Adler who rejected the heavy emphasis on sex in Freud's theorizing. Instead, Adler proposed his *individual psychology*, in which there is an indivisible contribution to personality from both internal and external factors.

During childhood, *styles of life* are established; that is, patterns of behaviour are created which appear in adulthood and depend upon social development within the family and society. Human relationships, however, are not equal. Infants automatically feel inferior because at that age they are inadequate compared with others around them. This establishes the necessity for *compensation*, or finding positive ways to improve and be more effective/superior through

*Alfred Adler (left).*

*Carl Jung.*

application and hard work. In this way, there is continuous, progressive development from feeling inferior to achieving suitable compensation.

The inferiority-compensation progression isn't problem-free, though. If compensation cannot be achieved satisfactorily, the sense of inferiority remains and in the adult this can manifest in an *inferiority complex*, *overcompensation* or a *superiority complex*. An inferiority complex is harmful because the individual feels exceedingly inadequate, so much so, that s/he becomes resigned to failure, ways to deal with challenges aren't sought and difficulties may be avoided. In contrast, overcompensation involves going to extremes to deal with the sense of inferiority. For instance, if a child were told s/he wasn't very good at history, s/he would overcompensate by working extremely hard to become very good at the subject. Great success can follow overcompensation, such as, in our example, the individual progressing to being a professional historian.

A superiority complex occurs when someone with an inferiority complex attempts to deal with their feelings of excessive inferiority. To deal with the unacceptable feelings of inadequacy, the individual compensates by endeavouring to appear more superior than s/he is. For example, s/he might exaggerate abilities or knowledge level.

Carl Jung was originally a follower of Freud but the two came to disagree on the nature of personality, with one of their divisions being the weight Freud gave to sexual motivation. Jung agreed that there is an unconscious aspect to personality, but divided it into the *personal unconscious* and *collective unconscious*, within his own theory, which he called *analytical psychology*.

The personal unconscious consists of lifetime experiences which have been repressed. The collective unconscious consists of concepts and experiences which are inherited from one generation to the next and which we all share. These shared concepts/experiences are

| EXAMPLES OF JUNG'S ARCHETYPES | |
|---|---|
| **Archetype** | **Brief Explanation** |
| The Self | The 'wholeness' of personality. |
| The Persona | The social 'mask' (or really masks) used in different situations. |
| The Shadow | Aspects unacceptable to the individual/society. |
| The Anima/ Animus | The anima is the feminine aspect in men, whilst the animus is the masculine aspect in women. |
| The Sage | An individual who possesses a 'whole' personality. |
| The Hero | A person of humble origins who defies and defeats evil. |
| The Trickster | An individual who can be malicious, self-serving, deceitful. |

represented in *archetypes* which are expressed in personality and can also be found in myths, folklore and fables. A healthy personality emerges as the individual gradually integrates their unconscious and conscious parts of personality. Integration allows a 'balance' to be achieved. Balance is important because it allows a person to become 'whole'. However, although this process is ongoing, the crucial time for psychological life is the middle years.

Jung also distinguished eight personality types which are formed from a combination of *attitudes* plus *functions*. Attitudes are associated with either inward or outward flowing energy. Inward flowing energy produces *introversion* whilst outward flowing energy produces *extraversion* and ideally, there ought to be a balance between the two. However, a person will be inclined to being more of an introvert or more of an extravert and this, coupled with the functions *thinking* versus *feeling*, *sensing* versus *intuition*, produces personality.

The reader is probably familiar with the idea of introversion and extraversion as these concepts have come into common usage. Characteristics of introverts include being contemplative, shunning attention and speaking carefully and quietly. An extravert on the other hand, turns outward towards other people, wants to be the subject of attention, speaks rapidly and very audibly. Jung's *thinking* entails engaging in deliberate, intentional thought; *feeling*, though, involves liking/disliking and therefore involves some kind of valuation. *Sensing* relates to information acquired from the physical environment and how it's perceived/interpreted, whilst *intuition* comprises having 'hunches', 'gut feelings' or a 'eureka moment'.

## Behaviourist Accounts

Strict behaviourism regards all behaviour as learned. Thus, it can be argued that if behaviour demonstrates personality, personality is also learned. For example, we all have likes and dislikes which feature in our personalities and these could be learned by association, or *classical conditioning*. Suppose you are someone who likes cold weather because it allows you to wear a sweater or cardigan. This preference may seem to be just one of your personal characteristics, yet it may have been learned. Suppose that as a child you were regularly comforted by a caregiver who wore a soft, cosy, sweater or cardigan. This pairing of comfort and clothing established an association between feeling better and the pleasing sensation of the garment. Consequently, later in life, you like wearing sweaters/cardigans because you find them comforting and the weather in which they are worn is cold.

Another way of learning personality characteristics is through *operant conditioning* which involves *rewards*. Suppose you've observed a child, on different occasions, out shopping with a caregiver. When the child arrives at a shelf full of treats, s/he always wants one. There's no problem when the treat is purchased but if the answer is a negative, complaints begin and grow worse until there is a full tantrum, which only disappears when the treat is bought. The child's personality appears to be very demanding and bad tempered. Learning applies here because whenever protestations ultimately yielded the treat, this behaviour was *rewarded*, or *positively reinforced*. That is, the child has learned certain behaviours are successful for achieving the desired goal. If, on the other hand, complaints and even tantrums do not produce the treat, these behaviours are likely to reduce and stop because they are unrewarded. Rewards can produce positive behaviours too. If a child is praised for a desirable behaviour, the positive attention reinforces the good behaviour; it is more likely to be repeated and become an established pattern. (Conditioning and key figures in this area are discussed further in Chapter 6).

Other theories have added a *social* or environmental element to learning theory. Julian Rotter's social learning theory proposed the concept of *locus of*

*Julian Rotter.*

| AN EXAMPLE OF LOCUS OF CONTROL | |
|---|---|
| A promotion opportunity arises at work. For the application to be successful, appropriate research regarding the post and well thought through ideas are required. One applicant has an internal locus of control and another applicant has an external locus. | |
| *Internal locus of control* – *successes and failures are the product of my attributes and efforts to achieve.* | Conducts thorough research into the relevant issues associated with the post. Organizes the research results logically and thinks through how these apply to the promotion. Includes this information carefully in the application. |
| *External locus of control* – *successes and failures are the product of chance, fate or powerful others.* | Does some research to have an idea of what's involved. Fills out the application. As the outcome is deemed beyond personal control the candidate goes to limited effort to address what the post requires. |

control, which refers to how much power a person believes s/he has over her/his life. Some people possess an *internal* locus because they consider their successes and failures to be the product of their own attributes and efforts to achieve. Other people, though, have an *external* locus, believing that what happens to them is due to chance, fate or powerful others. If someone believes that they possess control over success/failure, that individual can also cause a reward to occur. However, if what happens is the product of external causes, it's impossible to bring about a reward. Internal locus of control has been found to be related to life areas such as academic and career success plus coping ability.

Another form of social learning was proposed by Albert Bandura who contended some aspects of personality are acquired through *observational learning*, or *modelling*. In other words, watching other people and also noting whether the model is rewarded for what s/he does. Learning in this way is not restricted to childhood but it commonly occurs during this period. For example, a child may observe a parent or older sibling cope with a situation in a particular way and then behave likewise in a similar circumstance, such as slamming a door when frustrated. Similarly, if we observe a model being rewarded by receiving praise for a particular behaviour (e.g. being thanked for holding open a door; admired for a hairstyle) we may repeat that behaviour because it brings about positive outcomes.

## Humanistic Approaches

Abraham Maslow adopted a quite different perspective to personality from those discussed thus far. He argued that behaviour results from motivation to meet particular needs, which is usually experienced as a hierarchy. At the lowest level of the hierarchy, we are motivated to meet immediate, physiological needs which allow us to survive, such as food, water, clothing and shelter. Once these requirements have been met, we progress up the hierarchy where we are motivated to feel safe and secure. This involves needing to keep safe, healthy and secure and so might involve attempting to eat healthily, getting a job, saving and buying a house, for instance.

*Abraham Maslow.*

Moving up the hierarchy, the motivation for behaviour becomes love and belonging. These social needs can be met by engaging in relationships with family members, friends, different kinds of groups (such as those associated with religious beliefs, hobbies, sports, other personal interests) and romantic relationships. Next, we are motivated to gain esteem and respect. These can be realized in a variety of ways, such as educational and professional success, accomplishments in sport, music or other hobbies and personal interests. Attainments of this kind not only lead to a personal sense of achievement, but also to recognition and respect from others, such that the individual builds in self-esteem.

Self-actualization is often cited as the last stage of the hierarchy. Here, the person meets their full potential, makes the most of their abilities and talents and becomes the best they can be. Achieving self-actualization is not easy; it may take a lifetime and then be achieved by very few. If it is achieved, Maslow signalled that the stage beyond self-actualization is motivated by issues which are not related to the self, such as beauty, truth and goodness.

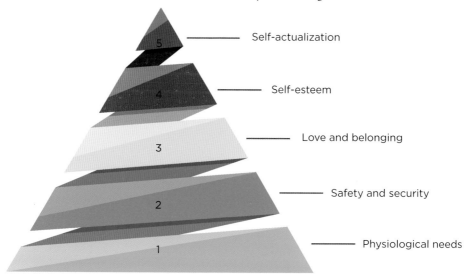

*Maslow's hierarchy of needs. The hierarchy represents different levels of needs which we are motivated to achieve. Once the lowest level (physiological needs) is met, we move up the hierarchy and are motivated to feel safe and secure. Progression up the remaining levels of the hierarchy operates in similar fashion. Not many people achieve self-actualisation and reaching this level may take a life-time*

Carl Rogers also maintained that people constantly strive to actualize. However, unlike Maslow, for whom self-actualization occurred high in his hierarchy of needs, Rogers saw people as being in the process of becoming a fully functioning person.

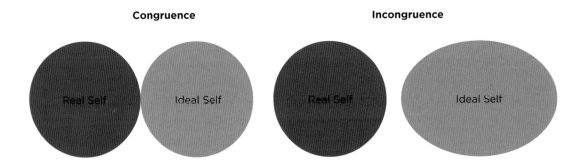

**Congruence**            **Incongruence**

*When the real self and ideal self are very alike there is congruence and there is an accurate self-concept. When the real self and ideal self differ significantly, incongruence occurs leading to discontentment.'*

Rogers noted that the *self* is an important aspect of a person's experience. It captures an individual's beliefs about him/herself; it affects how a person sees him/herself; and it influences how someone sees the world and behaves. The self, however, is divided into the *real self*, or what the person is actually like and the *ideal self*, or the person the individual would like to be. When the self and ideal self are very similar, there is *congruence*, and there is an accurate self-concept; the individual relates to their world appropriately and there is greater satisfaction with

---

### AN EXAMPLE OF INCONGRUENCE

Early in their child's education parents decide their child will inevitably be a professional. This will require good grades and thus there is an early emphasis on academic success; praise is only forthcoming if their child gets the top grades. This is highlighted in association with major exams through gifts. When there is a complete set of top grades, the bigger and better the gift; if though, the grades don't meet the top grades condition, the poorer the gift, or perhaps no gift at all.

Of course, only a limited number of students will achieve a top grade in every subject studied. Students know this and, in our example, the individual is aware that s/he does not belong to that small group. Incongruence is present here because the real self recognizes 'I can't get the highest grade in everything' whereas the ideal self succeeds in this way. When the ideal self's achievement level is not reached, discontentment arises and the student considers that s/he is a failure. The student thinks, feels and behaves like this because s/he has been attempting to live by others' standards rather than her/his own.

life. In other words, the person has self-actualized and is fully functional. In contrast, if there is a substantial mismatch between the self and ideal self, *incongruence* occurs. Incongruence gives rise to discontentment; instead of the world being related to appropriately, the individual may feel the need to distort experiences or even avoid them. This can lead to unrealistic thinking, feeling the world is unsafe and behaviours associated with this.

Incongruence between the real self and ideal self can be brought about in childhood. If caregivers give *unconditional positive regard*, the child sees that s/he is valued and accepted as s/he is. This allows the child to develop *self-regard* and s/he can move forward in the self-actualizing process and be psychologically healthy. If, instead, caregivers supply *conditional positive regard*, such that the child is valued and accepted only if s/he meets particular conditions, problems arise. The need for self-regard is still present but now has to be achieved by meeting the caregivers' conditions. Consequently, successful self-actualization and psychological health may not follow.

## Trait Theories

### PERSONALITY TRAITS

How would you describe yourself? Would you describe yourself as any of the following, for example: outgoing, reliable, moody, confident, optimistic, mean? Think of a few words that you believe capture what you are like.

By answering these questions, you have generated what you believe to be some of your own personality traits. Trait theories assume personality can be represented in terms of behaviours which are stable across situations and time, but which also differ from one person to another. These behaviours are personality traits.

### CATTELL'S 16 PERSONALITY TRAITS

| | | | |
|---|---|---|---|
| warmth | liveliness | vigilance | openness to change |
| intellect | rule-consciousness | abstractedness | self-reliance |
| emotional stability | social boldness | privateness | perfectionism |
| dominance | sensitivity | apprehension | tension |

*Gordon Allport.*

Gordon Allport was an early trait theorist and he, along with Henry Odbert attempted to establish all possible personality traits. They did this by going through an English language dictionary and identifying those words which described people. The original list of 18,000 words was whittled down to 4,500 by excluding synonyms and antonyms. This revealed three different kinds of individual trait: *cardinal*, *central* and *secondary* traits.

Cardinal traits govern an individual's whole personality and are responsible for virtually all behaviour, such as Lady Macbeth's ambition in Shakespeare's *Macbeth*. These kinds of traits are, however, quite unusual as most people do not have a personality consistent with just one trait. Central traits are characteristic behaviours which comprise an individual's essential personality, such as being kind/unkind, friendly/ unfriendly etc. Secondary traits are associated with specific circumstances and therefore do not appear as

*Lady Macbeth, a character defined by the cardinal trait of ambition.*

## A SIMPLE EXPLANATION OF FACTOR ANALYSIS

Factor Analysis is a sophisticated statistical procedure. Put very simply, when researchers have gathered large quantities of information (e.g. from people who've completed personality questionnaires), the technique reduces the data to the fewest factors present. There are though, different factor analysis methods and researchers choose which one they think is most appropriate.

consistently as central traits; for example, a normally placid person who becomes angry when traffic backs-up.

A list of 4,500 traits is very large and the variations in how the traits applied to people made comparisons difficult. Consequently, Raymond Cattell used a statistical technique called factor analysis, to reduce the number of traits and ultimately, this led to his establishing 16 personality traits on which people score high or low.

Personality was reduced to two traits and then three, using a different kind of factor analysis, by Hans and Sybil Eysenck. (All trait theories discussed below have used factor analysis to establish their traits.)

The Eysencks' three traits, *extraversion*, *neuroticism* and *psychoticism* were proposed as personality dimensions. This means extraverts appear at one end of the extraversion dimension, whilst introverts appear at the other. Emotionally sta-

*Hans and Sybil Eysenck.*

## EXAMPLES OF HEXACO TRAITS AND HIGH AND LOW SCORES

### H
#### Honesty-Humility

**Includes:** sincerity, fairness, modesty, whether or not the person is concerned with wealth.

**High:** not interested in extreme wealth and luxury; won't manipulate others or break rules for what's wanted; don't feel they deserve high social status.

**Low:** concerned with wealth and signs of status; prepared to be insincere and to twist rules for what they want; self-important.

### A
#### Agreeableness

**Includes:** compromise, forgiveness, anger.

**High:** willing to compromise with, forgive and be lenient to others; not swift to anger.

**Low:** swift to anger and holds grudges if misused; stubborn; critical of other people's flaws.

### E
#### Emotionality

**Includes:** anxiety, fear of physical danger, emotional support needs, empathy, emotional attachment.

**High:** experience anxiety to daily life stress; frightened of physical danger; need emotional support; empathize and emotionally attach to others.

**Low:** little anxiety even in stressful circumstances; not put off by physical danger; do not need others' emotional support or to emotionally attach.

### C
#### Conscientiousness

**Includes:** organization, thoughtfulness, accuracy.

**High:** organizes time and arranges their setting; thinks things through; orderly approach to objectives.

**Low:** organizing time and setting aren't priorities; decisions given little or no thought; happy including some errors; avoids anything considered too demanding.

### X
#### eXtraversion

**Includes:** sociableness, confidence in association with others, enthusiasm, optimism.

**High:** enjoy social occasions; confident when the focus of attention; energized, enthusiastic, positive about themself.

**Low:** not enthusiastic about social occasions, uncomfortable when the focus of attention; not as much energy and enthusiasm as others; believe they are unpopular.

### O
#### Openness to Experience

**Includes:** imagination, enquiring mind, appreciation of natural and artistic beauty.

**High:** uses imagination regularly; curious about various types of knowledge, out of the ordinary people and ideas; becomes engrossed in the loveliness of nature and art.

**Low:** uncreative; intellectually uncurious; not drawn to unconventional thinking; uninterested in art.

## SOME EXAMPLES OF OCEAN TRAITS AND EXAMPLES OF THE HIGH AND LOW ENDS OF THESE TRAIT DIMENSIONS

### O

### Openness

**Includes:** open to new experience, curiosity, varied interests, imagination, creativity, ideas and actions.

**High:** creative, tries out new experiences, has different interests.

**Low:** prefers routine and what s/he knows, conventional.

### C

### Conscientiousness

**Includes:** self-driven, goal-oriented, planning, organizing, can delay gratification.

**High:** works hard, organized, careful, reliable.

**Low:** procrastinates, disorganized, careless, impulsive.

### E

### Extraversion

**Includes:** sociability, talkativeness, assertiveness, social confidence, emotional expression.

**High:** Outgoing, gregarious, energized by others, prone to action.

**Low:** quiet, thoughtful, reserved, introspective.

### A

### Agreeableness

**Includes:** kindness, helpfulness, can be trusted, good-natured, altruistic, amiable.

**High:** helpful, kind, sensitive to others' needs, can empathize.

**Low:** can be less liked & less trusted; rude, unhelpful, antagonistic, uncaring towards others.

### N

### Neuroticism

**Includes:** emotional stability, anxiety, being moody, being sad.

**High:** Significant swings from one mood to another, anxious, sad.

**Low:** emotionally stable, calm, relaxed, not prone to feeling sad.

ble and emotionally unstable people appear at either end of the neuroticism dimension, whilst psychoticism has low and high ends. Most people appear somewhere towards the middle on extra-version–introversion and neuroticism–emotional stability but are at the low end of psychoticism. Some examples of the extreme ends of the first two dimensions are given in the box overleaf along with some examples of the high end of psychoticism.

Of course, there is a substantial difference between 16 and 2–3 personality traits. Hans Eysenck argued 16 were too many, yet others argued that his minimum of two was insufficient. A mid-point between the two is the *Five Factor Theory*. Having explored Cattell's 16 traits, a number of different people came to the conclusion that there are five traits, or personality dimensions. These were given labels such as those applied by Paul Costa and Robert McCrae: **O** – openness to experience; **C** –conscientiousness; **E** – extraversion; **A** – agreeableness, and **N** – neuroticism: OCEAN. Most people lie towards the middle on each of these dimensions.

The five factors approach has been extremely influential in terms of trait-based personality psychology. However, its cultural and language background was European, usually employing English as the language of choice. This led Michael Ashton and Kibeom Lee to broaden the cultural and language perspective, which resulted in their including an honesty/humility trait in their six-factor approach to personality: HEXACO: **H**onesty/humility, **E**motionality, e**X**traversion, **A**greeableness, **C**onscientiousness and **O**penness to experience.

## EXAMPLES OF THE EXTREME ENDS OF THE EXTRAVERSION AND NEUROTICISM DIMENSIONS PLUS EXAMPLES OF HIGH PSYCHOTICISM TRAITS

| *Extraversion* | | *Neuroticism* | | *Psychoticism* |
|---|---|---|---|---|
| **Extravert** | **Introvert** | **Emotionally stable** | **Emotionally unstable** | **High Psychoticism** |
| Outgoing | Retiring | Even tempered | Anxious | Antisocial |
| Talkative | Reserved | Calm | Worries | Hostile |
| Lively | Quiet | Controlled | Moody | Lacks empathy |
| Carefree | Plans ahead | Emotionally constant | Very emotional | Insensitive |
| Many friends | Prefers books to people | | | |

## Social-Cognitive Accounts

Walter Mischel proposed that a person's behaviour is not caused by a personality composed of fixed structures, as per trait theories. Instead, he drew attention to the way in which behaviour can differ across situations. If two situations are largely similar, behaviour is likely to be consistent, whereas, if the situations are quite different, behaviour changes. Furthermore, situations are subject to individual, cognitive processing: people take in and interpret information from the same situation differently. Consequently, they behave differently according to their particular appraisal of the situation.

Having theorized that learning occurs through observation, Albert Bandura later produced a social-cognitive theory of personality. Central to the theory is the idea that our cognitions and personality, behaviour and social context all influence each other, known as *reciprocal determinism.*

For example, if your social context is one in which you are exposed to books and reading, you too may read, be praised for doing so and value reading as important. This may encourage you to seek out other, like-minded people by joining a book club. The new people you encounter reinforce your belief that reading is important; they expand the subject matter you read, so that now you seek out and read a greater variety of books. Furthermore, this leads to your receiving positive comments and engaging in rewarding conversations.

Bandura also maintained that people possess *agency* and *self-efficacy.* Agency refers to the ability to exercise control over the nature and quality of life, whereas self-efficacy

*Bandura's Reciprocal Determinism.*

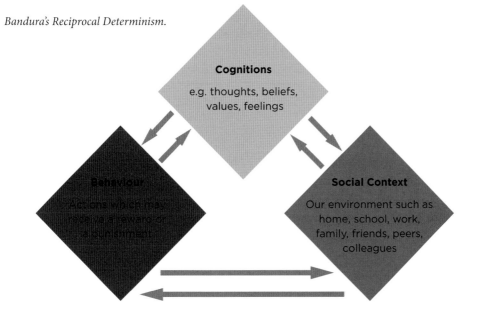

**Cognitions**

e.g. thoughts, beliefs, values, feelings

**Behaviour**

Actions which may receive a reward or a punishment

**Social Context**

Our environment such as home, school, work, family, friends, peers, colleagues

*A book club. Following Bandura's social-cognitive theory, those who value reading may seek out others who also enjoy the activity. Book club members reinforce the belief reading is important; increase the kinds of subject matter read; supply positive comments and supply rewarding conversations.*

refers to a person's belief that s/he has control over life's situations. People differ in their levels of self-efficacy and therefore also differ in the way in which they deal with their life's goals and challenges. A strong belief that control can be exercised over life-events leads to a willingness to tackle difficulties, rapid recovery if things don't go well and becoming heavily invested in chosen pursuits. In contrast, a weak belief that control can be exercised over life-events leads to concentrating upon weaknesses and likely failure. Difficulties are avoided because it is unlikely they will be mastered and when things don't go well, the person rapidly loses confidence in their ability.

## Biological Approaches

Although not discussed above, we have already met trait theorists who linked personality to biology. Cattell, for example, linked traits to heredity, while Hans Eysenck connected them to heredity and biological systems. Generally speaking, other biological accounts of personality involve the brain, behavioural genetics and evolution.

One illustration of personality being linked to the brain comes from research by Richard Depue. As we know, extraversion is associated with being more positive and enthusiastic and Depue has discovered that being so is linked to the neurotransmitter, dopamine.

(Neurotransmitters are chemical messengers that allow nerve cells to communicate with each other; see Chapter 2). When dopamine levels are high, or when the brain is especially responsive to dopamine, we are more likely to be sensitive and responsive to rewards – we are more positive and enthusiastic.

The behavioural genetic approach links personality characteristics to genetics. One example of this comes from Alexander Thomas and Stella Chess who considered temperament to be inborn and who distinguished three, general types of temperament in children: *easy*, *difficult* and *slow to warm*. Easy children are active, positive, happy, function in a regulated way (e.g. eating, sleeping routines) and are good at adapting to new situations. Difficult children are negative, often react quite intensely, don't function regularly, and have problems adjusting to new situations. Those who are slow to warm aren't as active as easy children; aren't always positive and have difficulty with new situations but they 'warm up' to changes after time. This is not to imply that such inborn characteristics fix personality. Instead, whilst temperament can play a role in personality, it is also influenced by experience, such as the kinds of interactions that take place with family members and the effects of becoming increasingly mature.

An alternative genetic account of personality development was forwarded by Arnold H. Buss and Robert Plomin, and it also proposed three different types of children's temperament: *emotionality*, *activity* and *sociability*. Emotionality is the equivalent of distress; that is, the tendency to become easily and intensely upset. Activity is effectively movement as it refers to the total amount of energy that is put out. Sociability refers to whether the child prefers being with other people and so seeks them out, or whether s/he prefers to be alone.

At this point, it is worth highlighting that any genetic contribution to personality will not be so simple as to be the product of a single gene. Rather, personality will result from multiple genes which will interact with each other. Furthermore, developmental experiences will also influence whether genes are switched on or switched off.

Evolutionary proposals have addressed personality in terms of Charles Darwin's theory of natural selection. Briefly, this means that

*Robert Plomin.*

*David M. Buss.*

personality traits have evolved which lead to our reproductive success and survival. One expert in this area, David M. Buss has discussed a number of issues which relate evolution to personality, including *life-history theory* and *costly signalling theory*.

Life-history theory views personality from the perspective of individuals possessing a finite amount of time and energy. Consequently, trade-offs, or compromises have to be made as to what receives energy. For example, one man might expend his energy on ensuring he has many encounters with the opposite sex and expends no energy on acting as a parent. In contrast, another man's energy might initially be spent on winning-over one, long-term member of the opposite sex. Once this has been successful, his energy might later be spent between the roles of acting as a parent and providing for his family.

Turning now to costly signalling theory, in order to reproduce, a mate is required; furthermore, the opportunity to survive can be enhanced through having friends and cooperating with others. The most desirable friend, mate or individual with whom to cooperate is the one who possesses the best attributes for these roles. However, obtaining one of these valuable others isn't automatic because they can choose from whomever is available. Thus, to be chosen by a valuable other necessitates sending out signals which indicate that the signaller is suitable to be chosen as a friend, mate or somebody with whom to cooperate. The most effective way to signal this suitability is to deliver a message which makes clear that the signaller also has the best attributes. To do this honestly, though, is typically costly. To signal a characteristic such as outstanding generosity, for instance (e.g. when buying presents; treating others; giving to charity etc) requires the funds to do this – outstanding generosity costs. Naturally, these resources are not available to all of those wishing to attract valuable others. When this is so, D.M. Buss argues it is possible for life-history theory to apply. Using the example of the man who prefers many encounters with the opposite sex: this man is now in a position where he lacks the finances to succeed in attracting many women (mates). To resolve this problem, he may decide to devote his financial and energy resources to winning one member of the opposite sex.

## SUMMARY

- Freud conceived personality in terms of id, ego and superego. In a healthy personality, the ego balances the id and superego; if it cannot do this, the ego uses defence mechanisms to protect itself which, long-term, produce unhealthy behaviour.

- Freud also described personality developing through psychosexual stages. Too much or too little gratification at these stages produces fixation which can be seen in behaviour.

- Adler proposed feeling inferior requires compensation. If this isn't achieved, this may lead to an inferiority complex, overcompensation, or a superiority complex.

- Jung described the personal unconscious and the collective unconscious with its associated archetypes. Personality consists of attitudes, extraversion and functions.

- In strict behaviourism, personality is reflected in learned behaviour; learning occurs through classical conditioning's association and operant conditioning's rewards. Social elements have been added by Rotter (locus of control) and Bandura's observational learning.

- Humanistic approaches include Maslow's hierarchy of needs, the highest level of which is self-actualization. Rogers' theory emphasizes congruence, when the real self and ideal self are very similar.

- Trait theories examine personality traits – behaviours which are stable across situations and time but differ from person to person. Trait theories were proposed by Allport (cardinal, central and secondary traits); Cattell (16 traits); H. and S. Eysenck (extraversion, neuroticism, psychoticism). More recent trait theories include OCEAN (Costa and McCrae) and HEXACO (Lee and Ashton).

- Mischel highlighted behaviour differs across situations which are subject to individual differences in cognitive processing. Bandura argued cognitions and personality, behaviour and social context all influence each other (reciprocal determinism) and that people have agency and self-efficacy.

- Biological approaches include dopamine levels being associated with extraversion (Depue); genetics influencing children's temperament types: Thomas and Chess's easy, difficult and slow to warm temperaments and A.H. Buss and Plomin's emotionality, activity and sociability temperaments. D.M. Buss discussed personality in terms of evolution including life-history theory and costly signalling theory.

# CLINICAL PSYCHOLOGY

**Clinical psychology involves assessment, treatment and research related to psychological distress/wellbeing. Clinical psychology addresses issues such as: anxiety, depression, psychosis, eating disorders, personality disorders, neurological disorders, addiction and learning difficulties.**

In Britain, clinical psychologists work in a number of different settings such as hospitals, clinics, health centres, community mental health teams, Child and Adolescent Mental Health Services, schools, prisons and social services. Usually, clinical psychologists are employed within the National Health Service but others may be in private practice and some teach and conduct research in universities. With further training it is possible to become a clinical neuropsychologist (involved in the assessment and rehabilitation of those who have a brain injury or neurological disorder), or to qualify in particular psychological therapies.

Techniques used to assess problems include observation, interview and psychological tests. Interventions can then be put in place to help with the problem. Sometimes a problem can be overcome but where this is not possible, intervention can improve quality of life, for example, by reducing psychological distress and enhancing psychological wellbeing.

| EXAMPLES OF PSYCHOLOGICAL TESTS | |
| --- | --- |
| Psychometric tests | tests which assume stable, underlying traits are present in everyone, at different levels |
| Intelligence tests | *Intelligence Quotient* or IQ tests estimate intellectual ability |
| Neurological tests | perceptual, cognitive and motor (movement) tests which allow assessment of whether the brain is functioning properly |

## A Brief History of Clinical Psychology

For some time, accounts of psychological disorder attributed symptoms to the person being *possessed by a demon*. In an era when treatments such as bleeding and purging were typical, other reasons were supplied for the symptoms (e.g. too much blood or bile) and mental health care could include chains and beatings. Instances of more enlightened approaches arose too, though. For instance, in response to what he witnessed at York lunatic asylum and other establishments, Quaker merchant William Tuke, opened the York Retreat (1796) in which patients were treated with compassion and dignity.

*William Norris restrained at Bedlam.*

*The York Retreat.*

By the 19th century, links were made between physical illness and symptoms of mental illness and psychiatry became a recognized field within Medicine. This brought a medical approach to mental disorder along with a determined effort to establish its biological underpinnings in a scientific manner. By 1883, Emil Kraepelin had produced a classification system in which he distinguished different syndromes, or groups of symptoms, associated with a disorder. Kraepelin also proposed two main groups of disorder: *dementia praecox* (an early term for *schizophrenia*) and *manic-depressive psychosis*. Furthermore, this era also saw advances being made in establishing the link between behaviour and regions of the brain (see Chapter 2).

*Emil Kraepelin.*

Towards the end of the 19th century, Sigmund Freud had begun to develop *psychoanalysis*; James McKeen Cattell attempted to measure intelligence and in 1905 Alfred Binet and Theodore Simon produced the first effective scale for measuring intelligence. However, it was Lightner Witmer, who, in 1896 established the first psychological clinic and was the first person to employ the term *clinical psychology*.

The psychological approaches to explaining and treating psychological disorder began with Freud's psychoanalytic model, with other major perspectives – behavioural, cognitive and humanist (discussed below) emerging in due course. Today, psychiatry and the biomedical approach still contribute to the understanding and treatment of psychological disorder: consequently, clinical psychology includes biomedical factors within its remit. However, given that disorder is not always biomedical in origin, clinical psychology looks to psychological processes for understanding

*Lightner Witmer.*

and treating disorder. Today, the biopsychosocial model has been adopted in which biological, psychological and social (environmental) factors should all be taken into account where appropriate.

## Psychological Functioning: Determining Normal Versus Deviation from Normal

If behaviour departs substantially from the *social norms* of a given society, that society often construes the behaviour as deviating from normal. In other words, the person is behaving in a way which the culture regards as undesirable, unexpected and unacceptable. However, using *deviation from social norms* as a means of determining whether or not psychological disorder is present is unsatisfactory for a number of reasons:

A.  If there has to be a 'substantial' departure from social norms, what exactly constitutes 'substantial'?

B.  Cultures aren't identical: what is normal for one, isn't necessarily normal for another, therefore assessing somebody from a different culture by your society's standards is problematic.

C.  Even within the same culture, social norms can shift with the passage of time and thus normality changes accordingly.

D.  Culture itself impacts psychological functioning.

Behaviour which deviates from normal occurs infrequently, hence, *statistical infrequency* (deviation from the statistical norm or average) can be used to determine if an individual meets diagnostic criteria. For instance, IQ scores in a standard population follow a bell-shaped curve (see overleaf). The arithmetic average (*mean*), the most frequently occurring score (*mode*) and the middle score (*median*) all fall at the mid-point of the curve: this is an IQ of 100. Most people (68 per cent) have an IQ between 85–115. Rare behaviour is found in the tails of the curve: very few people have an IQ of 70 or below (2 per cent) and very few people have an IQ of 130 or above (2 per cent).

The diagnostic point for Intellectual Developmental Disorder is an IQ of 70, plus/minus 5 points which allow for error. If, for ease of explanation, we look at an IQ of 70, we can see from the bell-shaped distribution overleaf, that only a small percentage of the population have this level of IQ and it therefore reflects the rarity of Intellectual Developmental Disorder. However, here we see a problem with using statistics: an IQ of 130 or above is also statistically rare, yet only the lower figure would be associated with psychological intervention. Moreover, the numerical value of an IQ of 70 isn't entirely helpful by itself: a person may have an IQ above 70 but still function akin to someone with a lower IQ score.

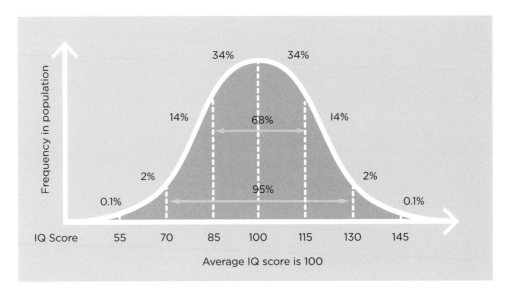

*IQ follows a bell-shaped curve. Most people have an IQ between 85-115; an IQ of 70 or below and an IQ of 130 or above are rare and found in the tails of the distribution of scores.*

Consequently, clinical judgement must supplement an IQ score.

Personal distress and impaired ability to cope at home, in the workplace, at school or socially can indicate deviation from normal functioning. For example, someone with clinical depression can experience great personal suffering and find it difficult or impossible to study, work, or go about usual daily tasks. Alternatively, a phobia (an anxiety disorder) which badly affects the ability to meet work demands, may mean the phobic foregoes applying for certain roles. On the other hand, though, psychological disorder can be present without personal distress, or recognition that behaviour patterns aren't those usually found in regular functioning. For instance, psychopaths do not feel distress at the way in which they treat others, whilst anti-social personality disorder is associated with no recognition that there is a problem with behaviours that are not only harmful to others, but to the disordered person him/herself. Additionally, sometimes behaviours which appear to be unproductive for daily living can be argued to have a positive purpose. In the phobia example above, the disorder is possibly interfering with successfully meeting a potential life goal, but it's also possible that it protects the person from harm. For instance, a height phobia might interfere with taking certain posts but protect from the consequence of falling from a height.

In summary, determining what is normal and what is deviation from normal is not always clear-cut.

# Approaches to Psychological Disorder

## BIOMEDICAL APPROACH

The biomedical model views psychological disorder as the product of biological processes.

Genetic inheritance is used to account for disorder by looking at whether the chance of a given disorder arising increases if a relative is similarly disordered. The *family method* considers genetic predisposition to psychological disorder by looking at first-degree and second-degree relatives. The former (parents, children, siblings) share 50 per cent of their genes, whereas the latter (e.g. nieces, nephews) share 25 per cent of their genes. If a psychological disorder is inherited, it should be more common where more genes are shared. The *twin method* follows the same rationale. Identical (or monozygotic, MZ) twins are genetically identical but fraternal (or dizygotic, DZ) twins share 50 per cent of their genes, as do other non-twin siblings. In these cases, if a psychological disorder is inherited, it should be more common between MZ rather than DZ twins. Where there is a high incidence of a particular psychological disorder within a family, attempts can be made to identify which gene is responsible.

However, a problem accompanies genetic evidence. Since families typically tend to live together, family environment has the potential to influence psychological disorder. This means that family environment effects can go on to make up a component of any apparently inherited element to disorder. Consequently, the *adoptee method* can be used to try and rule-out these

*If a psychological disorder is genetic in origin, then it should be more common in identical twins than fraternal twins. This is because identical twins have more shared genetic inheritance than fraternal twins.*

kinds of effects. It does this by assessing whether adopted children who have a biological parent with a psychological disorder, but whose adoptive parents are disorder-free, are more prone to having the same psychological issue as the biological mother/father.

Neurological explanations link psychological disorder to problems within the brain and to abnormal levels of neurotransmitters, the chemical substances that allow nerve cells to communicate with each other (see Chapter 2). Indeed, the most common biological intervention is drug therapy to influence neurotransmitter levels.

Although biology has its role to play in addressing psychological disorder, it is not necessarily the best or only way of explaining and treating all psychological problems.

## PSYCHOANALYTIC APPROACH
### (Associated with Sigmund Freud)

Freud linked psychological disorder to conflict between his proposed components of personality and fixation during the stages of psychosexual development (see Chapter 5). According to Freud, personality consists of:

| ID | EGO | SUPEREGO |
|---|---|---|
| Instinctual needs, e.g. food, water, warmth, sexual gratification. Driven by the *Pleasure Principle* which strives for immediate gratification. | Rational part of personality. Operates on the *Reality Principle* that aims to meet the id's needs realistically and in a socially appropriate way. | Our conscience/morality. It contains our parents' and society's ideals/morality. |

The ego has to balance what is realistic against the desires of the id and the superego's morality. If there is imbalance, the ego uses *ego defence mechanisms* to reduce the conflict and the anxiety that goes along with that conflict. This is when signs of psychological disorder can be observed. Personality develops as children progress through the five stages of psychosexual development: oral, anal, phallic, latent and genital (see Chapter 5). If a conflict arising at a given stage isn't resolved, *fixation* occurs and a person remains fixed at that developmental point. For example, the oral stage is associated with weaning an infant; during this process the child learns to become more independent of his/her caretaker(s). If the conflict associated with weaning is unsuccessful and fixation occurs, one result could be a person who is overly-dependent upon others.

Psychoanalytic therapy is a form of 'talking therapy' which explores how previous experiences are influencing the client now. Modern psychoanalysis has advanced considerably since Freud, but even so, psychoanalytic accounts are not necessarily drawn upon for explanation and treatment of psychological disorder.

## BEHAVIOURAL APPROACH
### (Associated with Ivan Pavlov, Burrhus F. Skinner)

This approach proposes that the behaviours associated with psychological disorder can be learned. Learning can occur through *classical conditioning* and *operant conditioning*. The former involves repeatedly pairing two stimuli. In Pavlov's research, he repeatedly sounded a bell when giving dogs food. This had two results: (1) the dogs' natural response to the food, which was to salivate and (2) the dogs learning to associate food with the sound of the bell. This learned association then led the dogs to salivate purely on hearing the bell. From this learned behaviour pattern, it has been proposed that phobias could be acquired in a similar way: for example, a bad, anxiety-inducing experience, with a dog (a pairing) could lead to dogs being feared (having a dog phobia).

Operant conditioning involves behaviour occurring and being repeated because it is reinforced through a reward. Skinner found that if a rat were placed in a box with a lever, it discovered that pressing the lever delivered a food pellet. The pellet reinforced the rat's behaviour so that lever presses became more frequent. Similarly, if someone who has learned to fear dogs now avoids them, s/he too experiences a reward because dog-induced anxiety does not occur (thus the dog phobia is maintained).

Treatments based upon the principles of classical and operant conditioning have been devised so that someone with dysfunctional behaviour can learn functional behaviour. It is even possible to use relevant treatments even if the disordered behaviour was not acquired through conditioning initially. However, behavioural accounts and treatments are not suited to all disorders.

*Ivan Pavlov.*

## CLASSICAL CONDITIONING

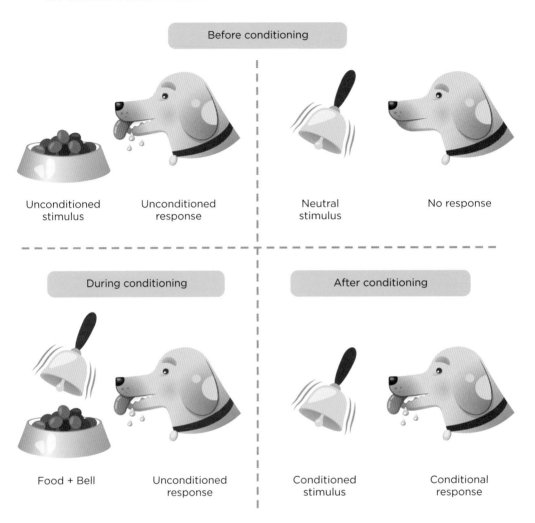

*How Pavlov conditioned dogs to salivate at the sound of a bell.*

## COGNITIVE APPROACH
### (Associated with Albert Ellis and Aaron Beck)

The cognitive approach links thoughts and feelings to behaviour. *Cognitive biases* (faulty thinking, beliefs, perceptions and interpretations) contribute to psychological disorders by producing symptoms and keeping them in place.

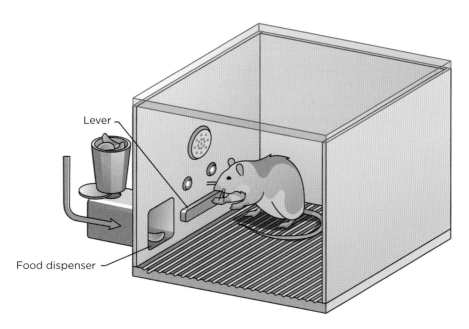

*The Skinner box. When a rat discovers that pressing the lever releases a food pellet, lever presses become more frequent. This is because the food rewards the lever-pressing behaviour and this behaviour is thus reinforced*

Ellis proposed an A-B-C-D-E-F model to explain and treat disorder. The explanation involves: an activating event (A) causes beliefs (B) that lead to consequences (C).

How an individual thinks about the event is captured in their beliefs (B), whilst emotional reaction to those beliefs and resulting behaviours are found in the consequences (C). However, since it is possible to control and change faulty thoughts and feelings, new, healthier beliefs, feelings and behaviours can be produced.

*Rational Emotive Behaviour Therapy* (probably the oldest cognitive therapy) involves disputation (D) leading to an effect (E) which yields new feelings and behaviours (F). Disputation entails questioning and challenging the beliefs (B): for example, examining the evidence for the thoughts held; considering an alternative view. Learning to dispute successfully produces effective or healthy, helpful thoughts and beliefs (E). New feelings and behaviours can then follow (F).

Beck's cognitive theory explains psychological disorder with reference to *automatic thoughts*. Such thinking is negative, spontaneous and habitual, though the precise character of automatic thoughts differs according to the kind of psychological problem a person has. The thoughts derive from *cognitive schemas*; that is, the mental frameworks we create from life events and which we then use to interpret our experiences. For example, if a person develops an 'I am useless' schema (perhaps from being repeatedly told this as a child), they might consistently interpret matters going wrong within this framework rather than attribute them to other causes. Beck also identified particular types of unhealthy thinking and proposed that in depression a *cognitive triad* exists. That is, the individual thinks negatively about themselves, the world and the future.

*Aaron Beck.*

Beck's therapy is called *cognitive therapy / cognitive behaviour therapy* (*CBT*) and is a goal-oriented, collaborative therapy designed to change thinking and behaviour patterns. Together, patient and therapist decide on the goals to be achieved and those that are designated the most important are addressed first. Each therapy session is organized to provide continuity from the last meeting to the present one and includes the following features: therapist and patient determine the content of the session; homework set in the previous session is considered; problems are discussed and further homework is set. Homework tasks involve behavioural tasks to benefit the patient.

One critique of the cognitive model is that faulty thinking may not be the cause but the product of having a psychological disorder.

*Carl Rogers.*

## HUMANISTIC APPROACH
### (Associated with Carl Rogers)

The humanistic approach focuses on therapy rather than explaining the origins of psychological problems. A person's free will is central to therapy. Although free choice can lead to a fulfilling life, this is not inevitably so, for free choice can also produce a painful life. Nevertheless, free choice must be exercised but if this challenge is too great, humanistic therapy can help. It does this by looking at the person as a whole; encouraging him/her to be aware of their needs and motivations and helping them to self-actualize, or fulfil their potential.

There are several types of humanistic interventions but Rogers's *client-centred* (or *person-centred*) *therapy* is probably best known. Its assumptions include that people are innately good, goal-directed and must be understood via how they experience life events. Therapists use techniques to create a positive environment for the client. *Unconditional positive regard* involves accepting the client as s/he is and being fully supportive, whilst through using *empathy*, the therapist accepts and understands what is communicated and reflects-back the client's thoughts and feelings. Ultimately, the client becomes more self-aware, can make independent decisions and can self-actualize.

## Classification and Diagnosis of Disorder

Guidance on the classification and diagnosis of disorder are provided in:
(a) the World Health Organization's *International Classification of Diseases*, currently in its 11th revision, *ICD-11*;

**BRIEF EXAMPLES OF HOW ICD AND DSM ORGANIZE THEIR INFORMATION**

This box gives a very brief idea of the way in which ICD-11 and DSM-5-TR cover psychological disorder. As ICD covers many other topics as well as mental disorder, it has a specific heading for the latter.

The examples provided below firstly show how the two systems list different types of disorder. Although they are very similar, some phrasing is different and ICD includes 'Bipolar or related disorders' under 'Mood Disorders'. Secondly, the examples give a brief indication of how a given type of disorder has lists of specific disorders under its heading; (the same type of disorder has been chosen for comparison purposes). DSM lists Schizotypal (Personality) Disorder but discusses it in the section devoted to personality disorders.

**ICD-11's Mental, behavioural or neurodevelopmental disorders**
Five examples of types of disorder are listed here, but there are many more:
Neurodevelopmental disorders
Schizophrenia or other primary psychotic disorders
Mood disorders
Anxiety or fear-related disorders
Personality disorders and related traits

> **Schizophrenia or other primary psychotic disorders**
> Three examples of these types of disorder listed here, there are more:
> Schizophrenia
> Schizoaffective disorder
> Schizotypal disorder

**DSM-5-TR**
Six examples of types of disorder listed here, but there are many more:
Neurodevelopmental disorders
Schizophrenia spectrum and other psychotic disorders
Bipolar and related disorders
Depressive disorders
Anxiety disorders
Personality disorders

> **Schizophrenia spectrum and other psychotic disorders**
> Three examples of these types of disorder listed here, there are more:
> Schizotypal (Personality) disorder
> Schizophrenia
> Schizoaffective disorder

(b) the American Psychiatric Association's *Diagnostic and Statistical Manual of Mental Disorders* now in its fifth, text revised edition, *DSM-5-TR*.

Overlap occurs between the ICD and DSM systems with reference to mental disorder but the ICD's overall content is broader because it covers human diseases and medical conditions too. Both systems list different types of disorder, then increase in specificity to particular disorders: descriptions are provided plus diagnostic criteria and other important information.

Although the systems may give the impression that all disorders are quite distinct from each other, it's possible for disorders to occur together (*comorbidity*). For example, depression and anxiety have been found to be comorbid with a number of other disorders.

## Psychological Disorders

### NOTE TO READER

Different mental disorders are discussed below including their symptoms. Some symptoms may be found in other disorders which are not considered here. If the reader is concerned, it may be appropriate to seek professional advice. In the UK, useful information can be found online from sources such as: the *NHS* and the charities, *Mind, Mental Health Foundation* and *Young Minds*.

### SCHIZOPHRENIA: AN EXAMPLE OF A PSYCHOTIC DISORDER

The term *psychosis* describes a loss of contact with reality in which the individual finds it difficult to distinguish between what is and isn't real. The term *schizophrenia* derives from Greek roots meaning 'splitting' and 'the mind' and was first used by Eugen Bleuler in 1908. Although it is not uncommon for people to think schizophrenia involves a split personality, perhaps something like Robert Louis Stevenson's characters, *Dr Jekyll and Mr Hyde*, this is not the case, and not what Bleuler intended. Instead, he was attempting to capture what he saw as a clear splitting of psychological functions such that personality loses unity.

Today, schizophrenia is characterized as having *positive* and *negative* symptoms. Positive symptoms reflect

*Eugen Bleuler.*

*'Some people with schizophrenia experience hallucinations; these can occur in any of the senses but auditory ones are the most common.'*

an addition to, or distortion of normal functions, whilst negative symptoms reflect a reduction or loss of normal functions.

Positive symptoms include delusions, hallucinations, disorganized thinking revealed in speech, grossly disorganized/abnormal motor behaviour and catatonia. Negative symptoms include diminished emotional expression, alogia (speech poverty), avolition, asociality and anhedonia. For a diagnosis of schizophrenia, it is not necessary to have all symptoms. In fact, it has been pointed out that it is possible for people with the same diagnosis of schizophrenia to be quite different in what they experience. Additionally, those diagnosed with the disorder do not respond identically to medications. Consequently, clinical psychologist, Richard Bentall has argued that schizophrenia's symptoms should be regarded as different disorders with their own causes and associated treatments. At present though, if someone meets the criteria for diagnosis, the diagnosis is schizophrenia.

The biological approach provides evidence that genetic inheritance contributes to schizophrenia. However, this does not mean genetic inheritance is the cause of the disorder, nor that having such an inheritance will inevitably give rise to schizophrenia. Instead, genetic inheritance produces a vulnerability, which, when coupled with a stressful environmental

## EXAMPLES OF SCHIZOPHRENIA'S POSITIVE AND NEGATIVE SYMPTOMS

| Positive Symptoms | Negative Symptoms |
| --- | --- |
| *Delusions*<br><br>False, firmly held beliefs despite conflicting evidence; they include:<br><br>Persecutory – person believes s/he's being persecuted, harmed, harassed.<br><br>Grandiose – believes s/he is someone famous; has special abilities or wealth.<br><br>Referential – believes external occurrences are directed at her/him.<br><br>Nihilistic – believes part of the individual or the world no longer exists.<br><br>Control – thoughts / actions / feelings are being controlled by an outside force.<br><br>Erotomanic – belief that someone of high social status is in love with him/her; this delusion is not common. | *Diminished Emotional Expression*<br><br>Emotional expressions reduced, including: eye contact, face movement; speech intonation; hand and head movement used to signal emotion when speaking. |
| *Hallucinations*<br><br>Vivid, clear experiences in one of the senses without any external stimulus to cause the experience. Hallucinations can occur in any of the senses but auditory ones are the most common. The individual hears familiar or unfamiliar voices which are distinct from their own thoughts. The voices may issue commands, hold a conversation or commentate on the individual's thinking. Voices can be malicious or benevolent. | *Alogia (Speech Poverty)*<br><br>Reduced speech; may be only 'yes / no' in reply to questions. |
| *Disorganized Thinking (Speech)*<br><br>Disorganized thinking is detected in | *Avolition*<br><br>Reduced motivation to engage in |

| | |
|---|---|
| speech. Speech may exhibit: Derailment/loose associations – switching quickly from topic to topic. Tangentiality – questions' answers are unrelated, or only indirectly related to the query. Incoherence – severely disorganized speech. This may include made-up words; speech produced based on words' sounds; no evident connection between phrases. | activities with a purpose; this can include work/social activities. |
| *Grossly Disorganized/Abnormal Behaviour* Behaviour may be: silly like a child's behaviour; inappropriate for where the person is; agitated; unpredictable. Day to day tasks may not be completed, or completed inappropriately (e.g. dressing, personal hygiene). | *Asociality* Lack of interest in / involvement in social activities. |
| *Catatonia* Decreased reaction to the environment. May include rigid posture; excessive movements. | *Anhedonia* Reduction in ability to experience pleasure from what is normally pleasurable; reduction in recalling pleasurable events. |

circumstance, leads to the emergence of the disorder. The kinds of environmental stressors related to schizophrenia are varied but include childhood sexual abuse, dysfunctional family relationships and deviant communication within the home (i.e. communication which the average person would find difficult and hard to follow and to understand).

The neurotransmitter dopamine and brain abnormalities have also been linked to schizophrenia. The *dopamine hypothesis* proposes that schizophrenia's symptoms arise either from the individual having too much dopamine, or, alternatively, from having normal dopamine levels accompanied by neuronal receptors (see Chapter 2) which are extremely sensitive to the neurotransmitter. Different brain abnormalities have been associated with schizophrenia's different symptoms. One example involves the prefrontal cortex (see Chapter 2). This area is involved in decision making, planning, purposeful behaviour, working memory (Chapter 1) and speech, all of which are affected in schizophrenia.

Biological treatment for schizophrenia involves antipsychotic medication. Antipsychotics fall into two types, first generation, or *typical antipsychotics* and the newer, second generation, or *atypical antipsychotics*. The older medications have been successful in treating positive symptoms but are associated with side effects, especially ones which produce symptoms like those of Parkinson's Disease (tremors and slurred speech). Second generation antipsychotics have improved positive symptoms, been better with negative symptoms and reduced the Parkinsonian side effects. Medications do not cure the disorder and second generation drugs can have their own side effects. However, they have significantly reduced the need for hospitalization of those with the disorder.

Behavioural accounts link schizophrenic symptoms to learning, through operant conditioning, in which rewards reinforce behaviour. For example, when someone with schizophrenia focuses on inconsequential aspects of the environment, it makes his/her behaviour appear very strange and unusual and thus attracts attention. As attention acts as a reward for the behaviour, the behaviour is both reinforced and repeated.

Learning via positive reinforcement has been used to eliminate undesirable schizophrenic behaviours and to foster desirable ones. The individual is not provided with a reinforcing, rewarding response when behaviour is inappropriate but is supplied with such a response when behaviour is appropriate, such as desirable self-care (e.g. hair combing) and socializing. Better socializing skills can also be taught through *social skills training*: this uses positive reinforcement, modelling (another behavioural technique in which learning occurs through watching another's behaviour) and role-playing. Skills such as how to behave in particular situations, make suitable eye contact and produce appropriate facial expressions can all be learned.

There are several cognitive explanations of schizophrenia's symptoms and just three of these are discussed below. First to be considered is Chris Frith's *Theory of mind* (TOM) account. TOM refers to a person's ability to understand their own cognitive processes (e.g. beliefs, attitudes, intentions, feelings) and the ability to use this knowledge to understand others' actions. When TOM isn't properly operational, this can produce symptoms found in schizophrenia. For instance, delusions of control arise through an inability to represent the person's own intentions to act, whilst persecutory and referential delusions come from an inability to understand other people's mental state.

'Hearing voices' is an auditory hallucination associated with psychosis. However, some

*Chris Frith.*

healthy people also hear voices, and there are cognitive differences between these individuals and those with psychosis. For example, 'hearing voices' has been attributed to activation of the brain's auditory areas and those with psychosis cannot detect that they themselves have generated the voices. Additionally, those with psychosis have more negative experiences with their voices. This has been ascribed to those with schizophrenia having a cognitive bias to interpreting their voices negatively. Unfortunately, the resultant negative interpretations make the person anxious, impact their mood and create physical changes which lead to yet more hallucinations. Other cognitive issues (e.g. problems with working memory) mean the voices cannot be controlled successfully. In turn, the uncontrolled nature of the voices yields distress which contributes to negative interpretation of the voices.

David Hemsley has proposed that hallucinations arise from attention failure. Essentially, he argued that experience teaches us what to expect and how to interpret our current situation. Subsequently, we use what we've learned to know what does and does not require attention and this happens automatically and swiftly. However, in schizophrenia, automatic focusing of attention does not occur. Instead, attention is given to everything, resulting in the individual's senses being inundated with information. As all sensory stimuli are treated as equally important and superfluous information isn't rejected, hallucinations arise. For example, 'hearing voices' occurs because a distinction cannot be made between internal thoughts and external stimuli. Delusions, on the other hand, stem from an attempt to derive meaning from the volume of external and internal stimuli. Negative symptoms are also addressed by this account in that they could result from the flood of sensory information, or emerge as a means of coping with this information.

Cognitive behavioural intervention can be used to address schizophrenia's symptoms in a number of ways. Cognitive challenges can be used to address: low expectations associated with negative symptoms; whether hallucinations may have another meaning from the one the individual believes they have, and whether delusions may have alternative explanations. If the therapist's verbal challenge is insufficient for a faulty belief to be rejected, its inaccuracy can be demonstrated via reality testing. This is a behavioural test as to whether the individual's beliefs fit with reality.

Where memory, attention and problem-solving difficulties are present, someone with schizophrenia may take part in a cognitive enhancement therapy to help improve these abilities. As daily living requires a variety of cognitive and behavioural skills, personal therapy can help ensure appropriate skills are available for the individual to cope. For instance, s/he might learn how to ensure s/he takes prescribed medication, how to recognize indicators of a relapse and what to do.

Schizophrenia has also been linked to how much negative, expressed emotion (EE) is present in the family of the person with the disorder. High EE has been connected to relapse. It occurs when the individual is subject to hostility and criticism from family members who blame him/her for, and are intolerant of, the disorder's symptoms. They also see their family member's symptoms as stemming from causes that mean improvement is unlikely and deal with the symptoms in fixed ways. High, negative EE is thought to be very stressful for the person with schizophrenia and the resultant stress leads to biological consequences that ultimately influence the neurotransmitter, dopamine.

Fortunately, family interventions based on *psychoeducation* are available to both assist family members and help prevent relapse. The interventions inform the family about the nature

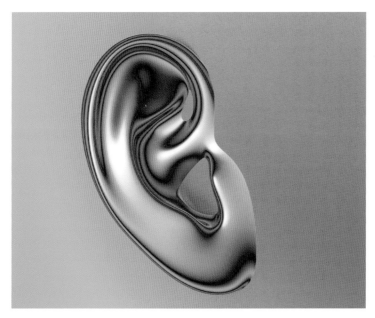

*Some people with schizophrenia experience hallucinations. An hallucination is an experience in one of the senses in the absence of an external stimulus to cause that experience. Audtiory hallucinations are the most common*

of schizophrenia (e.g. causes, symptoms) and provide information on courses of action when difficulties arise. Psychoeducation can involve learning about how low EE communication operates; how different experiences in the family can be discussed in a blame-free manner; how to encourage the family member to take prescribed medication; how to identify stress-inducing factors that might give rise to relapse and behaviours associated with relapse.

## MAJOR DEPRESSIVE DISORDER: AN EXAMPLE OF A MOOD DISORDER

Major depressive disorder is not the same as feeling down, unhappy and/or sad for a short period. Instead, it has symptoms associated with clinically significant distress along with impaired social or occupational functioning or impaired functioning in other significant areas of life. The disorder leads to emotional, cognitive, motivational, physical and behavioural problems.

Biological evidence indicates that genetics and their interaction with environmental factors (maltreatment in childhood; important events which have a significant effect on

*Major depressive disorder is associated with clinically significant distress, emotional, cognitive, motivational, physical and behavioural symptoms..*

| EXAMPLES OF THE EMOTIONAL, COGNITIVE, MOTIVATIONAL, PHYSICAL AND BEHAVIOURAL SYMPTOMS OF MAJOR DEPRESSIVE DISORDER WHICH MAY OCCUR | |
|---|---|
| **Symptom Type** | **Examples of Characteristics Which May Occur** |
| Emotional | Low mood; feeling hopeless, helpless, sad, miserable, worthless, dejected, discouraged, anxious, guilty. May often cry or be close to tears. Few positive emotions or facial expressions. Loss of sense of humour. May feel intolerant of others. |
| Cognitive | Difficulty paying attention, concentrating, thinking, remembering, making decisions. Negative beliefs about themselves, the world and the future; beliefs that the future can't be changed contribute to feelings of worthlessness, guilt and shame. Some people may believe it would be better if they were dead and some have suicidal thoughts. |
| Motivational | Lack of pleasure or interest in usual daily activities or things that brought pleasure such as hobbies. Lack of initiative which may begin by not wanting to spend time with others. Desire to stay where they are. Appetite can decrease noticeably (but it may increase too). Sexual desire can reduce markedly. |
| Physical | Changes to sleep such as sleeping too much; waking during the night and finding it hard to get back to sleep; waking in the early morning and being unable to go back to sleep. Unplanned increase/decrease in weight. Women may find their menstrual cycle is affected. Headaches, digestive issues, cramps, aches and pains that don't have a clear cause. |
| Behavioural | Slow movements; slow speech. Lack of energy and tired; reduced physical activity; may stay in bed for stretches of time. |

the quantity/quality of interpersonal relationships) influence whether someone experiences major depression.

Depression has also been connected to neurotransmitters and different proposals have been forwarded regarding the nature of this relationship. For example, motivational, cognitive and behavioural symptoms have been linked to serotonin and norepinephrine (also called noradrenaline) because they are required for messages to pass successfully

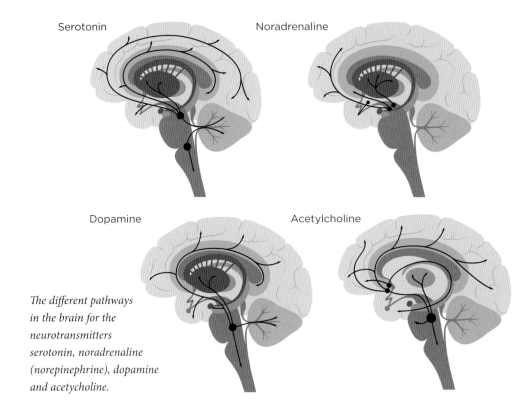

Serotonin

Noradrenaline

Dopamine

Acetylcholine

*The different pathways in the brain for the neurotransmitters serotonin, noradrenaline (norepinephrine), dopamine and acetycholine.*

between neurons. Reduced pleasure, motivation and initiative, on the other hand, have been linked to low dopamine because this neurotransmitter plays a role in the brain's reward systems. However, more recent accounts have argued that depression arises from an imbalance between neurotransmitters. Liborio Rampello and colleagues proposed mood is produced by an imbalance between a number of neurotransmitters including dopamine, serotonin, norepinephrine and acetycholine.

Brain abnormalities and impaired brain functioning are found in depression too. One example relates to the prefrontal cortex, which has been found to have less grey matter and reduced activation in people who are depressed. Since the prefrontal cortex is important for goal-directed activity, these anomalies may be related to reductions in this type of behaviour. Another example concerns the high levels of the stress hormone, cortisol, found with depression and which is associated with abnormality of the hippocampus (Chapter 2).

A comparatively new biomedical theory proposes that at least in some people, depression may be associated with changes in the immune system which trigger inflammation in the brain. When the body is invaded by something harmful and this is detected by an immune cell, the immune cell sends out *cytokines*, or messages, which signal the invader's presence and that an immune response is required. Inflammation is one of the immune responses cytokines produce. This relates to depression because physically ill people, and physically healthy people with depression, share some symptoms (e.g. extreme tiredness) and they both have increased cytokine levels. Moreover, cytokines are known to affect dopamine, serotonin and norepinephrine levels, and to reduce appetite and activity levels. These behaviours are, of course, observed in depressed people, but they occur too, when our bodies are fighting an invading organism. Hence, another link exists for the proposal that there is a connection between depression and inflammation.

The most common biological treatment is using medication to relieve major depressive disorder. Certain medications increase serotonin and norepinephrine levels in the brain, whilst others increase only serotonin. Evidence indicates that drug treatments can be beneficial though they are also reported to have side effects. A second type of intervention available when medication and psychological therapies have not been successful is *electroconvulsive therapy* (*ECT*). Treatment by ECT originally resulted from observation that psychosis and epilepsy rarely occurred together and that mood frequently improved after epileptic seizure. Today, ECT involves passing an electric current through the head for approximately half a second to induce a controlled seizure like those observed in epilepsy. Although ECT has been found to help severe depression, it is a highly controversial treatment; it is unknown precisely how it benefits severe depression, and it has side effects, the most common one being notable memory loss. A newer

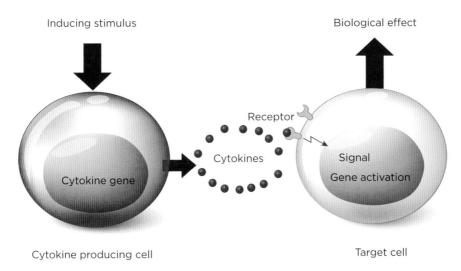

*When an immune cell detects something harmful, it sends out cytokines which signal the presence of an invader and that an immune response is needed.*

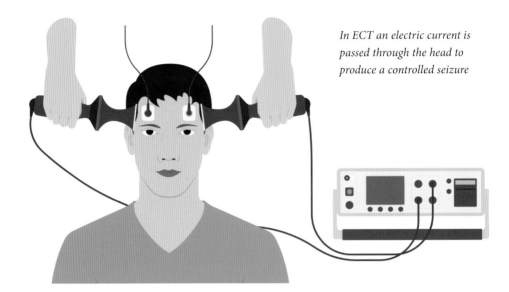

*In ECT an electric current is passed through the head to produce a controlled seizure*

alternative to ECT is *transcranial magnetic stimulation* (*TMS*). This involves passing a magnetic field into the brain to increase activity in a particular region of the prefrontal cortex. Evidence indicates it can improve major depression without ECT's memory side effects but it is not as yet fully clear how TMS influences mood.

Freud proposed depression relates to loss and grieving and the processes he described operate unconsciously. He argued that during grieving (e.g. the death of a parent) the mourner *regresses*, or returns, to the earliest stage of psychosexual development: this is the oral stage, which a child goes through between 0–18 months. At this time, the child was dependent on others and regression to this stage helps cope with the distress felt at the loss of a loved one. Through *introjection*, the mourner incorporates or identifies with the loved one. However, as negative feelings are often unconsciously held about the loved one, the mourner becomes the object of their own negative feelings. Successful mourning work allows mourner and loved one to separate and loosens the effects of introjection. However, if this does not occur, negative feelings such as anger are still directed inward causing self-hatred and depression.

Not all depression is caused by the death of a loved one though. Instead, it can be the product of another kind of loss event coupled with *fixation* at the oral stage. Oral fixation leads to a person being excessively dependent on others for love, approval and self-esteem. If these features are then subject to an imagined or symbolic loss (such as via withdrawal of love, affection, or esteem by significant people; a child's separation from a parent; job loss), introjection follows. Negative feelings felt toward the person associated with the loss event are directed inwards, and depression follows.

Freudian psychoanalysis requires that unconscious conflicts are worked through. With depression, therefore, the individual would be helped to gain insight into their conflict and to work through it; for example, dealing with inwardly directed hostility. However, modern, psychodynamic therapy focuses on personality's dynamic forces, which shift and change to produce behaviour.

Behavioural theories account for depression in terms of learning via operant conditioning. Peter Lewinsohn and colleagues contended that depression arises where there is a lack of reinforcement for productive behaviours. The lack of rewards causes the productive behaviours to stop (*extinction*) which is followed by social withdrawal and inactivity. Initially, this may produce more attention and therefore greater social contact but because these function as rewards, the individual's behaviour is further reinforced. When this ultimately leads to receiving less attention/low positive social reinforcement, the person's mood is affected and depression arises. Furthermore, as the symptoms of depression do not attract positive social reinforcement, depression can become long-lasting.

*Behavioural activation therapy* has people engage in pleasant activities so that they receive positive reinforcement and thus improve their mood. It might involve the individual highlighting

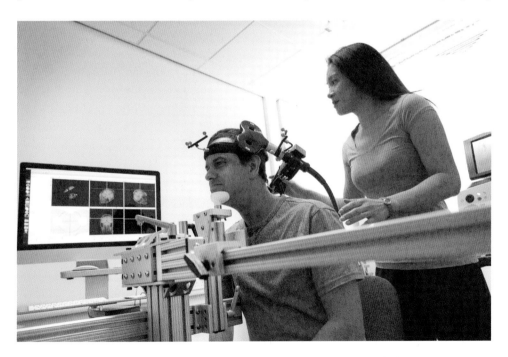

*Transcranial Magnetic Stimulation involves a magnetic field being passed into the brain.*

where they would like improvements in life, such as friendships, so that reinforcement in these areas can be focused upon. Additionally, improved interactions with others can be fostered through social skills training, which might involve improving conversational ability, or assertiveness training, for instance.

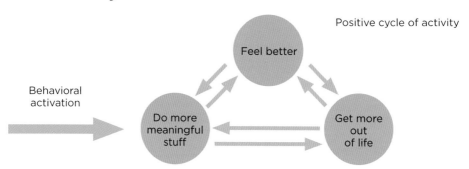

*Behavioural activation therapy improves mood by having people engage in pleasant activities from which they receive positive reinforcement.*

Beck's theory of depression proposes that the disorder arises from, and is maintained by, an interaction between *negative schemas, cognitive biases* and the *negative triad.*

Negative schemas (or life's organizational frameworks) are established during childhood and adolescence. Various events can create negative schemas/beliefs (e.g. the loss of/rejection by a parent, rejection by peers and teachers' criticisms) and these become crucial in adulthood when a stressful experience occurs, especially one that resembles an earlier circumstance. Mood lowers, negative schemas are activated, biased thinking occurs and the symptoms of depression follow. Cognitive biases, or negative ways of thinking feed into and are fed by the negative schemas. Together the biases and schemas support the negative triad. The negative triad relates to *the self, the world* and *the future*, each of which is viewed negatively.

Other cognitive accounts of depression focus upon helplessness and hopelessness. Originally, Martin Seligman proposed that if a person has several negative, uncontrollable and inescapable life experiences, this can create a negative mindset in which the person believes 'bad things' will happen no matter what they do. In turn, this gives rise to hopelessness and depression. From this, Lyn Abramson, Seligman and John Teasdale developed the *attribution model* in which they argued helplessness derives from an individual's attributional style, or the way in which they explain an event's cause. Causes can be:

(1) internal / external     (i.e. personal / environmental)

(2) stable / unstable     (i.e. unlikely to change soon / temporary)

(3) global / specific     (i.e. affecting many areas of life / restricted to one area).

| EXAMPLES OF BECK'S COGNITIVE BIASES | |
|---|---|
| **Overgeneralization** | drawing a sweeping conclusion based on a single incident. |
| **Arbitrary influence (jumping to conclusions)** | drawing a conclusion based on insufficient evidence/no evidence. |
| **Selective abstraction** | drawing a conclusion based on one aspect of a situation and ignoring all the others. |
| **Personalization** | tendency to interpret an event personally rather than objectively. |
| **Dichotomous (all or none thinking)** | everything is categorized in absolutes ('black or white' thinking) with no middle ground. |
| **Magnification** | exaggerating an event so that it is perceived as wholly bad. |
| **Minimization** | exaggerating an event so that it is perceived as irrelevant or neutral. |

| AN EXAMPLE OF AN INTERACTION BETWEEN A NEGATIVE SCHEMA, COGNITIVE BIASES AND THE NEGATIVE TRIAD | | |
|---|---|---|
| **Negative Schema** | 'I am incompetent' | |
| **Cognitive Biases Examples** | | |
| overgeneralization | makes one mistake in doing something and concludes 'I can't get anything right' | |
| selective abstraction | looks at a set of 10 exam results in which 9 are excellent and one is average and feels academically inept based on the one result | |
| arbitrary influence | on a busy street a work colleague gives no greeting; this leads to the conclusion of being deliberately ignored because 'I'm incompetent' | |
| **Negative Triad** | *self* | 'I'm useless' |
| | *world* | 'Everything is too difficult for me' |
| | *future* | 'I'll never be any good' |

Depression is more likely to occur with internal, stable and global attributions. This can be seen in the box below, where the combined effect of these attributions can be seen to lead to negative, gloomy thinking and poor self-esteem compared with external, unstable, specific attributions.

Abramson and other colleagues revised the helplessness attribution account in their *hopelessness theory*, which addresses the cause of hopelessness depressions. Such depressions are the consequence of either: expectation desirable outcomes won't occur; or, expectation of undesirable outcomes, for which the individual has no responses to change the situation. That is, the depression is caused by being in a state of hopelessness, which is brought about through vulnerability interacting with stressful life events. One vulnerability involves attributing negative events to stable and global causes; other factors that could be involved include low self-esteem and presumptions that negative life events will produce serious, negative results.

Cognitive therapy aims to correct the negative thinking found in those who are depressed. The individual is taught to identify and challenge the kind of thinking that leads to a low mood: for example, if s/he were to say, 'I'm no good, I can't get anything right', this can be challenged by the therapist. The second half of the statement is an overgeneralization; this is identified, then challenged, ideally using examples from the client's life which illustrate the overgeneralization's inaccuracy, such as a time when there was success. The client will also be asked to monitor their thoughts and identify thinking patterns which contribute to being depressed. The therapist teaches the client to think through negative, automatic thoughts and to seek alternative, more balanced assumptions. If appropriate, negative-stable-global attributional style can be addressed via *reattribution training*. This helps the client to view their situation in a more positive way than their attributional style affords.

Beck also included behaviour in treating a depressed person. Physical activity for severe depression could involve getting out of bed, going for a walk, or going to a shop. Alternatively, a lower level of depression might involve an activity the individual finds agreeable.

---

### EXAMPLES OF ATTRIBUTIONAL STYLE

A person is made redundant along with several colleagues whilst others are retained. The attributions could be:

| | |
|---|---|
| internal / external | 'I'm no good' / 'this was due to the economic climate' |
| stable / unstable | 'This fits with all my other losses and it won't change' / 'I will be able to find employment elsewhere' |
| global / specific | 'I fail at everything' / 'my department was over-staffed'. |

*In addition to changing cognitions, Beck included behavioural interventions in treating a depressed person. Walking is a physical activity that can be used to help someone with depression.*

## SPECIFIC PHOBIAS: AN EXAMPLE OF AN ANXIETY DISORDER

A specific phobia involves a consistent, persistent, marked fear or anxiety about a specific object or situation which is usually immediate. The fear/anxiety is out of proportion to the actual danger posed, and although the phobic person is typically aware of this, s/he reacts according to the beliefs s/he holds about the phobic stimulus. Symptoms last for several months; the object/situation is actively avoided or endured in association with intense fear and anxiety and there is significant distress or impairment in important areas of functioning (e.g. personal/family life; work; education). As children do not necessarily express fear/anxiety in the same way as older individuals, they may cling, cry, have a tantrum or freeze.

DSM distinguishes five subgroups of specific phobias: animal, natural environment, blood-injection-injury, situational and other. Common phobias include animals, water, height, blood-injury-injection, dental phobias along with claustrophobia.

Evolution has been used to explain specific phobia development from a biological perspective. Phobias to guns, motorcycles and electricity are less likely to be developed than phobias to animals, water, heights, injury and blood despite their presenting a genuine danger in current society. This difference can be attributed to animals etc having posed a threat to our prehistoric ancestors. According to Seligman, phobias which develop more readily due to their previous evolutionary usefulness, have led us to be *biologically prepared*, or to have a built-in, evolutionary predisposition to produce fearful reactions to what threatened our ancient ancestors. The fear isn't inborn; we are just much more ready to develop such phobias following a conditioning experience. This readiness to develop animal phobias etc exists because when our ancestors successfully avoided an animal etc, they survived, and thus the predisposition could be transferred to the next generation.

Another biological account links specific phobias to a structure in the brain called the *amygdala*. Specific phobias involve emotion (anxiety, fear) and the amygdala is important in memory for emotional events and its activation increases as subjective fear increases. Phobias also involve avoiding the feared object/situation. Once the amygdala has processed a phobic stimulus, it communicates with other parts of the brain which send responses. This information is integrated by the amygdala and supplied onwards, ultimately leading to muscle movement.

Freud proposed that the subject of a phobia symbolizes the original source of a person's anxiety. Anxiety is created when a feared id impulse is *repressed* (i.e. deliberately forgotten). The anxiety is dealt with by *displacement* (i.e. moving it) onto an object or situation with a symbolic connection to the id impulse, such as a horse, or enclosed space etc. Avoiding the phobic stimulus protects the individual from dealing with the anxiety induced by the id impulse. In this way, a phobia is a deep, psychological problem which must be addressed by finding its cause and lifting the repression.

 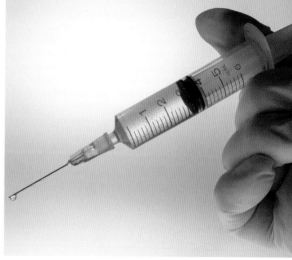

*Common subjects of phobias: a spider and a needle.*

| DSM PHOBIA SUBGROUPS, EXAMPLES OF PHOBIAS AND EXAMPLES OF PHOBIA NAMES | | |
|---|---|---|
| **DSM Phobia Subgroups** | **Examples** | **Examples of Phobia Names** |
| *Animal* | spiders<br>cats<br>dogs<br>snakes<br>mice<br>insects | arachnophobia<br>ailurophobia<br>cynophobia<br>ophidiophobia<br>musophobia |
| *Natural environment* | heights<br>storms<br>water | acrophobia<br><br>aquaphobia |
| *Blood-injection-injury* | needles<br>invasive medical procedures | trypanophobia (injections) |
| *Situational* | aeroplanes<br>lifts (elevators)<br>enclosed space | aerophobia / aviophobia (flying)<br><br>claustrophobia |
| *Other* | situations that may lead to choking or vomiting<br>in children, loud sounds or costumed characters | masklophobia (masks, people in costumes) |

However, modern psychodynamic theories would not automatically view specific phobias in quite this way. Instead, they might consider the phobia to be symbolic of something else that is occurring or has occurred in the person's life.

Hobart Mowrer's, behavioural, *two-factor theory* contended that phobias are acquired through classical conditioning and maintained by operant conditioning. In 1920, John Watson and Rosalie Rayner reported research which, it must be stressed, would now be unethical. They classically conditioned 'Little Albert', a nine-month-old boy, to fear a white rat. At first, he wasn't frightened of the animal, but by repeatedly pairing it with a loud noise, Albert learned to associate the noise with the rat and ultimately cried upon seeing the rat and without the

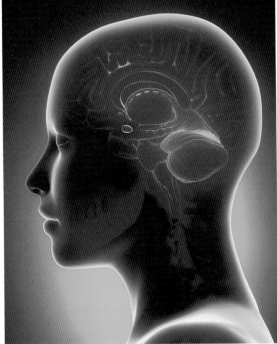

*The amygdala. This structure in the brain has been associated with specific phobias.*

noise. Albert's experience conditioned him to produce an emotional response to the rat; he cried and attempted to avoid the animal. Albert had acquired a phobia.

Operant conditioning maintains a phobia in two ways. Firstly, when the phobic stimulus is avoided, this reduces anxiety; anxiety reduction is rewarding and therefore the phobia is reinforced and maintained. Second, when the object/situation is avoided, this means the individual never encounters the phobic stimulus under circumstances where they feel safe. In turn, this means the fear cannot 'die out'; or, to use the relevant classical conditioning terminology, the fear cannot become *extinct* (extinguished).

To reiterate the behavioural account in very blunt terms: an anxious/frightening experience with an object/situation creates a phobia. The phobia is reinforced through avoidance and avoidance means the individual doesn't learn the stimulus can be encountered safely. Hence, the phobia persists.

More recent behavioural accounts have highlighted other ways in which phobias may be acquired. *Modelling* or *vicarious learning* involves watching somebody else's fearful reaction and then subsequently manifesting the same fear in the presence of the model's phobic stimulus. *Information transmission*, on the other hand, consists of fear developing towards a stimulus because a person has been told about how dangerous or disgusting something is.

Behaviour therapies employ *exposure* techniques to create *extinction* of anxiety/fear towards the phobic stimulus. Classical conditioning's learning principles are employed

*The Little Albert Experiment. Albert is seated between John Watson and Rosalie Rayner.*

to break the phobic stimulus-anxiety association by having the individual experience their feared object/situation without any anxiety. Thus, the person learns it is possible to encounter their phobic stimulus free from anxiety/fear.

Since those who have a phobia typically recognize their fear is excessive or unreasonable, a purely cognitive approach to addressing their disorder is unsatisfactory: they already think

| EXAMPLES OF CLASSICAL CONDITIONING BASED THERAPIES USED TO TREAT SPECIFIC PHOBIAS | |
|---|---|
| **Treatment** | **Procedure in Brief** |
| *Systematic densensitization* | Delivered using real stimuli, imagination or virtual reality. <br><br> The person being treated creates his/her fear hierarchy for the phobic stimulus running from its lowest fear grade to its highest. S/he is also taught how to perform deep muscle relaxation; relaxation will replace the anxiety response. <br><br> Whilst relaxing, the individual is exposed to the lowest level of the hierarchy. <br><br> When it is fully ensured the person is relaxed in association with this level and there is no anxiety response, the next fear grade above is dealt with in the same way. <br><br> When no anxiety occurs to the phobic stimulus, the anxiety response is extinct; it has also been replaced with relaxation (counter-conditioning). |
| *Flooding* | The individual encounters the phobic stimulus at its most frightening level and stays in its presence until it's no longer feared. Remaining until the fear isn't present is very important; if the person being treated leaves before this point, anxiety/fear may be reinforced. <br><br> Anxiety can't be maintained over a long time and so it returns to a normal level. <br><br> Now, the situation/object is associated with a normal anxiety level. |

their fear is inappropriate. Instead, what is crucial to note, is the way in which strong, unhelpful beliefs affect the perception of danger posed by the phobic stimulus, such as, the phobic stimulus may cause the individual harm. Faulty cognitions relate to why the stimulus is frightening (e.g. it's automatically thought, 'it will bite me'); these cognitions sustain fear and guide behaviour, such as avoiding the object/situation. Avoidance means situations never arise where the beliefs can be tested and shown to be mistaken. Consequently, more realistic thoughts do not develop, and it does not become evident that an alternative to the fear response is possible.

Cognitive behavioural therapy alters thinking via exposure to the feared object/situation. Exposure tests whether the individual's beliefs concerning their phobic stimulus are accurate. When the beliefs are shown to be incorrect because the expected consequences don't arise, the individual's anxiety reduces and accurate information about the threat posed by the situation/object can be established.

A comparatively new intervention, One-Session Therapy (OST) uses behavioural therapy's exposure technique and also addresses negative cognitions concerning the phobic stimulus. However, as its name implies, OST involves a client going through the therapy in a single (three-

*One-session therapy uses graduated exposures to the phobic stimulus; modelled non-anxious behaviour towards the stimulus and also challenges faulty cognitions.*

hour) session. The therapy involves encountering the phobic stimulus via graduated exposures; the therapist models non-anxious behaviour towards the stimulus (so the client can learn from this behaviour) and faulty cognitions are challenged. In this way, the client has a graduated but prolonged encounter with their phobic stimulus; physical avoidance is prevented and negative beliefs are demonstrated to be inaccurate and replaced with more helpful beliefs.

## SUMMARY

- Clinical psychology involves assessment, treatment and research related to psychological distress/wellbeing.
- Deviation from social norms, statistical infrequency plus distress and impaired ability to cope at home/work/school/socially have been used to assess deviation from normal functioning.
- The biomedical approach to disorder includes genetic inheritance, neurological problems in the brain and neurotransmitters. Biological interventions most commonly influence neurotransmitter levels.
- Freud's psychoanalytic approach explains disorder in terms of id, ego, superego and psychosexual development. Psychoanalysis addresses psychological problems by addressing how previous experiences influence the client now.
- Behavioural accounts contend psychological disorder is learned through classical conditioning and operant conditioning; treatment is based on learning functional behaviour.
- The cognitive approach links thoughts, feelings and behaviour; psychological disorder is addressed by dealing with faulty thinking and behavioural tasks.
- The humanistic account focuses on therapy and the difficulties which can arise from having free will. Client-centred therapy helps increase self-awareness so that a person can make decisions independently and reach their potential.
- The International Classification of Diseases and Diagnostic and Statistical Manual of Mental Disorders provide information for the classification and diagnosis of disorder.
- Biological, psychoanalytic, behavioural and cognitive accounts and treatments have been provided for different disorders including the psychotic disorder, schizophrenia; the mood disorder, major depressive disorder and the anxiety disorder, specific phobia.

# HEALTH PSYCHOLOGY

**Whilst mental health issues are the province of clinical psychology (Chapter 6), health psychology is concerned with the psychological processes related to physical health/ illness and how physical health impacts psychological wellbeing. Consequently, health psychology is involved in maintaining and promoting health as well as preventing illness or disability and improving an illness's outcome.**

Psychological knowledge can be used to promote a healthy lifestyle (such as healthy eating, going for vaccinations) and to encourage health improvement (such as weight management, stopping smoking). People can be helped to manage illness (e.g. diabetes, rheumatoid arthritis); adjust to a serious illness (e.g. spinal damage), manage their pain, and to rehabilitate (e.g. after a heart attack).

Academic health psychologists work in universities: teaching, conducting research and completing other duties associated with being a lecturer. Practitioner health psychologists can work in primary care, hospitals and rehabilitation centres as well as non-medical settings, such as community groups and organizations. Patients may be children, adults and older adults, as well as sometimes the patients' family or carers, as illness can have effects on those close to a patient. A practitioner may work one-to-one, or with groups, whilst some may approach health through online or media methods. The role of a health psychologist can also include advising organizations, national and local government plus working with health professionals and providing them with advice.

## A Brief History of Health Psychology

Health psychology's existence as a separate specialization is comparatively recent. This is perhaps surprising, given that the discipline of psychology can be dated to 1879 and certain of its pioneers had medical training, such as Wilhelm Wundt and Sigmund Freud. Early attention to health, though, fell upon mental health. In the UK, this can be seen in medical men who developed an interest in psychology's ideas and who had an influence upon British psychology. For example, during World War I, William H.R. Rivers, addressed shell shock

*US shell shock patients in a hospital in France, January 1918.*

– originally thought to be a contagious psychological reaction – from the perspective that soldiers needed to face painful memories, in moderation, and used a 'talking cure' in this process.

As time progressed, both the psychoanalytic movement and medical psychology grew. Later, the role of clinical psychologist developed and by the second half of the 20th century, whilst psychoanalytic influence waned, health issues outside clinical psychology's traditional remit were being examined. Focus on physical health grew considerably, with cognitive and social psychological accounts being drawn upon to explain health-related behaviour. Additionally, behavioural medicine developed and psychology contributed to this sphere. Behavioural medicine applies behavioural theories and methods to health by taking an interdisciplinary approach that uses psychosocial, behavioural and biomedical information.

*Wundt was one of psychology's pioneers; he established the first psychology laboratory in 1879 but his background was originally medical.*

In this way, health and illness can be better understood and a broad knowledge can be applied to prevention, diagnosis, treatment and rehabilitation.

By 1987, there was a special section for health within the British Psychological Society. This followed the American Psychological Association by nine years: their Division of Health Psychology being established in 1978. Now, health psychology is a profession separate from clinical psychology.

## What is Health?

**Task** – Please answer the following question *yes* or *no*: *Do you currently have good health?*

To respond to this query, you must have used a definition of what constitutes good health or otherwise. Now, here is another question: *What is your definition of health?*

In responding to the first question did you do any of the following:

- Decide you have good health because you are not ill?
- Take a medical condition into account?
- Consider health-related behaviours such as smoking, alcohol consumption, diet or taking exercise?
- Consider your physical fitness or physical restrictions?

If so, you have considered one or more of the kinds of issues that people usually think about in relation to health.

However, the World Health Organization (WHO, 1948) defined health as a *'state of complete physical, mental and social wellbeing and not merely the absence of disease and infirmity.'*

How does your answer to *What is your definition of health?* compare with the World Health Organization's? If you think that you may not meet the requirement of *'complete'*, this is not surprising; criticism of the definition has targeted this word. On the other hand, it is also possible to see the different kinds of complete wellbeing as something to aim for, encouraging us to do what is needed to achieve them.

How then can we achieve health? If a person already has an existing medical problem, of course, it is necessary to provide relevant healthcare. If there isn't currently a problem though, helping people to adopt a healthy life now also helps them prevent a problem arising later. Examples of non-communicable diseases which can be reduced through a change in behaviour include cancer, cardiovascular diseases (ischaemic heart disease, strokes), respiratory diseases (e.g. chronic obstructive pulmonary disease), diabetes, chronic kidney disease and type 2 diabetes.

Health psychology takes a biopsychosocial approach in which health and illness result from an interaction between *bio*medical, *psycho*logical and *social* factors. Examples of biological factors include genetic inheritance, the bodily systems (such as the cardiovascular, respiratory, digestive, or neural systems, for example) and the effects of external organisms (such as a bacterium, a virus or parasite). Psychological factors involve aspects such as a person's beliefs, attitudes, ways of thinking, emotions, stress levels, learning and behaviours. Behaviours can include acts such as alcohol consumption, diet, smoking and taking exercise. Social factors include those people with whom we have direct contact, such as: parents and other caregivers; other family members; friends; peers; social and work group members. However, they also include factors such as where a person is born, grows up and lives; work environment; education; social class; financial resources; employment versus unemployment; politics; culture and sub-culture; world and more local events.

## Lifestyle

Keeping in mind that health psychology uses a biopsychosocial approach, let's now look at this in the context of behaviours with which everyone is familiar – eating, drinking and taking exercise. Please note, the perspective is being limited to those areas of the world where exercise is not an integral component of daily survival; where food and drink are readily available and where clean water can be accessed with ease.

Eating and drinking are something that we all must do; indeed, they are essential to survival. Consuming the appropriate nutrients and calories from food benefits us by maintaining essential bodily functions such as brain activity, a beating heart, breathing, digestion, strong bones, growth, tissue repair and ensuring the immune system can fight illness. Sufficient fluids are important for such bodily activities as allowing the kidneys to dispose of waste products; the blood to take glucose, nutrients and oxygen to the body's cells and to regulate body temperature.

*Healthy eating is essential to the body and the brain's proper functioning.*

Regular physical activity is important too for several reasons. These include its role in burning calories which contributes to managing body weight: being overweight can lead to type 2 diabetes, certain cancers, heart disease and stroke. Physical activity also helps strengthen muscles and bones and in older adults, its improvements to strength, flexibility and balance can help with falling and fear of falling and reduce the risk of being unable to perform and enjoy everyday activities.

## DIET

However, whilst eating and drinking are commonplace, essential activities, in order to be healthy, it is not a matter of consuming whatever we wish. What we eat and drink can affect our bodies and facilitate health, or instead, lead to ill health. Furthermore, the diet we should eat and calories we should consume can be affected by issues such as special dietary requirements, age, medications and activity levels.

In considering the *biological* part of the biopsychosocial approach, let's focus on what is occurring in the body in relation to what is mentioned in the box overleaf: stroke, heart disease, rickets, cancer, type 2 diabetes and high blood pressure.

**Note to reader** – the information here is not intended to be at all exhaustive. If the reader has concerns about their health, it is recommended advice is sought from a medical professional. Information can be found online from the NHS (*www.nhs.uk*); the stroke association (*stroke.org.uk*); the British Heart Foundation (*bhf.org.uk*); Cancer Research UK (*cancerresearchuk.org*) and Diabetes UK (*diabetes.org.uk*).

A number of factors can cause the build-up of fatty deposits (atheroma) in the arteries (blood vessels which carry blood away from the heart). These include factors such as an unhealthy diet, high in fat; high cholesterol; being overweight; insufficient exercise. Atheroma consist of cholesterol (and other substances) which is associated with saturated fats (and trans fats).

Narrowing of the arteries can lead to problems such as a *stroke* or *heart attack*. Ischaemic strokes, for example, can be associated with a clot forming when atheromas break down or

*Regular exercise promotes good health.*

| EXAMPLES OF DIET IN RELATION TO HEALTH | |
| --- | --- |
| **Fruit and vegetables** | Benefits include providing vitamins and minerals; high fibre for a healthy gut; can help reduce risk of some types of cancer, heart disease and stroke. |
| **Starchy foods** (e.g. high fibre, wholegrain, bread, pasta, cereals, potatoes with their skins). | Supply carbohydrates which provide glucose for energy to support bodily functions and physical activity. High fibre foods of this type provide vitamins, minerals and of course, fibre. Fibre can help reduce the risk of bowel cancer, stroke, heart disease and type 2 diabetes. |
| **Pulses** (e.g. beans, peas, lentils, chickpeas) Fish Meat Eggs | Examples of foods that provide protein which is involved in growth, maintenance and repair in the body. Pulses provide fibre and can be an option instead of meat because they are low in fat. Meat should be lean to limit fat (see below). Fish contains vitamins and minerals; oily fish (e.g. salmon, sardines) contain omega-3 which can contribute to a healthy heart. |
| **Dairy** (e.g. milk, cream, cheese, butter). **Dairy alternatives** (e.g. soya) fortified with calcium, other vitamins and minerals. | Provide protein, minerals and vitamins; for example, calcium is a mineral involved in building bones, blood clotting and muscle contraction (including the heart). Lack of calcium can lead to osteoporosis in later life and rickets in children. Dairy contains saturated fat (see below); cheese and butter can also have high salt content. Dairy alternatives can have added sugar and salt. |

**Cakes, biscuits, ice-cream, crisps (and similar snacks), soft drinks.**

Collectively these foods and drinks relate to high sugar, fat and salt.

Sugar – we need one form of sugar, glucose but the body can manufacture enough glucose without our consuming extra sugar. 'Free sugars' are extra sugars, that is: (a) sugar that's added to food and drink at any point; (b) sugar in syrups, honey, nectars, smoothies, unsweetened fruit juices, vegetable juices. Free sugars do not include sugar in fruit, vegetables and milk. Sugar contributes to weight gain (which increases the risk of health issues such as type 2 diabetes and heart disease) and tooth decay.

Fat – we need fat because it provides fatty acids which the body does not make; it also helps us absorb vitamins A, D and E. Unused fat becomes body fat, and even in small amounts fat is high in calories and energy. Saturated fats raise LDL cholesterol and increases the risk of stroke and heart disease. They can also be found in fatty meat, sausages, pies, butter, cream, cheese, palm oil and other foodstuffs. Unsaturated fats can help lower LDL cholesterol; they can be found in foods such as olive oil, sunflower oils and oily fish.

Salt – a small amount of salt is needed so the muscles can contract and relax, for nerve impulses and for a proper balance of water and minerals. Salt can be present in a number and variety of foods other than snacks; high salt consumption is associated with high blood pressure which can increase the risk of stroke and heart disease.

become inflamed. When the clot then blocks a blood vessel, preventing blood and oxygen getting to parts of the brain, brain cells die. The symptoms of the stroke are related to which brain cells have died. Heart attacks are mainly caused by coronary heart disease, in which atheroma clog the coronary arteries. When an atheroma ruptures, a blood clot is produced which, if it blocks the heart's blood supply, causes a heart attack that damages the muscle of the heart.

*Rickets* occurs in children's growing bones. It involves the bones being softened and weakened which can give rise to problems with the skeleton (growth, development and deformities), the teeth, bone pain and in severe cases, bones that break more easily. Typically, rickets arises from insufficient vitamin D, which optimizes calcium absorption in the intestines. However, one of the other causes of rickets can be low calcium level. *Osteomalacia* is a condition similar to rickets but it is found in adults. It too is associated with soft and weakened bones plus a number of symptoms, including pain in joints and bones; difficulty walking; more easily broken bones and muscle cramps. It is also associated with a lack of vitamin D and calcium in the diet can help with bone strength. Vitamin D is produced when the skin is exposed to sunlight but it can also be obtained in the diet from egg yolks, oily fish and foods fortified with vitamin D.

*Cancer* is a disease in which abnormal cells in a part of the body continue to divide and thus grow uncontrollably. These cells can affect healthy tissue around them and it is also possible for a cancer which starts in one part of the body to spread to another part. Being overweight can increase the chance of having cancer compared with being a healthy weight. A healthy diet assists a person to both achieve and maintain a healthy weight. Additionally, the risk of bowel cancer can be helped to reduce with high fibre foods. Diets high in red meat or processed meat (meat that has been preserved or changed) can increase the risk of bowel cancer.

The body is fuelled by glucose (sugar) in the bloodstream which comes from carbohydrate in our diet. Insulin (a hormone released by the pancreas) is responsible for glucose getting into the body's cells. Once it is there, blood glucose levels decrease and the pancreas reduces how much insulin it releases. In *type 2 diabetes*, this process does not work properly. It is essential that type 2 diabetes receives treatment and is managed since high blood glucose levels can give rise to complications, such as, stroke and heart attack; certain cancers; issues with the feet; kidney and eye problems. A healthy diet which leads to healthy weight can help with blood glucose levels.

*Blood pressure* refers to the pressure on the artery walls as the heart pumps blood through the arteries. High blood pressure (hypertension) occurs when a person's blood pressure is consistently above normal. High blood pressure increases the risk of a number of problems including a stroke and heart attack. Since carrying extra weight can lead to higher blood pressure because more is demanded from the heart as it pumps blood through the body, keeping to a healthy weight can be beneficial. Eating a healthy diet helps with having a healthy weight. It

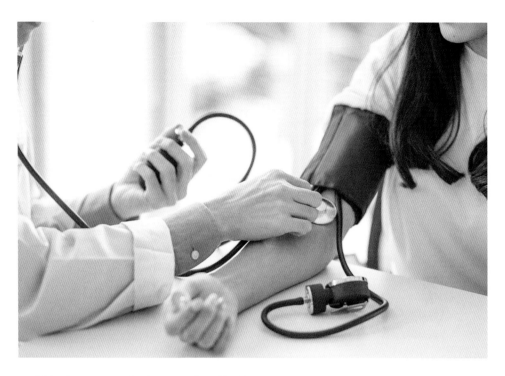

*High blood pressure can lead to a number of health issues.*

possesses other advantages too, in that a high fibre, low fat diet which does not have excessive salt intake can also help lower blood pressure.

Given that diet influences health, the question arises as to why some people do not regularly pursue a healthy diet? Keeping to the biopsychosocial approach, let's now look at some of the *psychological* factors which can affect consumption of food and drink.

Knowledge affects diet in different ways. If a person does not know what a healthy diet is, it cannot be followed. Furthermore, if the health reasons for pursuing the diet are not known, then a person may think there is no justification for switching their choices of food and drink. However, even when these aspects of knowledge are in place, it is essential that they are properly understood and that the individual knows how to apply the knowledge. Practical considerations relate to knowledge too: if someone does not know how to cook, this may limit their choices to less healthy options.

Learning also affects food choice. If a child lives in a family where lots of vegetables and fruit are a daily part of meals, alongside high fibre, low fat, low sugar, low salt, freshly cooked ingredients, this is the food the child will likely learn to prefer. Preference may increase the

*Children who grow up in households where fruit is common are more likely to prefer it when older.*

prospect of him or her opting for this kind of food in the future. For example, Helen Coulthard and colleagues found that children given home-cooked fruit and vegetables and raw fruit at six months old were more likely to be eating higher proportions of these foods at seven years of age. On the other hand, if family food consists of few fruits and vegetables, little fibre, high fat, high sugar, high salt items, it is likely foods which contain these contents will learn to be preferred.

It is not only the provision of food that affects learning; those we are around serve as models from whom we learn behaviour. Research indicates that children learn eating behaviours from parents and peers whilst adults can be influenced by other adults.

Learning via classical and operant conditioning can affect what we eat too. Suppose that whenever you deliberately settle-down to watch a film or a football match, you do so with a bowl of high fat, high salt snacks, or instead, something which is high in fat and sugar. The repeated pairing of these two events may become associated such that whenever you encounter a film or football match you get a craving for the associated food. Operant conditioning's role in eating behaviour can be observed regarding taste; for example, processed foods are tasty; tastiness acts as a reward and rewarded behaviours tend to be repeated.

Another psychological factor to affect dietary choice is emotion. Negative emotions and stress have been linked to an unhealthy diet which indicates unhealthy food may be used to cope with these states: daily hassles and negative emotion, for instance, have been linked to high fat, high sugar snacks. Indeed, when life's difficulties impact quality of life, some people may restore the balance by finding pleasure through consuming unhealthy foods. If you find this decision hard to understand, it may help to ask yourself whether you have ever eaten chocolate, a biscuit, ice-cream, or some cake to make yourself feel better?

Beliefs are important to health because they influence whether a diet is regarded as healthy, whether a person thinks they are likely to become unhealthy, and whether change is regarded as possible. The first two points relate to *optimistic bias*: that is, holding the belief that we are at less risk from a hazard than other people, such that risk from the hazard is underestimated. Consequently, it is possible for a person to believe that their current diet is healthy; that they eat a lot of fruit and vegetables and that they have low fat consumption, even when this is not actually the case. Over-optimism can also lead to a person believing they are at a lower risk than others from a medical issue, such as a heart attack. It is also possible to

*Some people turn to unhealthy snacks when suffering from negative emotions.*

believe that because to date, behaviour has not led to negative consequences, the same will be true in the future.

The final psychological factors to be considered here are *self-efficacy, attitude* to healthy eating and the *social influence* of others. The former relates to the extent to which a person regards herself or himself capable of pursuing a healthy diet; if self-efficacy is lacking, it is less likely a healthy diet will be adopted. Having a positive attitude to healthy eating has a direct effect on diet in terms of whether an individual will formulate an intention to eat healthily, whilst the influence of other people on food choice can be seen in the following sets of research. Tabea Huneke and colleagues reported that when a waitress with an apparently unhealthy lifestyle provided a menu, this led to earlier and longer attention being given to unhealthy food options compared with healthy ones. Additionally, Maferima Touré-Tillery and colleagues found that a healthy snack was more likely to be selected when people were observed by somebody from a different social group (i.e. an outgroup) compared with being observed by someone belonging to their own social group (i.e. an ingroup).

Turning now to some of the ways *social factors* contribute to eating behaviour, cost inevitably has a significant influence on what is purchased to eat and drink. How much has to be paid for what we consume is influenced by a variety of factors, including the cost of ingredients, materials and energy. Fossil fuel prices, for example, affect the price of food production (such as the cost of fertilizers) and food distribution. Demand for food; logistics; effects from weather and world events such as COVID-19 and the war in Ukraine all influence food costs too.

The lower a person's, couple's or family's income, the less money is available to spend on diet. Furthermore, what money is spent must be allocated to what will actually be eaten. Collectively, this means that if less healthy foods are cheaper, thought tastier, more satisfying and are those that will be eaten within the home, it is more likely that limited money will be spent on these goods. However, this is not meant to imply that higher income automatically guarantees a healthy diet because it does not. Higher income though, increases the kinds of places from which affordable food and drink can be purchased along with those options available to be part of a healthy diet.

Location of shops relates to food choices as well. A person may wish to purchase healthy foods but if, say, fruit and vegetables cannot be purchased at an affordable price locally, the only option is to shop further afield. Yet, this may not be possible due to transport costs being too high and if walking and carrying the goods home is not feasible. If either of these is the case, it is unlikely fruit and vegetables will be purchased.

Time available for both shopping and cooking impact diet. If time is at a premium, it may be more convenient to eat those products which provide a quick, tasty and satisfying meal rather than to cook from scratch. Being able to cook a meal from raw ingredients is not just affected

*Eating healthy food partly depends on having somewhere local where they can purchase it affordably.*

by time; it may be affected by age as well. Increased age is associated with health and mobility issues. Unless the older person can shop online, or has someone to shop for them, these issues may restrict where shopping can be done and what can be purchased. Within the home, health issues may also affect whether an older person is physically able to prepare food from basic ingredients: some standing may be necessary for too long a period; strength for lifting may be required along with the ability to carry items and peel or chop vegetables, for example.

## EXERCISE

Having considered diet in terms of the biopsychosocial approach to health, exercise will now be considered from the same perspective. Regular exercise affects health physically, or biologically, in many ways. Here, consideration is going to be given to certain medical issues considered above.

> **Note to reader** – Again, the following information is not intended to be exhaustive. If the reader has concerns, it is advised appropriate medical advice is sought. Information is available online through, for example, *www.nhs.uk*, *www.nhsinform. scot* and *www.who.int*.

The World Health Organization has stated that moderate-intensity and vigorous-intensity physical activity improve health and that physical activity is:

'any bodily movement produced by skeletal muscles that requires energy expenditure.' (WHO, *https://www.who.int/news-room/fact-sheets/detail/physical-activity*, accessed 14/12/22).

*Biologically*, exercise helps with weight loss and weight maintenance because it burns-up calories. Weight loss limits the amount of fat that a person carries, which in turn, can help reduce the risk of cancer because fat cells can send instructions to body cells to divide more frequently. Exercise's effects on weight is important for the heart too, as carrying too much weight puts stress on the heart. Physical activity though, strengthens the heart and also reduces blood pressure which is beneficial because high blood pressure increases the risk of both heart disease and stroke. Furthermore, exercise also helps cholesterol levels, raising 'good' (high density lipoprotein or HDL) cholesterol and lowering 'bad' (low density lipoprotein or LDL) cholesterol: the latter can clog blood vessels. Given that stress levels can influence dietary choices, it is worthwhile noting that physical activity can also help reduce stress. It does this by stimulating the production of brain chemicals called endorphins which raise mood and also by reducing stress hormones such as cortisol.

Regarding type 2 diabetes, exercise causes the muscles to require glucose for energy, which, in turn, means that there is less glucose in the bloodstream.

Exercise is also important for bones and muscles. Bone, like muscle, is living tissue and therefore, bone loss can occur in association with insufficient activity. Exercise builds strong bones in children and as we age, maintains bone strength by causing bone to become denser. Muscles are strengthened and increase in size through appropriate physical activity as muscle fibres increase in diameter. Both of these effects are especially important in the elderly because as we get older, muscle and bone density are lost. (Bone density relates to the density of bone minerals in a particular bone area; it is the minerals which make bones hard.) Reduction in bone density means that bones become weaker and are more prone to fracturing: osteoporosis is an example of where this can happen. When muscle and bone density are both lost, the chances of falling and having a broken bone are increased. Exercise, therefore, can help reduce both the chances of falling and the potential of having a broken bone, such as a hip fracture.

*Children are more likely to engage in exercise if it is part of an activity they consider fun.*

The *psychological* factors which affect physical activity are various but some are similar to those which we saw affect diet.

Life has many competing demands for time and attention which mean that exercise can drop down the list of things which must be done; or, it may simply fail to be thought sufficiently interesting to be pursued compared with more appealing alternatives. Knowledge about the necessity of exercise to good health may be lacking as may knowing how to exercise. Evidence indicates that sometimes people refrain from physical activity because they simply do not know how to start. Learning from models such as friends, family and teachers can influence whether exercise is instilled early in life. For example, if parents and other caregivers engage in physical activity and taking exercise in some form outside and/or within the home, it is more likely that children will learn that this is a behaviour to be adopted. Furthermore, given that children prefer fun activities, they are more likely to engage with exercise they consider to be fun.

Feeling insufficiently competent to exercise can also prevent physical activity. Self-efficacy issues may relate to fitness and skill levels, as well as a lack of body competence in older adults. Older people can sometimes feel that their age automatically means they cannot exercise. They may fear too, that health issues preclude them from exercise due to it potentially producing pain, discomfort and possible injury. Again, knowledge can play a role here, since the risk of falls and their consequences can be reduced through appropriate exercise and it can help with pain too. In arthritis, for example, appropriate exercise can help reduce pain and the symptoms of the condition.

Others also affect whether someone exercises. In children, adult support may be required for exercise opportunities whilst in adolescents, peer pressure plays a role. It has been reported for example, that girls may feel pressured to 'gender-appropriate' exercise, which may cause them to drop certain kinds of physical activity. In adults, lack of support from others can make

*Cycling functions as a means of transport and exercise; however, being able to engage in the activity can depend on being able to afford a bike, safety equipment and having somewhere safe to cycle.*

people disinclined to exercise, as can lack of having someone with whom to exercise. Senior adults have reported favouring physical activity when they have an exercise companion.

Confidence to exercise can be lost in other ways too. Those with a wish to exercise in order to lose weight may be prevented from doing so by the stigma attached to being overweight which makes them feel uncomfortable about taking action. Indeed, feeling embarrassed about taking part in physical activity prevents exercising in both men and women. Generally, though, women are more likely to refrain from exercising due to concerns about their appearance whilst doing so. Similarly, female adolescents can be affected by body dissatisfaction accompanied with a fear of looking foolish.

Direct comments along with the behaviour of others can intimidate and have negative effects on physical exercise too. Older adults have reported that discouragement from younger people can deter them from being more active. Comments may be directed at some people whilst they exercise, and women have reported incidents of sexual harassment when exercising both outdoors and indoors.

Regarding some of the *social factors* which affect physical activity, as with diet, the financial costs of exercise may prevent some taking part. Use of gyms and swimming pools incurs fees; it is affected too, by their locations and proximity influences transportation costs. When money is limited, purchasing clothes for exercise may be considered too expensive. Whilst cycling provides transport and exercise, it also necessitates outlay on a bicycle; safety helmet; potentially high-visibility gear and it requires that there is somewhere safe to cycle. If roads are the only option, the lack of cycle lanes in certain areas may be a deterrent to this activity.

Safety of the surroundings affects walking, running and children's play activities too. If available, parks, green spaces and playgrounds are safer than having to negotiate areas with traffic which, in many places, has physically increased over time and can affect pollution levels. Clearly, it is undesirable to take exercise if this must be done in association with breathing-in fumes. The parks, green spaces and playgrounds must also offer physical safety in other ways for them to be used. For example, the winter in the UK has short days and long hours of darkness; if exercise must be taken when it isn't daylight, poor lighting may make the potential exerciser feel unsafe. Moreover, if parks etc are unavailable, then physical activity can be affected by whether pavements and other urban features allow for, or prevent, safe exercise.

Increases in technology both in the home and at work have decreased how much physical activity is required by life, compared with what was necessitated historically, and it is easy to be unaware that this has happened. Examples of this include commuting to work in place of walking; lifts may be more readily accessible than stairs in offices and shops; the advent of efficient vacuum cleaners led to carpets and rugs no longer needing to be beaten by hand and whereas washing clothes was once a physical activity, it is now completed efficiently by machine.

*Parks offer a traffic-free environment in which to exercise but must also offer physical safety for them to be used.*

Even entertainment sources have changed: televisions once required channels to be switched by getting up from a chair, whilst now there are not only remote controls but various sources of entertainment – as well as information – conveniently available via home computer, or, even more readily directly in the hand, via tablet and mobile phone.

Ready access to varieties of entertainment which do not involve physical activity can mean that taking exercise faces stiff competition from alternative ways of spending time. Work, education, social activities with friends and family plus family responsibilities can also produce a lifestyle where people feel there is insufficient time for exercise. Women typically shoulder many of the responsibilities at home such as looking after children and elderly relatives along with completing many domestic duties. Although these factors may indeed add to how much activity a woman does, if her overall activity is less than a healthy level, she may well feel she does not have time for extra exercise.

## Psychological Models of Behaviour

Several psychological models exist which can be used to understand why people behave as they do with regard to health. Here, we will look at a small selection of those models which can be drawn upon by health psychologists to help people improve their health behaviours, such as, exercise and diet.

Although not explicitly mentioned previously, one of the psychological reasons people give for not exercising is that they do not feel motivated to do so. Lack of motivation to exercise can be seen in issues that were discussed above: (a) people are simply not interested in physical activity; (b) beneficial exercise is not allocated time in the same way as other activities; (c) self-efficacy along with (d) not maintaining regular exercise even though it was begun.

Motivation can be examined through Albert Bandura's *Social Cognition Theory* applied to health. Social Cognition Theory links behaviour to the expected outcome of that behaviour; self-efficacy; environmental factors and setting ourselves goals.

Before behaving in a given way, we try to foresee what the outcome of the behaviour is likely to be; that is, we construct expectations concerning the behaviour's outcome. If our expectation is that the outcome is likely to be positive, we will pursue the behaviour but if we expect it is likely to be negative, we are unlikely to pursue that course of action. In relation to exercise, this means that if a person expects the result of exercise to be an improvement in health, they are more likely to go for a walk, or cycling, or dancing and so forth. However, if what is foreseen is looking foolish or an injury, they are less likely to exercise.

When self-efficacy is present, a person believes his or her behaviour can either bring about a desirable outcome or prevent a harmful one. In other words, the person is capable of some control over what they do and over environmental factors. Belief in your own capability leads to more positive forms of thinking, too. All of this is important to

*Albert Bandura.*

motivation because believing you are capable has several effects: it prompts a person to take action; affects how much effort is applied; affects how long somebody will persist if an obstacle is encountered or if they experience failure; plus, it influences whether failure stimulates the person to further action or is discouraged. Furthermore, self-efficacy determines the goals people set and affects the expectations they have about a behaviour's outcome.

In the case of exercise then, those who believe they are capable are more likely to begin exercising; extend themselves whilst exercising; be motivated to continue exercising; set themselves higher goals; have favourable expectations about the resulting outcome and be more positively focused.

Why goals are important to behaviour is complex. Consequently, the discussion which follows is simplified and designed only to give the reader some idea about goals' significance in behaviour.

Let's suppose environmental influences have led to someone having developed the view, or personal standard, that being healthy is desirable and thus, this person wants to be healthy. However, the amount of physical activity which is part of the person's weekly routine isn't sufficient for a healthy lifestyle. The comparison between current behaviour and the individual's personal standard and goal produces discontent and incentive, or motivation to change. Conceivably, an overall, long-term goal is set: *'I want to take the appropriate exercise for good health on a regular basis.'* As a long-term aim, the goal is perfectly acceptable, but it is too far away in the future to motivate the person into doing something now, and, it doesn't provide a course of action for getting from the current exercise level to the one stipulated. Other, effective goals are needed which will ultimately lead to the overall aim being met.

Effective goals are specific, challenging and sufficiently short-term, in relation to when they must be completed, to yield immediate action. Goals with these characteristics motivate the individual to exercise and provide a framework for focused action straightaway. Furthermore, when the results of completing the first effective sub-goal are assessed in terms of improved health, the next effective goal can be set and so on. In these ways there is motivation to start and continue with health-improving physical activity.

Icek Ajzen's *Theory of Planned Behaviour* contends that intention (motivation) is the main element in producing voluntary behaviour. The greater the intention, the more likely a behaviour will take place and the more effort will be applied to that behaviour. Intention itself is formed from a person's *attitude* towards the behaviour, *subjective norms* and *perceived behavioural control.*

Relating this to diet and health, the voluntary behaviour would, of course, be eating a healthy diet. Before adopting this behaviour though, a person would have to form the intention to eat in this way. This would necessitate having a positive attitude towards healthy eating and such

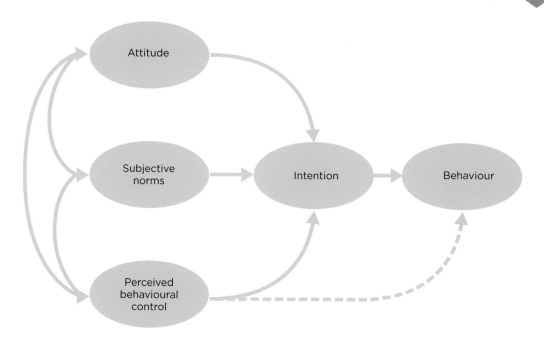

*Ajzen's Theory of Planned Behaviour. Behaviour is produced by intention and is also affected by perceived behavioural control. Attitude towards a behaviour, subjective norms and perceived behavioural control collectively produce intention.*

an attitude would stem from favourable beliefs and a positive assessment of its consequences. Additionally, intention would be contributed to by subjective norms. These comprise a person's beliefs about the extent to which others (such as friends and family), consider it important for the person to eat a healthy diet, along with motivation to act in a way which fits with these beliefs. The more somebody formulates the subjective norm that eating a healthy diet is right, the intention to do so will increase. Finally, perceived behavioural control involves how much control the individual believes he or she has over performing the behaviour. It captures the environmental and personal factors which affect behaviour and contributes not only to the intention to behave in a certain way but also directly influences behaviour itself. The more control a person perceives that they have, the greater the impact on formulating the intention to eat healthily and doing so.

Taking more exercise and eating a healthy diet involve a change from current behaviour to new behaviour. In James Prochaska and Carlo DiClemente's *Transtheoretical Model*, behavioural change involves a number of stages which a person can move into, leave, or go back to at any point. Change depends upon *self-efficacy*, *decisional balance* and the *processes of change*.

| THE STAGES OF CHANGE IN THE TRANSTHEORETICAL MODEL | |
| --- | --- |
| **Stage** | **Explanation** |
| Precontemplation | Not intending to make a change in behaviour. |
| Contemplation | Considering making a change in behaviour. |
| Preparation | Getting ready to change behaviour. An intention to change is formulated; ways to alter behaviour are planned; commitment to changing behaviour is present. |
| Action | Behaviour has changed over a short period. |
| Maintenance | The change in behaviour continues over a long period. |
| Termination | Enduring change in behaviour; no inclination to return to the previous behaviour. |

Self-efficacy refers to how much confidence a person has with regard to change and it is important for starting and maintaining change. There may be times when the individual is in a situation which may encourage relapse; if there is confidence that such situations can be dealt with, relapse is less likely. Decisional balance involves assessing the pros and cons of changing behaviour; if the pros are greater than the cons, then there is more to be gained than lost by changing behaviour. Regarding the processes of change, there are 10 of these through which the stages of change take place, five of which are experiential (thoughts and feelings) and five behavioural (doing) processes.

| THE PROCESSES OF CHANGE IN THE TRANSTHEORETICAL MODEL | |
| --- | --- |
| **Experiential Processes** | **Behavioural Processes** |
| *Consciousness Raising* <br> Becoming increasingly aware of facts and information about the health issue. | *Stimulus Control* <br> Managing the environment we are in so that the new health behaviour is helped rather than prevented; e.g. removing information on unhealthy take-away deliveries. |

| | |
|---|---|
| *Dramatic Relief* <br> Emotional response occurs to the risks to health from a behaviour. | *Helping Relationships* <br> Getting support from others (e.g. family, friends) for the health changes. |
| *Environmental Re-evaluation* <br> Evaluating previous and new health behaviours in terms of how they affect others and their physical environment. | *Counter Conditioning* <br> Using substitutes for the unwanted health behaviour. |
| *Social Liberation* <br> Noticing whether society supports the health behaviour change. | *Reinforcement Management* <br> Rewarding yourself when engaging in the new health behaviour. |
| *Self Re-evaluation* <br> A new self-image is created which fits with the new health behaviour; e.g. not exercising sufficiently makes me unhappy with myself. | *Self-Liberation* <br> There is a commitment to changing behaviour. |

### SUMMARY

- Health psychology is concerned with the psychological processes related to physical health/illness and how physical health impacts psychological wellbeing.

- Health psychology takes a biopsychosocial approach.

- Diet and exercise have direct effects on the body; they are also influenced by psychological factors (such as learning) and environmental factors (such as how much time a person has).

- Psychological models which help us understand behaviour include Social Cognition Theory, the Theory of Planned Behaviour and the Transtheoretical Model.

# FORENSIC PSYCHOLOGY

Forensic psychology draws upon psychological knowledge and applies this to the legal system. Areas that can be drawn from include cognitive, social, developmental and clinical psychology. Application can involve criminal investigations; the causes of offending; helping offenders find a means of avoiding future reoffending plus advising parole boards and mental health tribunals. In the UK, HM Prison Service is the major employer of forensic psychologists but they can also be found working in settings such as the Probation Service, police forces, social services, secure children's homes and secure hospitals, courts and university departments. In the latter, the individual performs customary academic duties – research, teaching, supervision and administration.

## A Brief History of Forensic Psychology

Forensic psychology has a longer history than its name because the field of law has employed medical expertise for centuries to assess a person's physical state and 'criminal insanity'. Psychology's status as an independent discipline is far shorter than either Law's or Medicine's. In 1879, Wilhelm Wundt founded the first experimental psychology laboratory in Leipzig, Germany and at this point, he established a methodological framework for research generally, thereby including forensic issues. Subsequently, a number of people pursued questions related to forensic psychology, for example, in the late 19th and early 20th centuries, James Cattell and Wilhelm Stern addressed topics related to eyewitnesses, as did Hugo Munsterberg, who also considered issues such as jury decision-making and false confessions. Modern forensic psychology began to grow in the second half of the 20th century as psychological research evidence increased and as courts became more willing to accept evidence from psychology and psychologists.

## Why Does Crime Occur? The Role of Stress-Inducing Events/Conditions, Neurological Factors and the Role of Genetics

Criminal behaviour does not have a simple explanation. Any complex behaviour stems from

*James McKeen Cattell.*

different factors which will interact with each other. However, several theories have attempted to provide reasons for criminality and a small selection of these are considered below.

Robert Agnew's *General Strain Theory* proposes that crime and delinquency can be a way of dealing with the negative emotions caused by *strains* or stress-inducing conditions or events. Strains can be *objective* or *subjective* and within each of these types, particular strains are more likely to lead to criminality.

Objective strain involves events or conditions most people belonging to a given group would not like. Whilst these can include factors that all people would probably find unacceptable (e.g. inadequate food, physical assault), they are also group-specific. That is, the events/conditions a particular group (e.g. defined by age, gender) finds unacceptable.

Subjective strain involves events and conditions that a particular person dislikes; consequently, this kind of strain can differ from person to person. It is particularly linked to emotional responses to events and conditions, such as anger, fear, disappointment and depression. However, the emotions felt by people under the same subjective strain may not be identical. Even if they are identical, the extent to which the emotions are felt will not be the same. Furthermore, different people will have different coping resources which affects how strain is dealt with.

Crime is more likely to result from (a) unjust conditions/events (b) severe events/conditions (c) where there is lack of social control and (d) where others model crime.

A.  Unjust strains (e.g. harm, disrespect, aggression towards an individual) can produce anger. Fury can be overwhelming, preventing someone from mentally accessing non-criminal coping behaviour. When a healthy way to deal with a situation is unavailable, crime is more likely to occur.

*Crime – a car thief attempting to break into a vehicle.*

B.  Strain severity is affected by the extent, recency and duration of events or conditions plus how much the strain affects a person's central values, needs, identity and activities. For example, prolonged lack of, or a recent loss of money may still allow one person to cope but put another in a position where it is hard not to commit crime.

C.  Social control can be exerted through feeling dedicated to a job or by parents who do not reject their child and discipline him/her in a consistent fashion. If social control is missing, the support mechanisms for preventing criminal behaviour can be missing too.

D.  Where events or conditions possess examples of people who hold favourable views towards crime, encourage it and provide illustrations of criminal behaviour, criminality can be fostered.

If you look at the box on pages 185–7, you will find examples of the events and conditions which are more likely to produce crime. Strains are not the only possible cause of criminal behaviour that psychologists have also considered though – other accounts have examined crime's potential biological origins.

Brain damage has been linked to offending given that injury to the brain can yield changes in behaviour. For instance, damage to the pre-frontal cortex (at the front of the brain) can lead to various issues including: diminished reasoning and problem-solving abilities; inability to control impulsive and emotional behaviours; inability to appreciate the consequences of actions; increased risk-taking and rule-breaking behaviours.

Early brain damage has been associated with violent crime. Additionally, evidence also exists that (a) offenders have incurred higher rates of head injury and (b) some offenders commit crime more after a head injury than before. However, the adult evidence is by no means problem-free: offenders may be more prone to being in situations which lead to a head injury. It is the case though that risks can exist to the developing brain even before birth and that the early years are crucial to brain development.

Another biological source of crime that has been considered is genetics. However, there is *no evidence* that all criminality is caused by possession of a specific gene. Instead, available data only *suggest* that there *may be* a genetic role in certain criminal behaviours. For example, a relationship has been found between genetic inheritance and property crime, and whilst this establishes a potential association between the two, it does not indicate the former causes the latter.

*Crime – in the UK it is illegal to use any knife in a threatening way.*

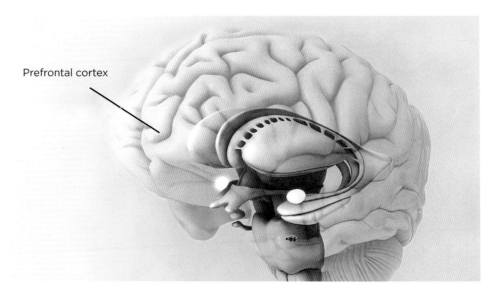

Prefrontal cortex

*Brain damage has been linked to offending; damage to the pre-frontal cortex has been linked to various issues including increased risk-taking and rule-breaking behaviours.*

Furthermore, genes should not be regarded as operating solely in isolation; they can interact with other genes and with the environment in which a person lives. For instance, there is evidence of a gene and environment interaction which can influence anti-social behaviour. An enzyme (enzymes accelerate chemical reactions) called monoamine oxidase A (MAO-A) is encoded for by the monoamine oxidase gene. It has been found that those who experience childhood abuse and have low MAO-A may be predisposed to anti-social behaviour. In other words, under the environmental influence of maltreatment in childhood, high MAO-A may protect the individual from later engaging in anti-social behaviour.

*The enzyme monoamine oxidase A.*

## EXAMPLES OF EVENTS AND CONDITIONS (STRAINS) LINKED TO CRIME

### Rejection by Parents

Unjust - Parents are supposed to show interest in, love and support for offspring. Parents should not be frequently hostile.

Severe strain – Endangers offsprings' central values, needs, identity, activities.

Lacks social control – Low social control.

Models – Offspring experiences aggressive behaviour; spends time with peers who offend.

### Poor Disciplinary Practice by Parents

Unjust – Harsh, strict, inconsistent and unpredictable discipline.

Severe strain – High level of strain: might include extreme physical/ verbal interventions.

Lacks social control – Low social control; undermines parent–child relationship.

Models – Parents exhibit favourable view towards and model aggression.

### Abusive Peers (Especially Youths)

Unjust – Peers are not official agents for imposing penalties.

Severe strain – Could include verbal and physical attacks, threatening behaviour.

Lacks social control – Typically occurs when those who could impose penalties (e.g. parents, teachers) aren't around.

Models – Often occurs in groups where members exhibit favourable views towards and model crime.

### Adverse Secondary School Experience

Unjust – Events and conditions may be regarded as unjust.

Severe strain – School plays a major role in young people's lives; hence, strain can be induced by being there: no choice in attending; an unequal relationship between staff and students; finding school pointless or receiving poor marks and/or unjust treatment from teachers.

Lacks social control – Low social control; will not feel dedicated to school.

Models – Can increase the likelihood of mixing with peers who offend.

**Poor Quality Employment**

Unjust – Events and conditions may be regarded as unjust.

Severe strain – Work plays a major role in adult life; hence strain can be induced by low status, tedious or exhausting work; poor pay, few decision-making opportunities. Could produce circumstances where crime may help cope with the situation.

Lacks social control – Low social control; unlikely to feel dedicated to the job.

Models – Can increase the chances of encountering those who commit crime.

**Failure to Easily Achieve Goals Legitimately but they are Easily Obtained via Crime**

Unjust – Failure to obtain goals easily not always seen as unfair, but may be seen as so if there is an evident discrimination based on factors the individual is born to, such as social class.

Severe strain – e.g. Person may want to experience something thrilling, be autonomous, have the finances to accomplish something now rather than save.

Low social control – Goals obtained easily through crime.

Models – Can be exposed to others who model relevant behaviours; can also be associated with individual characteristics such as being the kind of person who desires excitement.

# Offender Profiling

Sometimes the police may have difficulty in identifying potential suspects for a crime. The purpose of offender profiling is to establish the characteristics of the offender based upon scene of the crime information. However, profiling techniques are not identical.

Modern offender profiling began with the FBI. In the 1970s, the FBI formed its Behavioral Science Unit to investigate serial rape and murder cases. Originally, FBI profilers used their own skill and judgement to profile. In the late 1970s, 36 serial murderers were interviewed leading to the distinction between organized versus disorganized killers.

FBI profiling begins with gathering and organizing information from the case. This can include police reports, statements from witnesses; background intelligence about the victim; a chronology of what s/he was doing before death; crime scene photographs and the pathologist's report regarding relevant medical information such as time of death. These kinds of details are then used to establish the personality of the offender.

Classification of the crime scene as organized or disorganized is used to establish the likely psychological traits of the offender. For example, amongst other characteristics, planning and premeditation are associated with organized offenders: they know about police methods, leave behind little evidence, are controlled, may move the body and are likely to follow news media.

An organized offender is also typically above average intelligence, educated, employed, owns reliable transport and is married or lives with a partner. This offender's childhood is associated with inconsistent discipline and a father in stable employment.

Disorganized offenders leave a disorderly crime scene which is near to either home or work. Examples of their characteristics include lack of planning; forensic evidence such as blood, fingerprints and murder weapon may be left at the scene. The offender will have little to no interest in news media, may be below average

*Robert K. Ressler, who played a key role in the FBI's Behavioral Science Unit in the 1970s.*

*FBI profiling begins with gathering and organizing information from the case.*

intelligence, unskilled, have poor social and communication skills plus live alone. Childhood circumstances likely involve harsh discipline and a father with unstable employment.

Two other issues are also borne in mind: an individual offender may change their crime scene behaviour over time and, if there is more than one offender, this too can then be reflected in the crime scene.

The evidence gathered regarding the crime scene is used to build a picture of what took place in association with the crime. This can reveal attributes specific to the way in which the crime was committed, which, in turn, indicate the way in which the offender went about the crime, such as whether the victim was stalked.

The length of profile produced depends on how much information was originally available and it consists of a number of predictions concerning the offender. The predictions may be psychological, but they cover a variety of other issues too, some of which are listed below:

Psychological Factors – these include relevant personality traits; relevant psychopathology (e.g., is offending connected to a mental health issue such as depression?).

Demography – likely age, social class, whether the offender is in a job or not; if working, the type of job; likely area the offender is associated with.

Behaviour – whether the individual is sociable and good at mixing versus poor social skills and pursues activities/hobbies alone.

Lifestyle – whether the individual is isolated, living alone or married/in a partnership.
Strategies – potential ways in which the offender may be identified and caught.

The way in which FBI profiling originally developed has been criticized in terms of lacking scientific rigour. In general terms, criticism was related to how drawing upon investigative experience is not the same as extremely thorough, careful and verifiable research based on scientific principles.

Statistical offender profiling, developed by British psychologist David Canter, deliberately adopts a research-based, objective and scientific approach. It takes a given type of crime, such as murder, and applies statistical techniques to establish the patterns of behaviour that are associated with that type of crime. Statistical analysis can determine: (i) the probability that certain behaviours occur and (ii) the probability of particular behaviours occurring together. Where behaviours occur rarely, this is useful for distinguishing crime scenes. After crime scenes are differentiated, it is possible to pursue how these relate to offender characteristics.

For example, Gabrielle Salfati and David Canter were able to distinguish three types of murder crime scene, categorized according to the way in which the murderer interacted with the victim. The *Expressive (Impulsive)* scene exhibited wide-ranging, frenetic, impulsive behaviours; examples of offender characteristics included: married (when the offence was committed), female offender, previous offences such as drug, traffic, violent and sexual offences. The Expressive (Impulsive) offender was involved in conflict with people and potentially could not interact with them in the expected and appropriate way.

*Instrumental (Opportunistic)* murder was associated with offenders who exploited the immediate opportunities offered by a victim. Instances of their characteristics

*David Canter.*

included being familiar with the area where the crime took place, knowing the victim, being unemployed, having come to police notice and previous offences such as burglary, theft and vehicle theft.

The *Instrumental (Cognitive)* crime scene had considerable thought applied to the crime. Background characteristics of the offender were having served in the armed services and having served a prison sentence. This type of murderer's lifestyle is linked to violence and aggression and they regard people as meaningless.

Statistical profiling can be applied to crimes other than murder and rape. It could, for instance, be employed with fraud and arson.

## Factors Which May Affect Eyewitness Memory

**Task** – Imagine there is a street robbery in which the target of the theft is threatened with a knife. Two others are also in the vicinity of the offence and witness its events.

Here, all three people have witnessed the crime but only the victim of the robbery is directly involved, the others are effectively bystanders. Such a theft would be stressful and anxiety-provoking, especially for the victim. All witnesses would have to be questioned and recall what took place, such as, the thief, what was said and potentially other details such as how the perpetrator got away.

If, when interviewed separately, the bystanders provide consistent accounts, this can add credence to their accuracy. However, given that people often discuss shared events, it would not be surprising if our bystanders had talked about what had happened: co-witnesses have been found to discuss features of crimes. This is undesirable because our two witnesses would not have had identical viewpoints for the crime; one may have actually encountered, or believe they encountered a feature that is not part of the other person's experience. Discussion can lead to Witness A mentioning something that Witness B did not encounter and then B goes on to mistakenly recall this as a genuine memory of what occurred.

High stress compared with low stress events have been found to impair memory for crime scene details. Elizabeth Loftus and Terrence Burns showed experimental participants a film in which a boy was shot in the face. This mentally shocking event caused memory impairment for detail not only immediately before the event but for nearly two minutes previously. Additionally, the presence of a weapon can produce *weapon focus* in which attention is drawn to the weapon and thus memory for other details of the crime is reduced.

Description of offenders requires the translation of visually encoded information into verbal information. This can be psychologically challenging. For example, when supplying a verbal description of a face, it is impossible to address all features of the face simultaneously; one

*A robbery – will witnesses be able to recount the incident accurately?*

piece of information has to be delivered after another. Yet, when we look at and mentally process a face, we process it as a whole rather than as parts. Assessing weight and height can be difficult too without a comparison reference (for example, height in relation to a specified object such as a door frame).

Ability to identify an offender can depend too on the distance from which s/he was viewed: as distance increases between witness and offender, accuracy of witness identification reduces. Dates can be difficult to remember too if they are not recent.

Collectively, knowledge about issues which affect witnesses' memories helps us

*Elizabeth Loftus.*

Task – Can you recall the date of death of Queen Elizabeth II? Or the date of her funeral? Admittedly, these examples are artificial to our purpose here in that neither relates to an offence; they have been chosen simply because both events received extensive coverage in the Media and are therefore potentially accessible from memory for some readers. How much of the dates did you recall? The dates were 8 September and 19 September 2022.

to know when witness memory is likely to be more accurate, or less so. Furthermore, data gathering by experiment possesses the distinct advantage of being able to focus methodically and accurately on specific issues. Yet, no matter how realistic, experimental studies of eyewitness memory cannot fully replicate the genuine nature of an incident because provoking the kind of anxiety in a participant that is generated by a real crime is unethical. Where possible, this can be addressed by reviewing recall of real-life incidents. For example, in 1993 Christanson and Hubinette investigated 22 bank robberies that were between 4–15 months old. They interviewed 58 eyewitnesses including bank tellers (victims), other employees and customers (bystanders). Over time, memories for what occurred, the weapon and clothing were robust but memory for eye and hair colour plus details of the surrounding circumstances was quite low. However, compared with bystanders, victims had better recall of the robbery's day, date, time, plus customer numbers.

Think back now to the example of the knife-point robbery. Our three witnesses in the scenario are going to be questioned at different stages of the legal process and how they are to be questioned will matter.

Elizabeth Loftus and John Palmer demonstrated that a question's word choice influences responses and alters memory. Questions were posed about a film of a car accident. In the critical question, *About how fast were the cars going when they --- each other?'* the verb was one of *smashed, hit, collided, bumped* or *contacted.* Choice of word affected speed estimates, with higher speed estimates for *smashed* than any other verb. The greater force implied by *smashed* 'led' the witnesses. Using a similar experimental framework, including a critical question with *hit* and *smashed,* but testing memory a week later, Loftus and Palmer found more people claimed to have seen non-existent broken glass with *smashed* than with the less forceful verb. The choice of word altered memory for the event. *Smashed* set-up expectations and produced a memory that could not have been visually encoded.

Indeed, even using the definite article (*the*) or indefinite article (*a*) can influence reconstruction of an event. Again using a film of a car accident, Loftus and Guido Zanni posed the query, *Did you see -- broken headlight?* When the definite article was used, fewer witnesses reported uncertainty or 'I don't know' and there were more false recognitions of events that never occurred. Phrasing of questions matters if witness memory is to be accurate.

*A car accident: care must be exercised when questioning witnesses about the incident, so that their answers are not influenced, nor their memories altered, by the questions' wording.*

# Improving Eyewitness Memory Retrieval: The Enhanced Cognitive Interview

In our imaginary knife-point robbery, it would be ideal if the victim and witnesses could be encouraged to provide the best information possible about the crime. Naturally, this depends upon their memories of what they observed and psychologists have developed ways to improve witnesses' recall. Initially, Edward Geiselman and colleagues drew upon psychological research as to how memory recall operates and devised a technique called the *Cognitive Interview*. Some years later, Ronald Fisher and Geiselman added communication plus social elements designed to improve the wellbeing and comfort of witnesses, thereby yielding the *Enhanced Cognitive Interview*.

The Enhanced Cognitive Interview begins by building rapport between interviewer and witness. This includes introductions; using the witness's name; explaining why the witness is being interviewed and what will happen during the interview. Simple questions can be used to put the witness more at ease and verbal/non-verbal signals are used now and again throughout the interview to encourage increased recall.

Control of the interview is transferred to the witness by indicating s/he can report what happened in any order and stop whenever s/he wants. Additionally, it's explained that the witness is the person who is the most well-informed as to what happened, therefore s/he will be the one most active during the interview but the interviewer can help if required.

Information is now obtained from the witness in a number of ways. Initially, the witness is asked to freely recall what occurred. To do this, s/he is asked to mentally recreate the incident in detail (context reinstatement), including how s/he felt physically and emotionally plus what s/he was thinking about. For our street theft scenario, open-ended questions such as 'Tell me about the robber' can be used to recreate specific details.

Subsequently, follow-up questions concerning what the witness has mentioned can be asked. S/he is encouraged to report everything s/he remembers no matter how trivial and care is taken to ensure that the interviewer's questions fit the witness's recall (witness-compatible questioning). That is, if the witness were recalling a get-away vehicle, the interviewer wouldn't leap to asking about the driver but would stick with the theme of the vehicle.

Further retrieval occurs by asking the witness to recall what took place using different perspectives and timelines. Changed perspective might involve recalling using the way the witness was feeling prior to the incident, rather than at the point of the robbery itself, or recalling from the perspective of another witness, for instance. Recalling in a different temporal order alters the sequencing of events; e.g. our witnesses could be asked to recall the robbery in reverse order.

After these information-gathering methods have been employed, questions can be posed

## RECALL RESEARCH AND THE ENHANCED COGNITIVE INTERVIEW

| Interview Element | Psychological Reason for the Element |
| --- | --- |
| Building a Rapport | Helps to calm and reduce anxiety in the witness so more is remembered. |
| Control Transferred to Witness | Encourages witness to produce more information; even irrelevant information can trigger other, relevant memories of use to the investigation. |
| Context Reinstatement | Memory is better when there is an overlap between the circumstances of recall and the circumstances when the memory was formed (encoded). The greater the overlap, the more cues (memory jogs) available to help promote recall. |
| Witness-Compatible Questioning | In our street robbery example, if the witness is recalling a 'getaway' vehicle, then this is the route being pursued through memory. If now questioned about the driver, a new memory route has to be adopted and this switch can lose information. It is better to use open rather than closed questions. Suppose we are at a stage that it is now clear a knife was involved; open questions such as 'Tell me about the knife' are better than closed ones, e.g. 'Did the knife have a black or brown handle?' The latter limits the answer to black or brown; the handle could have been both colours or neither. The witness may not feel happy providing contradictory information, or the colour options may lead the witness and affect their memory. |
| Report Everything | Usually, a witness will only report what s/he believes to be relevant. However, because the witness does not know what is or isn't useful to the investigator, adopting this approach can exclude helpful information. Additionally, an apparently unhelpful memory could trigger another memory containing useful information. |

| Changed Perspective | An alternative perspective can increase the amount of information recalled. For example, in our street robbery, retrieving from the perspective of the other witness means considering their frame of reference rather than yours. This can lead to more peripheral information being supplied such as cars uninvolved in the robbery, that may have passed on the street. |
| --- | --- |
| Changing Temporal Order | We often have frameworks for how events operate such as how to place an order in a restaurant. These frameworks draw on knowledge and experience and they establish expectations, (e.g. the waiter/waitress will take the order). Although the witness may not have seen a street robbery in real life, s/he may have viewed one on television or in a film which has set-up expectations. In turn, the expectations can influence recall; information may be non-deliberately omitted because it wasn't expected. Using different chronologies such as reverse order disturbs expectations and reduces their influence. |

concerning issues that the witness did not raise but which the interviewer wishes to explore for the benefit of the investigation.

The next step of the Enhanced Cognitive Interview has the interviewer and witness review and check the evidence supplied. Lastly, what is likely to happen next is described to the witness and s/he is asked to get in touch if s/he remembers something else.

## Detecting Lies: The Face, Speech and The Strategic Use of Evidence Interview

When questioning a suspect, unless there is evidence to the contrary, dishonesty cannot always be detected. However, it is possible to look for signals that a person may be lying, such as those found in face and speech behaviours. It is essential too, to look for multiple indicators of deceit.

Faces are significant because they are our most important social stimulus. One of the reasons for this is that we regularly draw conclusions about how someone is feeling from facial expression.

Imagine – You see a colleague or neighbour unexpectedly and s/he smiles at you.

How would you go about interpreting the smile? Is s/he pleased to see you?

Would you look for signs of happiness/pleasure/enjoyment?

If the signs of happiness/pleasure/enjoyment are present, does this guarantee your colleague or neighbour is pleased to see you?

Does it matter whether the smile flashes quickly both on and off the face?

Does it matter if the smile is broad?

Facial expressions are the product of muscle movements and if these do not follow the appropriate pattern for an emotion, a person may be lying. Paul Ekman has written extensively on this topic and we will draw upon his expertise to explore this theme.

To assess the scenario in the box above, particular facial movements can be sought. Did the eyebrows lower a little along with the skin separating the eyebrow and the upper area of the eyelid? If so, the smile is definitely genuine. Unfortunately, though, this movement is not easy to detect so we may have to query: Did the cheeks move upwards and the eye narrow? Did the skin wrinkle on the outer corners of the eyes? If not, then the smile isn't genuine. However, a faked smile can also cause these changes, so we may still be dealing with dishonesty.

The eyebrows are also key to determining genuine sadness. Forehead muscles should be drawing the eyebrows towards each other and the brow areas nearest the nose ought to draw higher on the face. Fear should also cause the eyebrows to come together and move upwards, whereas anger ought to involve the lips' red edges narrowing. Another cue to emotional authenticity includes whether, if you were to draw a vertical midline down the face, the same emotion would be found either side of the midline. And, if an emotion appears too swiftly, this can indicate fabrication.

Turning now to speech information, consider the following question:

## *Where were you and what were you doing yesterday?*

Providing a truthful answer involves recalling your location(s) and actions plus reporting the information. Of course, the task increases in challenge should you be asked about a feature to which you didn't pay much attention or if a new question involves events from some time ago. Now, you may have to expend mental effort searching your memory.

In contrast to honestly, readily recalling your locations/actions, an on-the-spot lie is

*Paul Ekman.*

especially cognitively complex and demanding. The truth has to be recalled so that it can be swapped for untruth; successful deceit must be generated, sustained (which involves remembering the lie) and be credible. Some attention will also have to be devoted to ensuring the questioner finds you plausible. Consequently, if you know you're going to be quizzed, it makes sense to lighten the cognitive load and prepare a lie-script. A successful criminal would typically stick to the truth as far as possible without giving anything away. Additionally, potential questions are considered and responses planned, keeping the answers simple but sufficiently detailed to be convincing. Before reading further, please look at the box on page 200.

Without a pre-planned story/answer, the cognitive requirements of deceit may lead to less fluent speech. Research indicates that people speak more slowly and with a greater number of pauses when engaged in a cognitively complex task. 'Um' and 'uh' aren't distinctly associated with deceit and furthermore, these hesitations can be controlled if necessary. In contrast, voice pitch is hard to control and this has been linked to dishonesty.

To reduce mental load whilst constructing a lie, the speaker may avert their gaze from the questioner, though a successful deceiver may deliberately not do this to increase plausibility. Fewer body movements may be made with dishonesty in order to control behaviour and thereby avoid detection as guilty. In the box below, Person A could be telling the truth or have prepared well. Person B's behaviour fits with what people generally expect of a deceiver but perhaps at least some of it is typical of their normal behaviour. To improve deceit detection in interviews, a technique called the *Strategic Use of Evidence* (SUE) has been devised by Pär Anders Granhag, Leif Strömwall and Maria Hartwig.

SUE involves the suspect being unaware that the investigator holds some key evidence. In our street theft scenario, it could be that the robber left behind some forensic evidence, or doesn't know our two witnesses were there and saw/heard what happened. This key evidence is used to plan the interview in the knowledge that innocent and guilty parties behave differently.

*A police officer interviewing a suspect.*

An honest person is prepared to supply information such as having been in the location of interest, in our case, the street where the robbery took place. The details supplied will fit well with what the investigator already knows. An untruthful individual will avoid self-incrimination and deny having been at the robbery's location; statements will not fit as well with what is known.

It may become apparent during the interview that the investigator knows something; or, towards the end of the interview, the key evidence can be used to require the suspect to account for why their version of events isn't compatible with what's known. Having to address this issue can increase the cognitive demands on the liar. Additionally, as the deceiver endeavours to change their original account in order to maintain 'innocence', this produces inconsistency with what was stated previously. More inconsistencies emerge with deceit than with truth. So, if our robber had denied being on the relevant street, they might change their story when it is revealed they were seen there. Now they may have to go to some effort to try to 'plausibly' account for their presence.

Here are descriptions of the way in which Persons A and B account for their whereabouts at the time of a crime. They are both seated. Who would you believe?

Person A – Speaks fluently with what you'd regard as a normal pitch to the voice. Their speech has some pauses but few 'uh' or 'um' sounds. This person maintains a steady gaze towards the interviewer and appears physically relaxed, casually readjusting position in the chair from time to time.

Person B – Speaks slowly with a high-pitched voice. Their speech has many pauses and 'uh' or 'um' sounds. This person often diverts their gaze from the interviewer and sits rigidly with very few movements in the chair.

## SUMMARY

- Forensic psychology applies psychological knowledge to the legal system.
- Stress-producing events/conditions can produce strains linked to crime.
- The early years are of critical importance to brain development and early brain damage has been associated with violent crime.
- There is no specific gene for criminality; where a relationship has been found between genetic inheritance and criminality this does not establish a causal relationship.
- Where childhood maltreatment occurs, high monoamine oxidase A could protect from later anti-social behaviour.
- FBI offender profiling uses organized/disorganized crime scene classification to establish the offender's likely psychological traits.
- Statistical profiling analyses data to establish likely offender characteristics.
- Eyewitness accounts can be affected by violence, weapon focus and question phraseology.
- The Enhanced Cognitive Interview improves witness recall using psychological research.
- Deceit can be assessed using the face and speech.
- Strategic Use of Evidence Technique can reveal if an interviewee is honest/dishonest.

# SPORT PSYCHOLOGY

Sport psychology, on the other hand, includes: working with athletes to help them train, compete, enhance performance and cope with injury; helping coaches to bring about success and assisting referees with the difficulties associated with their duties. Exercise psychology, on the other hand, helps people for whom exercise will promote improved psychological and physical wellbeing.

In the UK, chartered psychologists in this field qualify in *sport and exercise psychology*. This means they can work across both areas but usually, they specialize in one or the other. However, both areas engage with the ways in which the mind and environment impact behaviour and there is, of course overlap, such as motivation and goal-setting. Furthermore, in addition to directly applying the principles of sport and exercise psychology, some psychologists in this field work in universities, teaching and conducting research.

Please note that in the discussion which follows, the term, *athlete* is used to refer to sportspersons generally and not only those whose chosen sport is athletics.

## A Brief History of Sport Psychology

The first sport psychology research and social psychology study are one and the same: Norman Triplett's 1898 investigation of cyclists' performance when alone or with others. This showed that racing speeds were notably faster when competition was present, even when this was provided by a pacemaker. By the 1920s, sport psychology laboratories were being established by Robert Werner Schulte in Berlin; Piotr Antonovich Roudik in Moscow and Avksenty Cezarevich Puni in Leningrad. In the United States of America, Coleman Griffith was a highly significant figure. Credited as the man who established sport psychology in the USA, Griffith conducted research and applied his expertise practically with the Chicago Cubs baseball team.

Later, during the Cold War, the Soviet Union and the USA drew on input from sport psychologists to improve athletic performance and from the 1960s onwards, sport and exercise

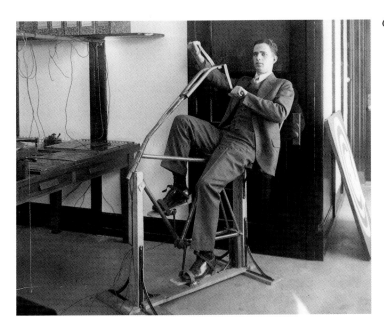

*Coleman Griffith.*

psychology grew considerably. Dedicated research journals were established; professional societies for sport and exercise psychology were formed and the area was recognized within psychology's professional bodies. For example, by 1965, The International Society of Sport Psychology existed; the *Journal of Sport Psychology* was published (1979; later becoming the *Journal of Sport and Exercise Psychology*). In the 1980s the British Association of Sport and Exercise Sciences was founded; the British Psychological Society created first a section (1993) and then the Division of Sport and Exercise Psychology (2004).

Advances in research and the application of knowledge has led to sport psychology becoming increasingly important, as is demonstrated by the number of professional athletes and sport organizations which continue to draw upon the area.

## Motivation

Motivation is a driving force which produces behaviour designed to achieve our objective. It is present in everyday behaviour, such as when we need to drink something: thirst drives us to seek out a drink and to continue to consume it until the thirst is quenched. Motivation is also an important factor in sport behaviour because it affects whether an individual does or does not participate; how much effort is applied to achieving an objective and whether that effort is ended.

Some people are motivated to engage in sport for no other reason than the pleasure they may derive from their chosen pursuit. They may have fun, acquire health benefits, enjoy spending time with like-minded people, forge new friendships and gain satisfaction from the sport. Other people may become involved in sport because there is some compelling, external motivation for doing so. This might involve, for example, pleasing others, such as parents or workmates, or prize-winning which can be associated with an obvious trophy, money and admiration from others.

**Task 1** – Take a moment to ask yourself who you think is most likely to continue with sport, the person being motivated by fun etc or the person who is motivated by pleasing others or prize-winning?

After being motivated to take up a sport, some people are happy to be non-competitive, whereas others may want to be better than others and win. Let's consider two people who have taken up cycling recreationally. One remains happy, purely enjoying the experience of going from A–B and the pleasures this provides such as nice scenery. The other cyclist, though, wants to be tested and thus shifts to competing against others and working to improve the times in which sections of road are completed. The second cyclist's approach is much more intense and competitive than the first one's. Cyclist Two is motivated to be successful but Cyclist One isn't. Certain people are motivated to be successful, whereas others are not and this contrast has been accounted for in different ways, some of which are discussed below.

One theory argued that motivation for success is driven by a personality trait associated with needing to achieve and drew on the work of David McClelland and John Atkinson. It was proposed that although we want to be successful, we also want to avoid failure and these two motivations drive whether we approach or avoid a situation. If we want to be successful more than we fear failure, we will go ahead and approach a situation. If, though, we fear failure and this motivation is greater than the motivation to approach, we will withdraw from the situation, or avoid it from the outset. Putting this in sport terms, an athlete who is more motivated by success will approach a challenge and want to play against someone or a team who offers this. On the other hand, a person who is more motivated by fear of failure will prefer to play against those who will be relatively easy to beat, or they will avoid taking part in a challenge.

John G. Nicholls's achievement goal theory, on the other hand, looked at motivation from the perspective of what is meant by 'success', or, achievement goal. It proposed that there are two orientations towards success, *task orientation* and *ego orientation*. If you are a task-oriented athlete, you are concerned with improving at your chosen sport whereas an ego-oriented athlete wants to outperform others.

*Motivation affects whether people participate in sport. Subsequently, some of those who participate will be happy to be non-competitive but others will want to win.*

**Task 2** – Consider how you think these two kinds of athlete will view success and how this might affect their behaviour.

A task-oriented athlete views success in the context of their own performance and whether they performed better than on previous occasions. Consequently, this person considers that they've been successful if a skill, such as completing a particular shot, has improved; they apply sustained effort to upgrading their abilities and want to play opponents who will let them become involved in realistic challenges. Evidence indicates too, that task-oriented athletes are associated with sportsperson-like behaviour.

An ego-oriented athlete, on the other hand, regards success from the perspective of how they have performed relative to other players. This means that irrespective of personal performance, what is critical is demonstrating superior ability compared with others. Hence, winning is very important to this sort of person. However, it isn't always going to be the case that this kind of athlete is sufficiently accomplished to be better than others. To deal with this

*David McClelland.*

position, one option is picking only those challenges where success is inevitable; another alternative is to deliberately take-on something so hard, failure is inevitable; or, thirdly, quit taking part all together. As being better than opponents and winning is so important to the ego-oriented athlete, it is perhaps unsurprising that such a person has been associated with unsportsperson-like behaviour.

Although the task- and ego-oriented athletes have been presented as two distinct types of sportsperson, this is not meant to imply you can't have aspects of both motivations. To be successful at the very top of their sport, an elite athlete will want to ensure that their individual skills are the very best they can be, yet the desire to win also combines to being one of, if not the best athlete in a given sport.

Coaches also create psychological environments which promote different kinds of motivation like those described just above. A *mastery motivational climate* creates an environment in which success is framed in terms of an athlete's improving, whereas a *competitive motivational climate* focuses on being better than others, competition and avoiding errors.

Task 3 – Do you think a mastery or a competitive motivational psychological environment has a better effect on athletes?

Research has demonstrated that a mastery motivational environment consistently produces desirable effects, such as increased effort and enjoyment, lower anxiety and improved coping abilities. A competitive emotional climate, however, has been found to produce undesirable effects, such as success being equated to ability and being assessed in relation to others along with higher levels of anxiety in the athlete.

Another way in which motivation has been considered is in terms of *attribution theory*, which comes from social psychology. Attributions are the reasons or explanations that we

*Elite athletes combine task- and ego-orientations.*

supply to account for our own and other people's behaviour and in sport these can relate to success and failure. According to Bernard Weiner, the causes that we attribute to achievement can be categorized in three ways: internal/external; stable/unstable; and personally controllable/ personally uncontrollable.

Attributional style matters because it affects whether we think we will be successful or otherwise in the future. If the attributions are associated with factors which encourage the athlete to trust in their own abilities and decisions as well as anticipate future success, motivation to take on other challenges will increase. In contrast, if attributions are associated with factors which reinforce the idea that failure stems from uncontrollable, stable, internal factors, such as a fixed lack of ability, motivation will decrease and the athlete may even give-up all together. If the

*Coaches create psychological environments which promote different kinds of motivation.*

latter negative attributional style occurs, it's possible to use attributional retraining to help the athlete. This could involve training the athlete to realize, for instance, that what is being thought of as uncontrollable and stable isn't entirely uncontrollable and can be changed.

*Self-determination Theory* comes from the work of Edward Deci and Richard Ryan. It proposes that we are naturally self-motivated towards personal growth. Optimum growth occurs when our three psychological needs for autonomy, competence and relatedness are met. In other words, we need: to feel we have a choice and are in control; a sense that we are effective at what we do, and we need to be connected to others. We also find success rewarding and satisfying. However, our desire for growth interacts with our social context and whether this fosters, or stands in the way of our natural self-motivation. It is this interaction which yields different kinds of motivation.

In sport terms, if people play their chosen sport because they find it interesting, derive satisfaction from just taking part and it provides them with a positive experience, they have *intrinsic motivation*. Intrinsic motivation is associated with autonomy because the athlete freely chooses to engage, they are in control and thus there is self-determination. The need for competence is met too since the athlete can set their own targets. The need for relatedness is

## ATTRIBUTIONS

**Player A –** This person has just won a match and afterwards considers the following to be the reasons for the success:

'I'm pretty good but even so I still wanted to give it my all.'

**Player B –** This individual has just lost a match and later identifies the following to be the reasons for the loss:

'My opponent was so much better than me, I'd no chance and the weather didn't help, there was no point trying.'

Using Weiner's different attribution types, we might analyse Player A's thoughts as follows:

*'I'm pretty good'* – concerns ability and so is *internal*; ability is often regarded as *stable*.

*'I still wanted to give it my all'* – refers to the effort applied and has an *internal* cause; however, as effort can be increased or decreased, it is also *personally controllable* and changeable, or *unstable*.

Before reading on, look again at Player B and think about how you would classify the different reasons given for the loss.

*'My opponent was so much better than me I'd no chance'* – overcoming the opponent was too difficult a task, so cause of the defeat is *external*; the defeat was associated with the opponent's ability which can't be influenced, therefore the cause is *external* and is *stable* and *personally uncontrollable*.

*'and the weather didn't help'* – weather is *external*.

*'there was no point trying'* – refers to effort, *internal*, *unstable*, *personally controllable*.

It is possible that you may be asking about 'luck' because sometimes chance plays a role, such as in a non-deliberate, extra bounce of a ball. Chance is *external*, *unstable* and *personally uncontrollable*. You may also be questioning whether ability is truly stable: ageing athletes may not be as fast or as precise as they once were and therefore their ability has dropped; similarly, practising improves skills and thereby must improve ability. You have a point. What is key though is the sportsperson's attribution: does the athlete regard ability as stable?

*Richard Ryan.*                                    *Edward Deci.*

found in the sense of security others provide, such as being part of a team or being provided with a secure base.

When the reason for engaging in sport is not wholly due to the enjoyment and satisfaction gained from the activity itself, the athlete has *extrinsic motivation*. This sort of motivation is linked to engaging in sport for its external benefits. Such benefits include any kind of reward such as money, trophies or beneficial contracts or a reward associated with avoiding punishment. A third form of behaviour is distinguished too – *amotivation*. An amotivated individual lacks intention to act and thus lack of motivation to play and little effort will be given to their sport.

Coaches create environments, or social contexts around athletes which can impact motivation. Behaviours such as enhanced persistence, effort, performance and wellbeing have been associated with self-determined, autonomously managed actions found with intrinsic motivation. Hence, a coaching environment which encourages intrinsic motivation can be desirable. This can be achieved by fostering the three needs of *autonomy*, *competence* and *relatedness*. Autonomy can be encouraged by allowing the athlete to make decisions whilst competence may be supported by focusing on developing skills and abilities which require improvement. Relatedness could be stimulated by making the athlete feel supported and part of a team. In contrast, a very controlling environment can negatively impact intrinsic motivation. If the athlete were made to feel as though their worth and group-membership depended upon winning trophies, for instance, the reason to play would be to win (lack of autonomy) and being

Extrinsic motives.

Intrinsic motives.

*Intrinsic motivation involves playing sport for the enjoyment and satisfaction the activity provides. Extrinsic motivation is associated with a sport's external rewards.*

part of the group would depend on trophies (relatedness is subject to certain requirements). Finally, should the coach criticize the athlete's ability in a way that undermined their abilities, this would reduce their feelings of competence.

## Anxiety

**Task 4** – This task refers to sport but if you struggle to put yourself in the positions of an amateur or professional athlete, think about the following in terms of sitting a test or an exam.

Imagine that you are an athlete and part of a team. Tomorrow, your team is involved in the final of a major tournament, do you think you'll be feeling nervous? What if the event is particularly significant, such as the Olympics or World Cup? Do you think you'll be more nervous just before the final?

Now imagine that instead of being part of a team, you're involved in an individual sport and tomorrow is the final of a major tournament. Are you nervous? Are you more nervous just before the event?

Which would make you more nervous, the final of an individual sport or a team sport? Do you think it would be a problem if you had no nerves at all, in either case?

Task 4 refers to 'nerves' and feeling 'nervous' but psychologists prefer to be more precise and distinguish between *arousal* and *anxiety*. Arousal refers to our energy or activity level and it differs along a continuum from low to high. When in a deep sleep, we are at the low end of the arousal continuum. If a smoke or fire alarm were triggered though, its sound would wake us and we'd be alerted to danger. Now, our arousal level is at the high end of the continuum which allows us to be ready to take appropriate action.

Anxiety arises when someone or something is *perceived as threatening*. In other words, the interpretation of the threat is what is important. If, for some reason we had to walk along a high roof without safety gear, our anxiety would, of course, be high because the task poses a genuine danger to life. Similarly, if you were a novice mountain climber, you could be anxious about the potential dangers, even when with experts and using appropriate safety equipment. You know you are inexperienced and that mountain climbing can be a high-risk activity. In contrast, it's quite possible to be physically safe but still experience anxiety. An amateur athlete who has to take a shot at a significant stage of a match may well feel anxious despite no physical danger

*Different athletes at the start of a race can have different levels of trait and state anxiety.*

being present. As each person in these examples has anxiety, it's reasonable to suppose they are all also in a state of high arousal. Where there is high anxiety, there is usually high arousal. However, high arousal does not automatically lead to anxiety.

Anxiety has different dimensions: *cognitive anxiety* involves worry and negative expectations; *physical (somatic) anxiety* relates to physiological signs whilst *behavioural anxiety* is revealed by changes in behaviour.

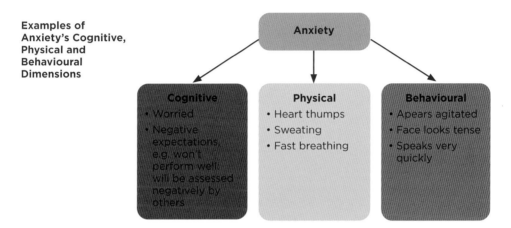

**Examples of Anxiety's Cognitive, Physical and Behavioural Dimensions**

*Trait anxiety* and *state anxiety* are distinguished too. Trait anxiety conceptualizes anxiety as a fairly stable personality characteristic which predisposes the individual to feel highly anxious in particular situations. State anxiety captures a person's mood changing from one situation to the next and it can be affected by trait anxiety.

An athlete high in trait anxiety may interpret sporting events as threatening and feel negative most of the time, whereas another athlete, low in trait anxiety, may typically feel less threatened and be less negative.

The sporting situation itself affects anxiety too. Suppose there is a swimmer with low trait anxiety: we know this person will be predisposed to be generally less anxious. There may be some state anxiety prior to racing, such as an amount of nervousness and apprehension, but our swimmer finds this typically changes as the race starts and pool lengths are swum. However, when the event is an international championship final, the swimmer knows this is a very important race, so it wouldn't be unusual for them to have heightened state anxiety compared with usual. Another athlete, though, who is high in trait anxiety will be predisposed to be anxious throughout. Contests themselves are also likely to produce high state anxiety unless involved in a swimming race which poses no kind of threat – let's say one in which a win was inevitable – this situation wouldn't generate high state anxiety as success is bound to occur.

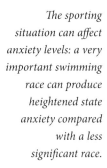

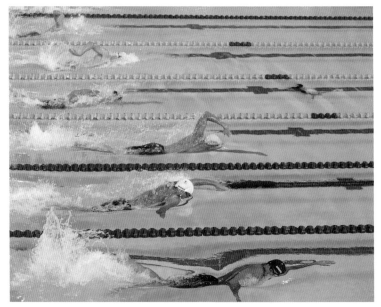

The sporting situation can affect anxiety levels: a very important swimming race can produce heightened state anxiety compared with a less significant race.

Precursors to an athlete being anxious are called *antecedents of anxiety* and a number of these have been identified. You have just met one antecedent – *trait anxiety* – and discovered it can affect state anxiety. However, knowing that athletes who are high in trait anxiety can go on to have more state anxiety doesn't identify the cause of this increase in state anxiety. To argue, 'this swimmer becomes more anxious in competitions due to already being anxious' gets us nowhere because we don't get to the root of the problem.

Another antecedent to anxiety involves *perfectionism* which consists of two types. If an athlete wants to be good at their sport so they can be successful, this is adaptive perfectionism. Excessive concern over mistakes constitutes maladaptive perfectionism and is linked to anxiety. *Self-worth* is also a precursor of anxiety. When self-esteem is strongly connected to winning, it becomes very important to avoid defeat and its possibility leads to anxiety. Additionally, if a person doesn't believe that their abilities are going to lead to success, this lack of *confidence* can induce anxiety.

All the antecedents discussed so far are related to athletes themselves but there are other precursors to anxiety which exist beyond the individual. One of these is *competition importance*: the more important a sporting event is considered to be, the more anxiety that accompanies the occasion. *Time to competition* influences anxiety in different ways. In the days before an event, cognitive anxiety is usually high and stable whereas physical, or somatic anxiety is low up to one or two days before the competition. At this point, it starts to increase and builds until competition begins. Finally, *sport type* can have an effect. More anxiety is induced by sports which involve physical contact and individual sports provoke more anxiety than those involving teams.

## PSYCHOLOGICAL THEORIES OF SPORTING ANXIETY

In what ways do arousal (energy level) and anxiety (perception of threat) affect an athlete's performance? Several theories have been used to answer this question but for brevity, only four are discussed below: two which address arousal and performance and then two which address anxiety and performance.

*Drive Theory* as proposed by Clark Hull, along with Janet and Kenneth Spence, linked arousal level, performance and skill. In sport, highly skilled athletes have learned to perform well, so will typically produce the best response in a situation and for these people, high arousal yields better performance. Less skilled athletes, such as learners, may not select the best response and instead choose one that they are more accustomed to employing. In this case, at best, there may be no change in performance as arousal increases but at worst, performance may decrease. Although initially appealing, Drive Theory had too many problems to be a satisfactory explanation of arousal and performance. To give one example – even highly skilled, professional athletes are sometimes known to 'choke' – anxiety suddenly affects performance and they experience the kinds of symptoms associated with high arousal levels.

*The Inverted U Theory* from Robert Yerkes and John Dodson took a different perspective from Drive Theory. It contended that as arousal increases, so does performance, until an optimal

*Clark Leonard Hull (centre).*

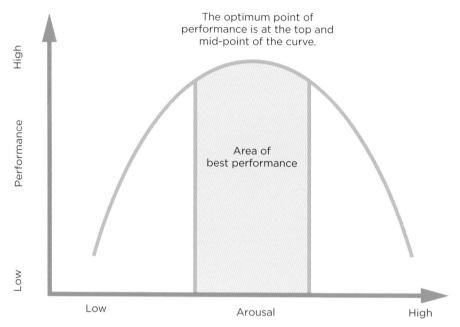

The optimum point of performance is at the top and mid-point of the curve.

Area of best performance

High

Low

Performance

Low        Arousal        High

*Inverted U Theory.*

point is reached. Beyond this point, as arousal increases further, performance decreases. If this pattern is plotted on a graph, the image produced looks like an arc (hence the name *Inverted U*), with the optimum point in the middle, at the top.

Different athletes have different optimal arousal levels. A highly skilled athlete's optimum performance point is, of course, quite different from a low skilled player's optimal point, since what is easy for an advanced athlete is hard for a less skilled player. (Think about how elite darts players regularly hit their chosen, relatively small areas on a dartboard, or how a professional footballer can pass a ball to another player, successfully at the right moment). Elite athletes require comparatively more arousal to hit their optimum point than less skilled

*Robert Yerkes.*

players because they are highly accustomed to performing and producing actions correctly, without having to think them through whilst manoeuvring. Low-skill players, on the other hand, have to think about what they are doing, therefore, to perform at their optimal point requires comparatively less arousal.

Task complexity combines with arousal to influence performance too. For simple tasks the optimal level of arousal is higher than for a complex task. Consider a snooker player who, faced with a difficult pot, has to use the rest, hit the cue ball at the right speed and angle whilst taking into consideration the position of other demandingly placed balls. The required manoeuvre is tricky and requires finesse, under these circumstances low arousal level is desirable, otherwise focusing and making the right movements will be too difficult. In contrast, taking part in a rugby scrum demands a lot of energy to provide the strength required for the player's team to win the ball. Under circumstances like this, low arousal wouldn't help gain the ball and a high arousal level is essential instead.

Inverted U Theory is not problem-free either, though. Whilst it describes the way in which arousal affects different kinds of performances, it fails to provide any understanding of what actually brings about the effect of arousal on performance. Moreover, as explained above, arousal consists of three types but Inverted U Theory treats it as if it is a single whole.

*Professional darts players regularly hit the necessary areas of a dart board. Their optimal performance point is quite different from that of a less skilled player.*

*Professional snooker: when faced with a difficult pot requiring finesse, a low arousal level is desirable.*

The problem of arousal being considered as a single construct does not exist in Lew Hardy and colleagues' *Catastrophe Theory* as this account addressed the interaction between cognitive anxiety, physiological arousal and performance. Catastrophe Theory's proposals are:

- When an athlete isn't worried – a state of low cognitive anxiety – physiological arousal's effect on performance creates an inverted U pattern, as described above.
- When an athlete is worried – a state of high cognitive anxiety – increased physiological arousal continues to improve performance until a particular point. This point coincides with the best performance and therefore, optimal arousal. If physiological arousal is increased further, there is now a sudden, swift, catastrophic drop in performance. The drop is so far, that the athlete is now performing at a lower level than before the catastrophe; recovery from here is difficult; physiological arousal has to drop considerably to get back to the original high performance level.

- Low physiological arousal coupled with high cognitive anxiety enhances performance. This means that if the athlete is physically relaxed, some cognitive anxiety will improve performance.
- High physiological arousal coupled with high cognitive anxiety reduces performance.

Catastrophe Theory is complicated because it is dealing with not one but three components. This also makes it difficult to test to determine its accuracy. Based on the research conducted so far, it is fair to say that more investigations are needed to confirm the theory's proposals.

The final theory to be discussed here is by Rich Masters and Jon Maxwell and is called the *Conscious Processing Hypothesis*. It is important because it looks at *how* anxiety may influence performance.

When we are new to a task, we have to think about the kinds of movements that are required in order to be successful. When we become proficient at the same task, we don't need to think about it in the same way because performing the task becomes automatic. A non-sport example of this is riding a bike. Initially, we have to think about getting on the

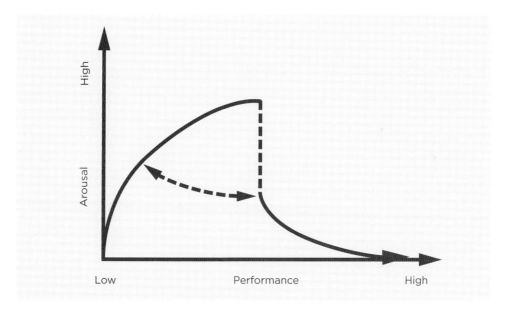

*Catastrophe Theory: when an athlete is worried, (high cognitive arousal), increased physiological arousal improves performance to a particular point. This point coincides with best performance/ optimal arousal. When physiological arousal increase further, there is a sudden catastrophic drop in performance.*

bike, depressing the pedal to move off, putting the other foot on its pedal and going fast enough not to wobble. We also have to think about what to do when slowing, stopping, turning corners etc and all this involves telling ourselves what to do and consciously controlling our movements. (If you don't ride a bike, similar principles apply to other tasks such as driving or learning to play an instrument.) As we gain experience though, complex tasks can be performed without conscious thought – we just hop on the bicycle and go. This same principle applies to sport, such as when a highly skilled athlete automatically performs a particular shot in football, cricket, rugby or tennis, for instance.

The Conscious Processing Hypothesis argues that when an expert athlete becomes anxious, instead of proceeding with their usual, automatic movements, they consciously process, or control these movements. In other words, anxiety makes athletes start to analyse what they are doing and they revert to conscious control of their actions where they tell themselves what to do. This means they are very aware of what they are doing and their movements do not have their customary, unconscious finesse.

Research has supported the Conscious Processing Hypothesis's account of anxiety's effect on performance and it can explain why even elite athletes can underperform through 'paralysis by analysis'.

## Using Psychology to Help Enhance Motivation and Reduce Anxiety

*Goal-setting* helps athletes in a number of ways, such as providing a focus for attention; improved motivation, effort, persistence and performance; along with helping the athlete to develop ways in which to problem solve and create action-plans. It does this by establishing the athlete's aims; means of achieving them; a time-frame and assessments of how goal-achievement is advancing.

Goals can be set based upon *outcome, performance* and *process*. Outcome goals are based on results and require comparison with others, such as winning a match or being one of the first three in a race and they depend in part on the quality of the opposition. Performance goals relate to athletes achieving their own, individual standard such as gaining or improving a particular ability. Process goals concern how an aspect of sport is completed and therefore concentrate upon a behaviour, such as always striking on a tennis racquet's 'sweet spot'. All three goals ought to be set for athletes to gain their desired results. Furthermore, individual goals must be specific so that athletes know precisely what they are trying to achieve – such as increasing the length of a long-jump by a precisely defined length – which allows for clear, measurable feedback. Each goal must also provide challenge but be realistic; if it is too easy, the goal will be achieved too readily, whilst an unrealistic goal will not be achieved at all. Well-developed, written action plans

*Goal-setting helps athletes. Individual goals must be specific so that the athlete knows precisely what must be achieved, such as increasing their distance in the long jump by a defined length.*

which clearly define what is required for athletes' short- and long-term goals usefully identify what must be done for a goal to be successfully achieved.

Another way athletes can be helped is to ensure that they interpret anxiety symptoms correctly. Although symptoms like an increased heartbeat and butterflies in their stomach could indicate something unpleasant is about to happen, they can also demonstrate that the athlete is motivated to succeed. Once it is recognized that the symptoms are evidence of something beneficial, they can be used constructively to promote performance.

A common source of anxiety in sport comes from the stress and pressure athletes experience when there is a disparity between their ability and what the situation demands from them. The inequality is perceived as a threat and this creates anxiety. Let's suppose that commonly, during matches, a golfer repeatedly takes too many putts to sink the ball on the green. There is a mismatch between needing to sink the ball in as few strokes as possible and the athlete's ability to do so. One way to tackle this issue is to train the athlete to change how the situation is perceived. Currently, our golfer perceives having to putt as a threat but if this is changed to perceiving putting as a challenge, the threat disappears. Instead of concentrating on the fear of missing the hole, the golfer needs to learn to focus on a particular aspect of their putting process that they can control and establish this as their challenge. For example, before putting it is important to establish what the ball's route to the hole is like, such as assessing the undulations on the green; consequently, our golfer could identify this procedure as their focus and challenge. In doing so, the anxiety of putting has been reframed as a challenge involving the golfer's preparation to putt skills. Of course, if our golfer has a genuine lack of ability in the processes required to putt, this can be addressed through a practical plan to improve these skills which will help produce greater equality between ability and task demand.

Competitions induce state anxiety and this can be prepared for by using *simulation training*. This involves practising under conditions which replicate – as closely as is practicable – what the conditions will be like during the event. Through these experiences the athlete becomes familiar with what might occur during the competition and can cope with its pressures successfully.

*Imagery* also assists athletes to deal with anxiety by helping them prepare for what their sport and competition require from them. Imagery consists of using memories of previous

*If there is a disparity between the requirement to putt successfully and the golfer's ability, this can create anxiety because putting is perceived as threatening. If this perception is changed to viewing putting as a challenge, the threat disappears.*

---

**IMAGERY TASK**

You are going to be asked to imagine something. When you do so, please find a quiet place, sit down and close your eyes whilst creating the images in your mind. The task is not related to a specific sport so that it can be performed by all readers; afterwards, though, you may want to imagine yourself taking part in an aspect of your chosen sport. Please note: (a) there are individual differences in imagery ability – don't worry if you find the task(s) hard; (b) the ease/difficulty of creating one image will not necessarily be replicated with all other images.

Please try to focus on seeing, hearing and feeling in your mind's eye, ear and hand.

Imagine that you are holding the kind of pen where, if you press its top, the nib is released and if you press it again, the nib retracts; that is, you 'click' it on and off.

- What does the pen look like?
- What does it feel like in your hand (e.g. hard/soft)?
- Click it on. What did that sound like? Was it one smooth sound? Two sounds? Three sounds?
- Imagine you are writing the letter 'P' – what are the movements associated with this?

---

sensory experiences to 'see', 'hear', 'feel', 'taste' and 'smell' in your mind, whilst *motor imagery* involves mentally performing actions.

Let's suppose a footballer has an important match ahead such as a competition, or a match which decides whether the player is selected or dropped from the team. The player could, for instance: visualize the stadium; visualize what it's like scoring a goal in real-time; mentally recreate the movements needed to score that goal and what those movements feel like; hear the excitement of the crowd as the player makes their run and the roar when the ball goes into the back of the net. Imagery helps because evidence has shown that certain brain areas relevant to vision and movement are also involved when using imagery. This means that when an athlete employs imagery, these areas and their nerve pathways are being tuned as if really playing.

*Self-talk* refers to making statements to yourself. When anxious, an athlete's statements can become negative and destructive causing performance to be worse instead of better. Consequently, the self-talk needs to be shifted to being productive to reduce anxiety. Helpful statements can also assist with poor performance itself and dealing with difficult issues during play. Suppose a snooker player is very anxious; this could be addressed by stating something encouraging and which focuses on what to do next, such as, 'Right, next point; red, middle

*Imagery helps athletes deal with anxiety by mentally creating potential experiences and what may be required from them whilst competing.*

pocket.' Similarly, if a goal defence player lets a ball through during a netball match and is stressed about this, a statement that helps maintain a positive frame of mind for later play could be 'I was in position quickly.'

Many athletes can be observed going through certain procedures before performing an action. This can be seen in tennis players before they serve; rugby players preparing to kick a conversion; footballers preparing to take a penalty and a golfer attempting to putt. In addition to systematic physical actions, players will also use a series of thoughts to help them prepare for their task. In other words, *pre-performance routines* are adopted. These frameworks provide a player with purposeful, focused attention on what they can control themselves and this helps reduce anxiety. Examples of procedural routines include golfers stepping back from the ball and practising the putt and tennis players bouncing the ball before engaging in their service action.

Finally, *relaxation techniques* can lower anxiety levels. However, there isn't a universally applicable technique as the circumstances of sports differ and what may be useful before play isn't going to be automatically equally valuable during play, when an appropriate level of arousal is desirable. To illustrate the former point: some sports are slow-moving between points, such as golf, whilst others are faster but have regular breaks, such as tennis, where professionals have 20 seconds between points and 90 seconds at the change of ends. Continuous sports like football may only have brief breaks for penalties during play, whilst other continuous sports are fast and without breaks, such as cycling. This means that even a relatively quick relaxation technique that only takes a few seconds can't be employed either with all sports, or at all times, within certain sports.

Although the focus here has been on just motivation and anxiety in relation to sport the techniques can be used more broadly too. Goal-setting could apply to daily exercise and to the person who wants to play just for fun, perhaps with a goal of a couple of times a week. Anxiety-related techniques can also help improve concentration, focus and performance more generally too.

## SUMMARY

- Sport psychology addresses how mind and environment affect behaviour in relation to sport. This includes working with athletes but also coaches and referees.
- Motivation is a force which drives behaviour to achieve an objective; in sport this affects participation and how much an individual extends themselves to achieve an objective.
- Motivation has been accounted for in terms of an achievement personality trait; whether a person's achievement goal is personal improvement or winning and whether coaches encourage an atmosphere focused on improving skills or winning. Focus on improvement typically leads to better results.
- Motivation has also been accounted for using attribution theory and the reasons an athlete gives to success/failure. Self-determination theory distinguishes intrinsic and extrinsic motivations; coaching environments which foster the former are beneficial.
- Arousal relates to energy level; anxiety involves perceiving a threat and usually having high arousal. Anxiety can be cognitive, physical or behavioural.
- Trait anxiety is a personality characteristic and is comparatively unchanging; state anxiety relates to mood and changes. Situations can affect anxiety.
- Anxiety antecedents include: trait anxiety, perfectionism, self-worth, confidence level, competition importance, time to competition, chances of physical contact and playing an individual sport.
- Arousal's effect on performance has been explained through Drive Theory and the Inverted-U Theory.
- Anxiety has been accounted for using Catastrophe Theory and the Conscious Processing Hypothesis.
- Motivation can be enhanced and anxiety reduced via: goal-setting; appropriate interpretation of anxiety symptoms; reducing the disparity between perceived ability and situation demands; simulation training; imagery; self-talk; pre-performance routines and relaxation techniques.

# OCCUPATIONAL PSYCHOLOGY

Occupational psychology is concerned with the people who work in organizations, the work which is done and how the organization operates. This includes selection, training and development of employees; how individuals, groups and teams behave; improved worker performance and ensuring that workers' welfare is looked after, such as stress levels. The nature of work itself is examined, too, along with the environment in which it takes place. This may consist of securing a healthy and safe workplace for the employee as well as finding ways for the work and organization to function better. Organizations may need to be considered in terms of their culture, structures and organizational change.

In the UK, what is now referred to as occupational psychology used to be called industrial psychology. Elsewhere, occupational psychology may go under the title of industrial-organizational psychology, or work and organizational psychology. You may even see reference to business psychology, or to industrial psychology alone, or organizational psychology alone. However, despite these differences, the focus is the same.

In the UK, occupational psychologists may work as external, independent consultants whose services are purchased by a client-organization, or sometimes they are direct employees of organizations. Those organizations which use the expertise of an occupational psychologist are typically in the private sector, though public services can require their services too (such as the National Health Service, His Majesty's Prison Service, the Home Office) as well as not-for-profit organizations. Occupational psychologists also work as academics in universities, often in management and business schools rather than in psychology departments.

Below we are going to look at four areas of occupational psychology which most workers will experience: how workers are selected; work–life balance and occupational stress; plus worker appraisal.

## A Brief History of Occupational Psychology

In the early 1900s European researchers were carrying out investigations in areas that we would now recognize as part of occupational psychology. By 1911, the American, Walter Dill Scott had written *Increasing Human Efficiency in Business* and Frederick Winslow Taylor had argued jobs could be analysed to improve efficiency so that the best people could be selected for different roles. Such 'time and motion' studies were also employed by Lillian and Frank Gilbreth to explore job efficiency, but Lillian was noted too for her work on time management and stress, fatigue and motivation. Just as Lillian Gilbreth is often considered to be the mother of modern management, Hugo Münsterberg, is commonly regarded as the father of occupational psychology, publishing, in 1912, *Psychology and Industrial Efficiency*. He pointed out the importance of linking people's jobs to their mental and emotional abilities because this improves job satisfaction and productivity.

World War I saw Agostino Gemelli use measures for selecting pilots in Italy; in the USA Robert Yerkes and colleagues developed tests for screening and selecting recruits, whilst Walter Dill Scott and Walter Bingham concentrated on selection of men suited to being officers. Indeed, Bingham had an expanded role during World War II in terms of using psychological knowledge in association with military personnel.

*Lillian Gilbreth.*

Between 1929–1932 Elton Mayo conducted a famous set of investigations known as the Hawthorne Studies because they were conducted at Bell System's Western Electric Hawthorne Works. Although alternative interpretations of the results were advanced later, at the time, this research drew attention to issues such as the importance of management–worker communication and how this affected productivity. Furthermore, by the 1940s, social psychologist Kurt Lewin was exploring group

*Walter Dill Scott.*

*American soldiers taking the Army Alpha test in November 1917.*

*Hawthorne Works of Western Electric, 1925.*

dynamics; he established a research centre in the middle part of the decade and collaborated with colleagues in the UK.

Later, occupational psychology was affected by changes to employment practices such as selection and recruitment due to legislative changes. For example, America's civil rights movement produced anti-discriminatory legislation and other shifts in the workplace occurred too, including those related to age and female employment. Management had to change too, as workers expected greater involvement in decision-making. By the 1980s, organizations were employing people on a global scale; in the UK, economic recession placed greater demands on those who were in work meaning that issues associated with stress in the workplace and the work–life balance were explored.

Currently, occupational psychology is responding to new changes within the workplace. Where older employees remain within the workforce (the UK has comparatively recently increased the age at which individuals can receive the State Retirement Pension), this sets new challenges, such as, how this affects job availability throughout the overall workforce; the physical practicalities of performing a role and employment opportunities for the older worker. There has also been an increase – especially since COVID-19 – in the number of those who work

*The rise in home working since COVID-19 has led to changes in evaluating personnel.*

at least some, if not all of the time, away from the office and now it is not unusual for recruitment interviews to be conducted online. All of these changes from traditional patterns of employment mean that how a person works with others, whether this be peers, managers, or those who are being managed is very different from what was previously the norm.

## Selecting Personnel

When you apply for a job, commonly, you first encounter the *advertisement* for the post. Next, you learn about the nature of the role from the *job description*, whilst the *person specification* tells you about the kinds of qualifications, abilities, experience and knowledge the successful candidate will have to possess. Occupational psychology can be involved in each of these elements of the recruitment process.

In order to have an accurate job description and person specification it is essential to have a thorough understanding of what the role necessitates and this is achieved through *job analysis*. Different methods are available for performing job analysis and only some of these are considered below.

*Observation* involves observing employees as they go about their work in order to establish what their job involves. Questions can be asked for clarification and the job analyst gets direct information about the job. However, it is not always possible to observe all key aspects of jobs: some roles involve cognitive processing such as thinking and problem-solving and these kinds of mental tasks can't be directly observed. Furthermore, whilst observation means the job analyst does not have to rely upon potentially biased reports from the employee, this methodology is open to bias on the part of the observer, who may give inappropriate significance to certain tasks.

*Interviews* can be conducted with reference to different kinds of work and allow for the collection of a lot of information. Follow-up questions can be asked if more detail is required or when clarification is needed; an interview can be conducted with individual workers if necessary but group-interviews gather information more quickly. Data collection depends though on interviewees providing accurate descriptions of what they do and it is always possible for something to be omitted unintentionally.

*Surveys* are a less time-consuming way of gathering data than interviews. They do not require the job analyst to be present whilst being completed and so information can be gathered

*Interviews are one way of gathering data about employees and job applicants.*

relatively quickly, as well as being in depth and covering a variety of issues. On the other hand, if a survey fails to include an important question, this information is lost entirely; there is also no way to ensure that all questions are completed and addressed properly and, of course, these matters cannot be pursued through follow-up queries.

Other methods of performing a job analysis include standardized techniques which can be directed towards: (i) what is involved in the job (job-oriented analysis); (ii) what knowledge, skills, abilities and other characteristics are needed to complete the work (worker-oriented analysis); or (iii) a combination of elements in relation to both job and worker (hybrid methods).

An example of a job-oriented approach is *Functional Job Analysis*. This method assumes that any job can be divided into three categories – Things, Data and People – each of which has different functional levels, or associated difficulty. 'Things' refers to interacting with equipment used to do the job; 'data' includes facts, ideas, statistics and other kinds of information; and 'people' refers to communication. Information can then be put together about a job's constituent tasks and how these tasks are completed in relation to the categories and their levels.

| EXAMPLES OF HIGH, MIDDLE AND LOW LEVELS OF FUNCTIONAL JOB ANALYSIS'S THINGS, DATA AND PEOPLE | | | | |
|---|---|---|---|---|
| **Categories** | | | | |
| | | **Things** | **Data** | **People** |
| **Levels** | **High** | *setting-up* e.g. installing/ repairing equipment | *synthesizing* e.g. conceives an original, new way of dealing with a problem by drawing together ideas | *mentoring* e.g. providing advice/guidance |
| | **Middle** | *operating* e.g. operating equipment | *compiling* e.g. collecting/ categorizing information | *persuading* e.g. influencing others regarding a product |
| | **Low** | *handling* e.g. carrying/moving items | *comparing* e.g. selecting/ sorting | *taking instructions* e.g. following directions/orders |

| THE POSITION ANALYSIS QUESTIONNAIRE AND ITS MAJOR CATEGORIES ||
| Major Categories | Explanation |
| --- | --- |
| Information Input | addresses how a worker acquires information to do the job |
| Mental Processes | refers to thinking and decision-making involved in the job |
| Work Activities | the job's physical activities, including any tool or equipment the worker uses |
| Relationships with Other Persons | the kinds of relationships that exist with the job such as colleagues and line-management |
| Job Context | the job's physical and social contexts |
| Other Work Characteristics | any other elements of the job not already taken into account |

A worker-oriented approach is found in the *Position Analysis Questionnaire* (PAQ). This begins with a job analyst first gathering background information; workers are then observed as they perform their role and subsequently, they are interviewed about the content of their work. Now, the job analyst is in a position to complete the PAQ.

The Position Analysis Questionnaire follows a structured format consisting of six major categories each of which is designed to gather detail under the relevant heading. Worker behaviour is captured by 187 items and the questionnaire is completed using a rating scale for each item. All together, six different rating scales are used which relate to: extent of use, importance, amount of time, possibility of occurrence, applicability, and special, item-specific scales. When completed, the questionnaire's information is scored by computer which also generates the results of the PAQ.

An example of a hybrid method is found in the United States of America's *Occupational Information Network* (O*NET) devised by the Department of Labor. O*NET is a dynamic system which collects, and gives access to, information about occupation and worker requirements. Originally, the information in O*NET came from job analysts but subsequently, this was expanded to include information from workers themselves. The job-related information the system contains relates to aspects such as generalized work activities, work context, organizational context and the sorts of tasks, equipment, machines and tools that

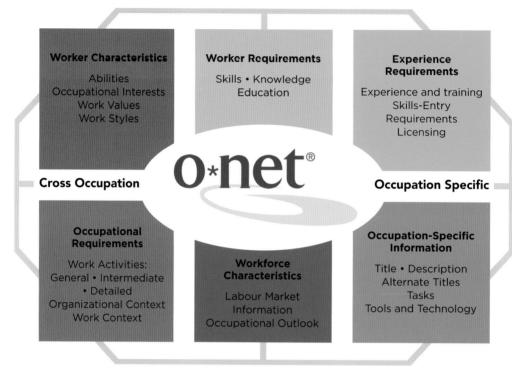

**Worker-oriented**

**Worker Characteristics**

Abilities
Occupational Interests
Work Values
Work Styles

**Worker Requirements**

Skills • Knowledge
Education

**Experience Requirements**

Experience and training
Skills-Entry
Requirements
Licensing

**O*net**®

**Cross Occupation**

**Occupation Specific**

**Occupational Requirements**

Work Activities:
General • Intermediate
• Detailed
Organizational Context
Work Context

**Workforce Characteristics**

Labour Market
Information
Occupational Outlook

**Occupation-Specific Information**

Title • Description
Alternate Titles
Tasks
Tools and Technology

**Job-oriented**

*The United States, Department of Labor's Occupational Information Network (O*NET) collects, and gives access to, information about occupations and worker requirements.*

an employee would use. Employee-related information includes abilities, interests, skills, education and knowledge. O*NET is available online and thus provides an easy-access resource of job analysis within the USA.

Upon completion of the job analysis, the job description and person specification can be drawn-up. A job description contains the characteristics of the job (its purpose, what it involves and how it is done) whereas the person specification details the knowledge, skills, abilities and other features that the role requires.

The organization is now in a position to advertise the post. The advertisement needs to cover information characterizing the organization, such as what it does, what it is like and its values. The specific role must be stated, what will be required of the person who is suited to the job, along with how to get in touch with the organization posting the advertisement.

| WHAT A JOB DESCRIPTION AND PERSON SPECIFICATION CAN CONTAIN ||
| --- | --- |
| **Job Description** | **Person Specification** |
| • Job title. | • Necessary qualifications. |
| • Organization, department, location of the post. | • Membership of professional organizations. |
| • Grade or level. | • Levels of knowledge and experience necessary for the post. |
| • Pay. | • Skills and attributes. |
| • Summary of what the role involves. | • Indication of whether all of the above are essential or desirable. |
| • Job purpose and duties. This information should contain sufficient information so that potential applicants have a clear idea of what they will be required to do. This might involve factors such as: lifting; assembling parts; planning; organizing; being responsible for others; evaluating; keeping records; using tools or equipment; following health and safety legislation; dealing with and communicating with customers or clients in an appropriate manner. | • Information on whether certain factors may make a potential applicant ineligible for a role. |
| • Information on who the post-holder will report to. | |
| • Information on working conditions. | |

However, it is not as straightforward as simply including these types of information to generate applications. The way in which the advertisement is framed can affect applicants in different ways. For example, who applies can be influenced by the kind of language the advertisement uses. Danielle Gaucher and colleagues' experimental work found that when an advertisement contains more stereotypically masculine wording, women found these jobs less appealing. Furthermore, the attitude that an applicant forms about an organization can be affected by the extent of their experience of work and seeking employment coupled with the

*Psychometric tests are often used in employment selection. They take 'mental measurements' relating to ability, aptitude, achievement and personality.*

advertisement. H. Jack Walker and colleagues reported that with low experience, applicants' attitudes towards an organization were more influenced by a more secondary feature of an advertisement: the physical attractiveness of individuals who appeared in the information. However, when there was greater experience of job applications, it was the content of the advertisement which affected attitudes towards the organization.

We are now at the point that many of us are familiar with: we've seen the advertisement, sought further details and have decided we meet the job description and person specification, so we have applied for the post. After this point there are a number of different ways of proceeding with selection of the right person, but we are going to look at just two: psychometric tests and interviews.

*Psychometric tests* are used to take 'mental measurements' and are often used in selection. They include tests designed to assess ability, aptitude, achievement and personality. Current abilities are assessed by completing tests of achievement which measure verbal and numerical reasoning. Future performance, on the other hand, is assessed through aptitude tests which give an indication of whether a skill is likely to be acquired by the individual. Consequently, aptitude tests are directed towards the kind of skills required for a particular role; this might include measures of specific kinds of abilities the job would require.

What constitutes personality and the different accounts of personality were discussed in Chapter 5. In a work setting, it is assumed that personality traits are related to whether a person is suited to a particular role and to predict how they will perform in the job. Commonly, the 'Big Five' personality traits captured by 'OCEAN', (openness, conscientiousness, extraversion, agreeableness, neuroticism) are used in tests. The tests themselves are obtained from test publishers.

*Interviews* are a common way of trying to select between different candidates for a post. Structured interviews allow for candidates to be asked about the same issues in very much the same way. Questions which focus on a candidate's behaviour on a previous, specific occasion, allow an assessment of how the individual would behave in a future, similar circumstance. Given that all candidates do not necessarily share the same levels of relevant experience, questions can be framed around hypothetical situations and what the candidate would do under those circumstances. Ideally, efforts should be made to ensure that each candidate's interview is as similar as possible which means taking care with prompts and any further questioning. It is important too, that interviewers are consistent in the ways in which they assess the candidates.

Psychological research has shown that the features described above are vital to the interview process because interviewers can be influenced by a range of factors. Examples of these include the candidates': race, gender, education, qualifications, social background and physical appearance. Other factors involve the impressions an interviewer has gained from pre-interview information; too much weight being attached to information supplied at the beginning and the end of the interview and to any negative information provided.

Choosing the right person for the advertised post is important because if the selected individual is wrong for the job this has negative consequences for both the employer and employee. Once all the information has been gathered to make a decision, that decision should be based upon those elements of the job which are considered most important being given greater weighting than less important elements. The person who has performed best can then be selected accordingly.

## Work–Life Balance and Work-Related Stress

Once in employment, a worker will want to have a good work–life balance. Of course, what this means will differ from one person to another. Balance does not automatically mean 50 per cent of your time is spent on work whilst the other 50 per cent is spent on life outside of work. Instead, it is more about getting the proportions right for you and what this may be in one stage of life could well be different at another stage.

Initially, a person may not have to consider having sufficient time for being a parent but as children are born this changes and will alter again as the children age and become more

*Working late and a poor work-life balance can lead to stress.'*

independent. Caring responsibilities may reappear later in life too as grandchildren arrive and as elderly relatives require more assistance. There may also be somebody in the family with long-term care needs who must be considered over many years. Even if a person is single and does not care for others, fairness and equality mean this individual too is entitled to a work–life balance.

At the same time, though, it may be necessary to work more than one job and work long hours to have sufficient income to live. Long hours may also be the culture of the workplace or have become a habit. Some jobs involve taking work home because it cannot all be completed at the workplace and technology can bring work into the home and leisure time.

The different responsibilities associated with home and work can make the individual feel pulled in different directions simultaneously. When this occurs and work–family conflict follows this is undesirable for everybody concerned. The worker can become distressed, dissatisfied with their job, less committed and less effective, for instance. From the employer's perspective, a worker who is in this position may be actively seeking to leave and be unable to contribute fully satisfactorily to the organization. This is where an organization can help by being supportive.

If working hours are more flexible, perhaps through flexitime, part-time working or reduced hours this can make for better work–life balance. It may be possible too, to make the job itself more flexible, perhaps through job-share; offering independent-working and extended leave options. Additionally, it could be established that there is no expectation to respond to emails outside given times.

Certain employers might be able to offer childcare facilities onsite, though for this to be beneficial across all workers, all employees must be able to afford any associated fees. Furthermore, where these kinds of options exist, workers must be made aware of them and to feel that they can use them. This means that managers and others responsible for workers should not only be supportive of improved work–life balance but also encourage this.

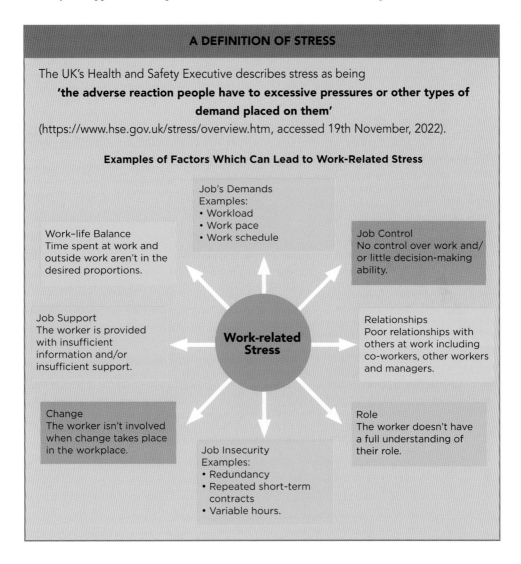

## A DEFINITION OF STRESS

The UK's Health and Safety Executive describes stress as being

**'the adverse reaction people have to excessive pressures or other types of demand placed on them'**

(https://www.hse.gov.uk/stress/overview.htm, accessed 19th November, 2022).

**Examples of Factors Which Can Lead to Work-Related Stress**

Job's Demands
Examples:
• Workload
• Work pace
• Work schedule

Work–life Balance
Time spent at work and outside work aren't in the desired proportions.

Job Control
No control over work and/or little decision-making ability.

Job Support
The worker is provided with insufficient information and/or insufficient support.

**Work-related Stress**

Relationships
Poor relationships with others at work including co-workers, other workers and managers.

Change
The worker isn't involved when change takes place in the workplace.

Job Insecurity
Examples:
• Redundancy
• Repeated short-term contracts
• Variable hours.

Role
The worker doesn't have a full understanding of their role.

Lack of a satisfactory work–life balance is one of several factors which can bring about work-related stress. Fixed working patterns and long hours relate to a person's work schedule, affect work–life balance and so are job-demand stressors. Other stressors of this type include the amount of work to be done coupled with the time available for it to be completed.

Stress can come about too when an employee has too little control over their job and can take too few decisions. It can also follow from issues surrounding the role, such as when a worker's understanding of what they should be doing does not agree with that of the management and when the role involves conflicting responsibilities. Fear of losing one's job, hours which can vary and repeated, very short-term contracts can lead to insecurity and therefore also constitute stressors. If changes are implemented without involving the relevant worker, this too can be stressful because it may make the individual feel as though they have no control, for instance.

Jobs also involve relationships with others in the workplace and these can be stress-inducing if there are issues such as:

- lack of sufficient appropriate support – which includes providing the means to complete the job;
- bullying – a worker may be directly targeted with verbal and/or physical abuse, for example, or the bullying may be comparatively more subtle such as finding ways to exclude the worker;
- sexual harassment – examples include verbal behaviours, such as sexual comments or topics of conversation and/or non-verbal behaviours such as touching;
- violence – this could be part of points above but can also be a separate issue.

There are various consequences of stress such as: headaches, impaired immune functioning, back pain, heart disease, anxiety, depression and disturbed sleep. If stress is prolonged, burnout can occur. It is associated with emotional, physical and mental exhaustion such that the individual experiences symptoms such as lack of energy, tiredness, irritability, hostility, inability to sleep and negative self-evaluations. Stress and burnout clearly have important effects on those who experience them and it is in organizations' interests to help prevent them. Worker absence through ill-health means that person is not contributing to the organization; even if the worker is present, stress can lead to reduced productivity due to reduced motivation, fatigue and impaired mental functioning. Furthermore, where stress is present, staff are more likely to want to leave and find new employment.

Different coping strategies can be adopted by workers to deal with the stress they face. Which method is adopted will depend on a person's own characteristics (such as whether the individual feels they have the relevant skills to deal with the situation) and the situation itself (factors which encourage or discourage a strategy). Some people may choose to avoid or ignore the problem; others may cope by doing something which helps them escape the stress, but in both

*Orgaizations can help with work-related stress by promoting stress-reduction activities such as lunch-time yoga classes.*

these cases the problem remains. Directly addressing the issue, on the other hand, specifically focuses on the stress. A worker may do this by seeking and receiving assistance with whatever is causing the stress. Alternatively, the issue may be cognitively reframed such that instead of thinking about the problem in terms of inability, a more 'can do' form of thinking is adopted.

Ideally, workers would adopt the best strategies for dealing with stress. Similarly, an ideal approach by an organization would be to help its employees cope with stress, or, even better, the organization may be able to eliminate the cause of the stress all together.

The kinds of actions that can help a worker cope with stress could include promoting stress-reduction activities, such as relaxation techniques, yoga, or other forms of exercise. These can be facilitated by offering lunchtime classes and providing access to a gym. Taking breaks and holidays can be encouraged too along with measures that help workers to cope with non-work-related responsibilities. Other ways of helping with stress would be to foster an atmosphere where discussing stress is accepted; training managers to identify signs that workers are stressed and to be supportive. The latter might involve, for example, permitting workers to attend appointments designed to help them deal with their stress and making alterations to the job itself. Changes to a job can follow from time management analysis which can determine the time required to complete tasks and whether: (a) this can be realistically shortened; (b) the quantity of work must be reduced; or (c) the job should be completed in another way. Other alterations to the job could involve managers adjusting deadlines to accurately reflect how much time tasks necessitate and appointing more staff.

## Performance Appraisal

A regular feature of working life is undergoing some kind of performance appraisal. Performance appraisals are used to determine whether it is appropriate to promote a worker, award a rise in pay or potentially decide that the worker should not be kept. Other reasons for appraisal include identifying strengths and weaknesses, goal-setting, providing feedback and determining what kinds of development and training are required so the worker is more effective in their role.

Jobs are, of course, different and therefore different kinds of appraisal techniques are required according to the role being performed. Appraisal methods fall into two types:

---

### EXAMPLES OF APPARENTLY COMPARABLE MEASURES BEING OTHERWISE

**Example 1**
Sue and Fred work together and are employed in identical retail sales jobs. By the end of a week, Fred has more sales than his co-worker. Using sales data alone, Sue appears to be less efficient in the job. However, this situation changes if we know that Sue has had a lot of customers who have been unsure of which product to purchase and have asked her many questions. It changes further too, if we also know that Sue is very approachable and therefore people choose to go to her if they have questions.

**Example 2**
Sunita and Ajay both work for the same organization and have very similar jobs. They both have had additional duties added to their roles which Sunita has completed satisfactorily but which Ajay has dealt with perfunctorily, or not at all. These different behaviours could be taken to signal Sunita is simply a better worker than her colleague because she gets things done to the required level. Yet, if we discover that Sunita has a permanent contract which means she can plan and organize her life, whereas Ajay's repeated short-term contracts mean that he cannot make long-term life-plans, a different picture emerges. Sunita is motivated because she has job security, whilst Ajay's motivation has dwindled due to lack of job security. He might be discouraged from adding to his workload by partially completing tasks he may not be able to see through. Furthermore, it would be unsurprising if he was seeking to leave the organization.

*Rensis Likert.*

*objective* and *subjective*. Objective assessments measure work behaviours that can be quantified in some way. Examples of objective measures include: how long it takes a worker to complete a task; the number of items produced in a given time; sales made; number of errors; deadlines achieved; absences; lateness incidents and accidents. Accurate objective measures are not always available for a given job though, and sometimes, what appear to be comparable measures may not be so.

When objective measures cannot be taken satisfactorily, subjective measures are used. These involve a worker's performance being appraised by those who are in a position to assess the individual's efficacy, such as a line manager or supervisor. Different subjective methods of performance appraisal exist and a selection are discussed below.

The *Graphic Rating Scale* method involves the person conducting the appraisal rating the worker. Using Example 1 (see box below), Sue and Fred might be rated on how many sales made, knowledge about the products on offer, approachability, reliability and other performance-related traits and behaviours relevant to the job. The ratings would be made using a Likert scale (named after the psychologist who created it, Rensis Likert). Different formats exist for Likert scaling but the one given below will give you an idea of what one looks like and what is involved. The rater goes through the behaviour and traits and gives a tick according to their appraisal.

A *Mixed Standard Scale* consists of a series of mixed, randomly organized statements which relate to different aspects of worker performance. Each aspect of performance has three

| AN EXAMPLE OF A LIKERT SCALE FOR RATING PRODUCT KNOWLEDGE | | | | |
|---|---|---|---|---|
| 1 | 2 | 3 | 4 | 5 |
| No product knowledge | Inadequate product knowledge | Satisfactory product knowledge | Good product knowledge | Excellent product knowledge |

| EXAMPLES OF MIXED STANDARD SCALE STATEMENTS |
| --- |

**Performance Level**

| High | He/she regularly shows excellent product knowledge. |
| Medium | He/she regularly shows adequate product knowledge. |
| Low | He/she regularly shows inadequate product knowledge. |

**The High Performance Level Statement Amongst Other Statements**

He/she has no issues keeping to the day's schedule.

He/she rarely completes work by previously established deadlines.

He/she can work collaboratively with colleagues.

He/she regularly shows excellent product knowledge.

statements associated with it which are designed to capture three levels of performance: high performance, average or medium performance and low performance. The rater indicates for each statement whether the worker's performance is higher, worse or at the level given in the statement. Subsequently, the appraiser's responses can be brought together and combined to produce a score for each aspect of performance.

A *Behaviourally Anchored Rating Scale* (*BARS*) assesses different worker behaviours by using a graphic scale accompanied by a definition of the behaviour associated with that point. In this way, it captures effective and ineffective behaviour for different aspects of a specific job. The BARS scale is developed in a series of stages. Firstly, the important elements (performance dimensions) of the job are established by using a job analysis as discussed above. Next, another appraisal technique called the *Critical Incident Method* is used to determine the occasions on which the worker behaved in an effective or ineffective way. The critical incident behaviours are categorized into performance dimensions, such as following procedures appropriately, product knowledge and completing work by the deadline. Finally, chosen behaviours are then assigned a number.

The *Management by Objectives* (*MBO*) performance appraisal originates in the work of Peter Drucker. This method involves manager and employee together developing and agreeing upon a set of objectives. The objectives should be written in accordance with SMART criteria, that is, they should be specific, measurable, achievable, realistic and time-bound. (Please note that the words used in association with SMART can vary: to give just one example, other words including attainable and assignable may be used for achievable.)

## AN EXAMPLE OF A BARS SCALE

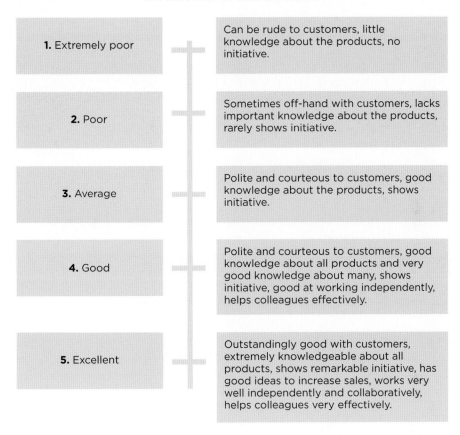

| | |
|---|---|
| **1.** Extremely poor | Can be rude to customers, little knowledge about the products, no initiative. |
| **2.** Poor | Sometimes off-hand with customers, lacks important knowledge about the products, rarely shows initiative. |
| **3.** Average | Polite and courteous to customers, good knowledge about the products, shows initiative. |
| **4.** Good | Polite and courteous to customers, good knowledge about all products and very good knowledge about many, shows initiative, good at working independently, helps colleagues effectively. |
| **5.** Excellent | Outstandingly good with customers, extremely knowledgeable about all products, shows remarkable initiative, has good ideas to increase sales, works very well independently and collaboratively, helps colleagues very effectively. |

- *Specific* – the objective must be clear, exact and well-defined.
- *Measurable* – the objective should have a measure, or outcome, that demonstrates that the objective has been met.
- *Achievable* – it must be possible for the employee to achieve the objective; the resources required for success must be available.
- *Realistic* – it must be possible for the employee to complete what is required by the objective and the objective must be relevant to the employee's responsibilities.
- *Time-bound* – the objective should have a deadline, or finishing point; this might be one, single specific point in time, or there may be a number of points at which progress is reviewed; it must be practical to complete the objective in the time allocated.

*Peter Drucker.*

Essentially, the SMART objectives function as goals which the employee has to meet. This means that when it comes to performance appraisal, a comparison can be made between the original objectives and whether the goals were met.

All of the methods we have looked at so far involve the individual being appraised by a superior. An alternative to this is *360 Degree Feedback*. This method gets its name from the more rounded assessment that is generated by gathering feedback from different, multiple sources. The variety of sources includes the person's immediate superior, peers, subordinates, customers but may be expanded to include self-evaluation, higher management or other relevant party. The various sources all provide different kinds of feedback perspectives and therefore a bigger picture is created compared with using one appraiser alone.

Which technique to use for appraisal will depend on the job a person does. Often, organizations use more than one performance appraisal method. Where ratings are involved, it is important that raters are properly trained due to the problems that psychologists have identified with this methodology.

When presented with a scale which runs from 1–5, or 1–7 (or whatever the chosen scale end-points are) and 1 represents something very negative and the top number something very positive, three kinds of distributional error can occur. A central tendency error arises when the rater repeatedly opts for the middle of the scale. This may be because he or she doesn't like to use the very ends of the scale and so 1–5 becomes 2–4 and 1–7 becomes 2–6. Another reason for selecting the mid-point might be that the rater doesn't feel there's sufficient information to go either way. Whatever the grounds for choosing an average response though, the full extent of the scale isn't employed.

This can occur too, if the rater is too lenient and gives too high ratings, or if s/he is too harsh and ratings are too low. In these examples, it is obvious that a person will be appraised as either better or worse at their job than they really are. However, these same appraisal mistakes occur with repeatedly selecting the mid-point of a scale – poorer than average workers are assessed as being better, whilst higher than average workers are appraised as being worse than they are.

Other rater errors involve primacy and recency effects. In the former, too much weight is given to the rater's early experience of the worker, whereas too much emphasis is given to the

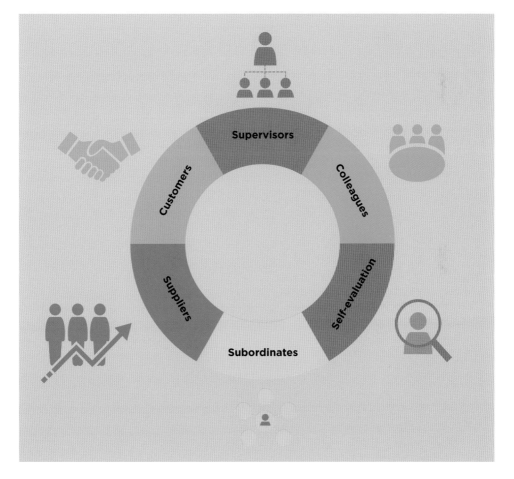

*360 degree feedback produces a more rounded assessment by gathering feedback from different, multiple sources.*

latest, or newest information, when a recency effect is present. Either of these emphases may be positive or negative for the person being rated; yet, what is actually required is an assessment of performance over the whole time which is under consideration.

Sometimes a rater may be disposed to giving more favourable ratings (the halo effect), or, less favourable ratings (the horns effect). These behaviours can arise for a number of reasons including favouring people who are like the rater; those who are good at expressing themselves well; or those who dress in a certain way. The horns effect could include judgements based on age, race or gender, for example.

| EXAMPLES OF THE ADVANTAGES AND DISADVANTAGES OF THE TYPES OF APPRAISAL | |
|---|---|
| **Appraisal Type** | **Examples of Advantages and Disadvantages** |
| *Graphic Rating Scale* | + Easy and inexpensive to develop.<br>− Raters may not use the scale in the same way. |
| *Mixed Standard Scale* | + If the appraiser is not being consistent, this can be spotted due to each aspect of performance being considered three times via the three statements.<br>− The appraiser can only respond based on the statements provided, so if these do not include an element of the job, this won't be covered. |
| *Behaviourally / Anchored Rating Scale* | + Desirable behaviours are clearly identified.<br>− Time-consuming to establish; can be costly to set up. |
| *Management by Objectives* | + Employee feels more involved as goals are established by manager and employee together.<br>− May not be appropriate for all jobs. |
| *360 Degree Feedback* | + Identifies those areas needing development.<br>− Can be time consuming and expensive as several people may be involved and their separate responses also have to be combined. |

Knowing that these kinds of errors may arise means that raters can be trained to endeavour to avoid them. Improved rating accuracy can be encouraged, for example, by ensuring that raters use scales in the same way and avoid distribution effects. Informing raters about the dangers of primacy, recency, halo and horns effects can be helpful for them to keep in mind when conducting the appraisal. However, physical notes on performance are essential so that there is evidence to draw from and there isn't reliance on what may well be a faulty memory.

Ultimately, because occupational psychology has identified different ways of conducting appraisal along with their advantages and disadvantages, the person being appraised and the appraiser can each benefit, as the process of performance appraisal can be made good and fair from both perspectives.

## SUMMARY

- Occupational psychology is also known as industrial-organizational psychology as well as work and organizational psychology.
- Selecting personnel involves job analysis, job description, person specification, advertising and identifying the right person for the role from those who apply.
- Work–life balance is about a person getting the proportions of time spent on work and on life outside work right for them. Organizations can help with this in various ways such as through flexible work opportunities.
- Work-related stress can be brought about by: job demands; little or no job control; poor work relationships; no full understanding of the role the job involves; job insecurity; lack of involvement in changes at work; insufficient support and a poor work–life balance.
- Organizations can help with stress in a number of ways such as training managers to identify it and potentially making alterations to the job.
- There are objective and subjective methods of conducting performance appraisals. Subjective measures include: Graphic Rating Scale, Mixed Standard Scale, Behaviourally Anchored Rating Scale, Management by Objectives and 360 Degree Feedback.
- Use of rating scales has a number of problems and subjective measures have their own advantages and disadvantages. Knowing about these issues means they can be taken into account when performance appraisals are conducted.

# FURTHER READING

## Sources that cover multiple topics in Psychology

- *30-Second Psychology: the 50 Most Thought-provoking Psychology Theories, Each Explained in Half a Minute*, by Christian Jarrett, Icon Books Ltd.
- *The Rough Guide to Psychology*, by Christian Jarrett, APA Publications.
- *A Degree in a Book: Psychology: Everything You Need to Know to Master the Subject – in One Book!*, by Alan Porter, Arcturus.

## Case Studies

- *Classic Case Studies in Psychology*, by Geoff Rolls, Taylor & Francis Ltd.

## Chapter 1 - Cognitive Psychology

- *Cognitive Psychology: The Basics*, by Sandie Taylor and Lance Workman, Taylor & Francis Ltd.
- *An Introduction to Cognitive Psychology: Processes and Disorders*, by David Groome with others, Taylor & Francis Ltd.
- *Cognitive Psychology: A Student's Handbook*, by Michael W. Eysenck and Mark Keane, Taylor & Francis Ltd.

## Chapter 2 - Neuropsychology

- *The Brain: The Story of You*, by David Eagleman, Canongate Books.
- *A Day in the Life of the Brain: the Neuroscience of Consciousness from Dawn Till Dusk,* by Susan Greenfield, Penguin Books Ltd.
- *The Tell-Tale Brain: Unlocking the Mystery of Human Nature*, by V.S. Ramachandran, Cornerstone.
- *The Man Who Mistook His Wife for a Hat*, by Oliver Sacks, Pan MacMillan.
- *A Student's Guide to Cognitive Neuropsychology*, Ashok Jansari, Sage Publications Inc.

## Chapter 3 - Developmental Psychology

- *An Introduction to Developmental Psychology*, Alan Slater and J. Gavin Bremner (Editors), John Wiley & Sons Ltd.
- *Developmental Psychology: From Infancy to Adulthood*, by Ann Birch, Palgrave Macmillan.
- *Developmental Psychology*, by Rachel Gillibrand, Virginia Lam and Victoria O'Donnell, Pearson Education Limited.

## Chapter 4 - Social Psychology

- *Social Psychology: The Basics*, by Daniel Frings, Taylor & Francis Ltd.
- *Social Psychology: A Very Short Introduction*, by Richard J. Crisp, Oxford University Press.
- *An Introduction to Social Psychology*, Miles Hewstone and Wolfgang Stroebe (Editors), John Wiley & Sons Ltd.
- *The Lucifer Effect*, by Philip Zimbardo, Ebury Publishing.

## Chapter 5 - Personality

- *Personality Psychology: The Basics*, by Stanley O. Gaines Jr, Taylor & Francis Ltd.
- *Personality: The Psychometric View,* by Paul Kline, Taylor & Francis Ltd.
- *Personality: What Makes You the Way You Are,* by David Nettle, Oxford University Press.

## Chapter 6 - Clinical Psychology

- *Clinical Psychology: A Very Short Introduction*, by Susan Llewelyn and Katie Aafjes-van Doorn, Oxford University Press.
- *Clinical Psychology: An Introduction,* by Alan Carr, Taylor & Francis Ltd.
- *Clinical Psychology*, Graham Davey, Nick Lake and Adrian Whittington (Editors), Taylor & Francis Ltd.

## Chapter 7 - Health Psychology

- *Health Psychology: The Basics*, by Erica Cook and Lynne Wood, Taylor & Francis Ltd.
- *Health Psychology*, by Karen Rodham, Palgrave Macmillan.
- *Health Psychology*, by Jane Ogden, Open University Press.

## Chapter 8 - Forensic Psychology

- *Forensic Psychology: A Very Short Introduction*, by David Canter, Oxford University Press.
- *Forensic Psychology for Dummies*, by David Canter, John Wiley & Sons Inc.
- *Forensic Psychology: The Basics*, by Sandie Taylor, Taylor & Francis Inc.
- *Forensic Psychology: Crime, Justice, Law, Interventions*, Graham M. Davies and Anthony R. Beech (Editors), John Wiley & Sons Ltd.

## Chapter 9 - Sport Psychology

- *Sport Psychology*, by David Tod, Joanne Thatcher and Rachel Rahman, Bloomsbury Publishing PLC.
- *Sport Psychology: The Basics: Optimising Human Performance*, by Rhonda Cohen, Bloomsbury Publishing PLC.
- *Sport Psychology: A Complete Introduction*, by John Perry, John Murray Press.

## Chapter 10 - Occupational Psychology

- *Work Psychology: Understanding Human Behaviour in the Workplace*, by John Arnold, Iain Coyne, Ray Randall and Fiona Patterson, Pearson.
- *Occupational Psychology: An Applied Approach*, by Gail Steptoe-Warren, Pearson Education Limited.
- *Understanding Occupational & Organizational Psychology*, by Lynne Millward, Sage Publications INC.

# INDEX

# PICTURE CREDITS

t = top, b = bottom, l = left, r = right